THE
CLASSIC
ITALIAN
COOKBOOK

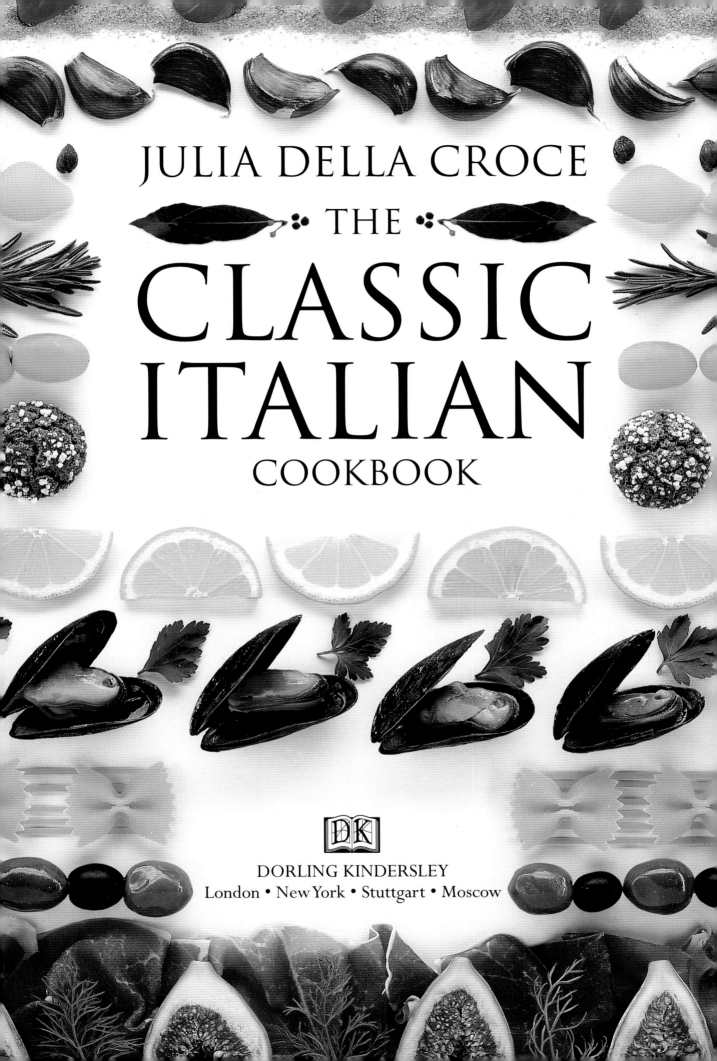

JULIA DELLA CROCE

THE
CLASSIC
ITALIAN
COOKBOOK

DORLING KINDERSLEY
London • New York • Stuttgart • Moscow

A DORLING KINDERSLEY BOOK

Project Editor
Lorna Damms

Art Editor
Sue Storey
at Patrick McLeavey & Partners

Senior Editor
Carolyn Ryden

Senior Art Editor
Tracey Clarke

Managing Editor
Susannah Marriott

Deputy Art Director
Carole Ash

Photography
Clive Streeter

Home Economist
Lyn Rutherford

Production Controller
Manjit Sihra

Production Manager
Maryann Rogers

For my mother, Giustina Ghisu della Croce

First published in Great Britain in 1996
by Dorling Kindersley Limited
9 Henrietta Street, London WC2E 8PS

A CIP catalogue for this book is available from
the British Library

ISBN 0 7513 0312 7

Reproduced in Italy by Scanner Services SRL
Printed and bound in Italy by A. Mondadori, Verona

CONTENTS

THE ITALIAN PANTRY 18
*A vibrant photographic guide to the key
ingredients essential for achieving
authentic Italian flavour*

CLASSIC DISHES 38
*An inspiring selection of some of Italy's
most distinctive classic dishes*

General Introduction

During the course of writing this book, I have been asked what is meant by the title "Classic Italian Cookbook". It is a question I have often asked myself, particularly in contemplating which recipes I should include. In formulating an answer, I offer a definition from the Random House Dictionary: "classic, of enduring interest, quality, or style…". The recipes in this volume have survived decades and even centuries, and are still much used in Italian cooking today. Their preparation is based on sound principles of using fresh ingredients of the highest quality, and turning them into a finished dish with the least amount of modification, thus preserving their inherent goodness and flavour.

Some writers of cookery books would have us believe that any departure from the way things have been done for centuries defies authenticity. On the contrary, cuisine is a living art, affected by historical events, popular trends and the introduction of new foods. While the names of dishes are unchanged, their preparation is typically lighter today than it was when people were more physically active. The current recognition of Italian food as one of the world's most healthy cuisines has been pleasing to those of us who have been nurtured on it. However, any reference to "the Italian diet" always leaves me cold. The Italian way of eating is much more than a sensible "diet": it is a way of life.

History has proved that where there is a great civilization, there is great cuisine. The roots of Italian cooking are in the ancient Mediterranean cultures. Italy's first-known inhabitants, the Etruscans, had a highly artistic and developed culture, amazingly advanced in agriculture. Over that are layers of influence from invading peoples, including the Romans, Phoenicians, Saracens, Goths, Normans, French, Spanish and Austrians.

For centuries, there was a distinction between what the wealthy ate and what was eaten by the poor. Meat-eating was a privilege reserved for very few until modern times, while the peasant class, with its close connection to the earth, had access to fruit and vegetables, and to the wild foods of the sea and forests. Thus with even comparatively meagre resources, the peasants developed rich cooking traditions. Through the courts and the religious communities, with their higher level of education and international connections, new foods and cooking ideas were gradually diffused. With the rise of the middle class at the time of the Renaissance, the concern for quantity was replaced with one for quality. It is in the middle class that a meeting of *cucina ricca* (the "rich kitchen") and *cucina povera* (the "poor kitchen") took place, brought together by a common reliance on local resources. Over the centuries it evolved until finally it blossomed into what we know as the classic Italian kitchen, an exceptional embroidery of diverse cultural, economic and historical influences. For the most part, great Italian food is found in the home. Even while the

task of cooking is still generally left to women, everyone understands the importance of good food. A case in point is my maternal grandfather, who was a gentleman farmer in Sardinia. An intellectual and a *padrone*, he never did manual work. Nor did he do any of the routine cooking. Yet, every Sunday, he prepared the spit over the open hearth, and roasted the lamb for the elaborate family lunch. My mother draws a vivid picture of him, sitting in front of the fire and patiently turning the lamb. Despite his limited repertoire, he was a passionate gourmet. Sixty years after his death, stories are still told in the family about his remarkable love of good food and wine.

Years ago when I was studying in Edinburgh, I would walk from one end of the city to the other to buy olive oil in the town's only Italian shop. I well remember those long treks in the chilly, blustery Scottish winter, but I felt as though every step was a step towards my roots, for in that bottle of deep golden oil were captured the sun, the earth and the centuries of my ancestors' lives. It was a real treasure, and not only because the cost of the oil was as much as a week's rent in those days.

The celebration of food and wine for an Italian is a daily event overlaid with spiritual significance, not one reserved solely for special occasions. The love of good food, the intimate connection to the craft of growing and making it, the joy of eating and sharing it, is passed from generation to generation. What shall we name this phenomenon? Is this not classic – classic Italian food of enduring interest, quality and style?

Julia della casa

Italy's Culinary Heritage

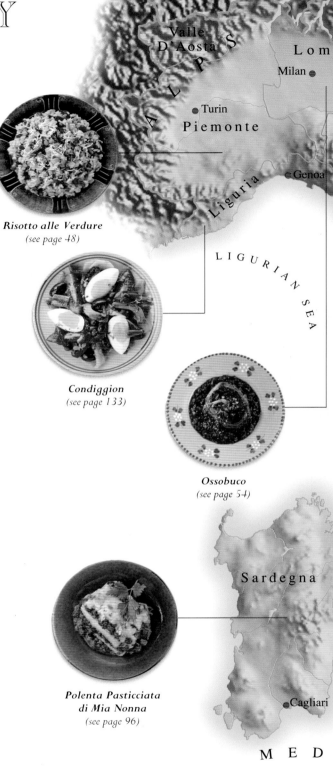

THE MOST DEEPLY ROOTED aspect of Italian cooking is that of its regional differences. After all, it wasn't until 1870 that Italy became a nation. While the Roman Empire had unified the peninsula in an official language and in political administration, engendering a feeling of universalism, its regions persisted in their local customs and provincial languages. In addition, each region has had its own embroiled history of foreign invasions and influences, which affected the culture and consciousness of its population.

After the fall of Rome, Italy had neither a capital nor a centre, but was a country of many capitals and centres. Even now, every region, city or village is still richly unique. This diversity is reflected in the cuisine. Each province and city has its own shape of pasta, its unique breads and pastries, its own selection of recipes. Italy's example shows that recipes are not created in a vacuum; they are the living records of the way in which a society lives, thinks and feels. In these pages I hope to begin to convey the unique character of each region's food culture and its part in Italian cuisine as a whole.

While Italian guide books always begin a discussion of the regions with Piedmont and then proceed south, in the brief gastronomical tour that follows, I have begun with Tuscany because that is where Italian civilization and cuisine began. From there, I move on to Rome and the Greek-influenced south, which also predates the north in the development of cuisine. Last appear the Italian islands, Sicily and Sardinia, because their remoteness has made them particularly unique in gastronomical terms.

Risotto alle Verdure
(see page 48)

Condiggion
(see page 133)

Ossobuco
(see page 54)

*Polenta Pasticciata
di Mia Nonna*
(see page 96)

ITALY'S REGIONS
This map shows Italy's regions and marks key towns and cities. Dishes typical of particular regions that can be found in subsequent chapters are also featured.

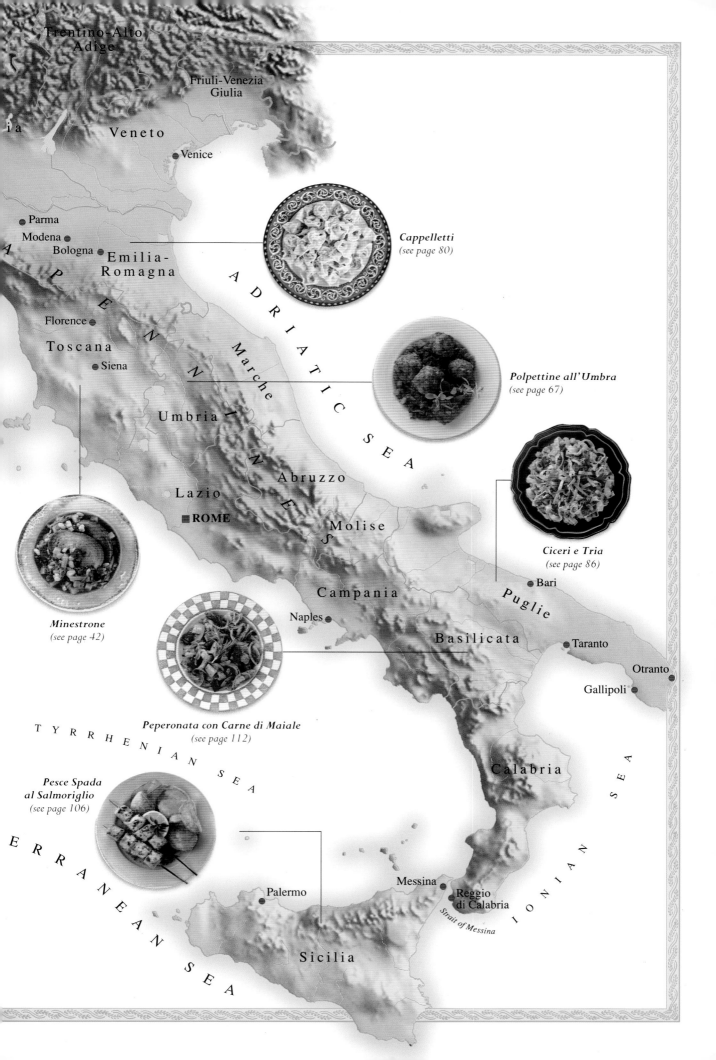

Trentino-Alto
Adige

Friuli-Venezia
Giulia

Veneto

Venice

Parma
Modena
Bologna
Emilia-
Romagna

Cappelletti
(see page 80)

Florence

Toscana

Siena

Marche

Polpettine all'Umbra
(see page 67)

Umbria

Abruzzo

Lazio

ROME

Molise

Ciceri e Tria
(see page 86)

ADRIATIC SEA

APPENNINES

Bari

Puglie

Minestrone
(see page 42)

Campania

Naples

Basilicata

Taranto

Otranto

Gallipoli

Peperonata con Carne di Maiale
(see page 112)

TYRRHENIAN SEA

Calabria

IONIAN SEA

Pesce Spada
al Salmoriglio
(see page 106)

Palermo

Messina

Reggio
di Calabria

Strait of Messina

MEDITERRANEAN SEA

Sicilia

TOSCANA (TUSCANY)

Minestrone (see page 42)

Tuscany is the heartland of Italy both in a geographic and a historical sense. Italian civilization began there. When Rome was no more than a muddy encampment, Etruscan civilization was already highly developed, and it is in Tuscany, ancient land of olive, wheat and vine, where Italian cooking began. Tuscan cooking is uncomplicated and natural; lavish in its use of raw materials, but straightforward in its preparation. It relies on bread and pasta, seasonal fruit and vegetables, high quality cheeses, cured meats and olive oil produced by skilled artisans whose craft is a result of personal pride and centuries of know-how. The westernmost provinces look to the sea for many dishes, while in the hilly regions, shepherds still tend their flocks and make good rustic cheeses. In addition, Tuscans have earned for themselves the nickname of *mangiafagioli*, "bean-eaters". This is also the land of *bistecca alla fiorentina*, which has been one of the highlights of the Florentine table for a hundred years. In fact, it is not a beefsteak, but a rib of young Chianina beef. The Chianina is a huge, imposing breed of white cattle whose flavourful meat is tender, lower in cholesterol and more digestible than other beef. A description of Tuscan cooking would not be complete without mentioning wine, a passion that began with the Etruscans, who developed techniques of viniculture; this is why Italians say that Tuscany was baptized in wine.

UMBRIA

Polpettine all'Umbra
(see page 67)

The culinary traditions of Umbria are tied to the mountains and valleys that dominate its landscape. The cooking, based on the region's superior olive oil, is honest and simple, flavoured with local herbs, especially marjoram, fennel and rosemary. A prevalent feature of the cuisine is the bountiful use of meats of both domesticated and wild varieties. There is beef, pork, kid, veal and baby lamb, raised naturally on a diet of grasses, wild thyme and sage. Hare and capon, many species of wild game birds, river fish, mostly giant carp and trout, vary the menu. The most striking Umbrian dishes are the grilled and spit-roasted meats, such as the famous *arista*, tender roast pork loin scented with rosemary or fennel seeds, and *porchetta*, luscious whole roast suckling pig flavoured with garlic and pepper. The finest *prosciutti* (hams) and dried and fresh sausages are also found here. Umbria produces several local pasta specialities of note: *ciriole alla ternana*, thick wholewheat noodles that are served with various sauces, and *umbrici*, handmade spaghetti. The hills abound with wild mushrooms; five varieties of truffles grow here and the black truffle is used generously in everything from risotto to spaghetti, meat and fish dishes.

MARCHE (THE MARCHES)

The Marches have been held at one time or another by the Etruscans, the Greeks, the Romans and the Gauls, but while each left their mark, none of these cultures has dominated. This is the most homogeneous region in terms of geography and natural resources. Fishing and agriculture are the area's only industries and its cuisine reflects sea and land traditions equally. Local waters supply the spectrum of seafood, including prawns, lobster, squid, cuttlefish, anchovies, sardines, sole and turbot. All go into the celebrated local *brodetto* (fish soup), of which each town has its own version. Every category of food is well-represented in the country cooking. There is excellent farmed meat and game of every description. The local olive oil, cured meats, sausages and cheeses are laudable. The Marches are blessed with white truffles that rival the celebrated ones of Piedmont, and with wild mushrooms of many varieties, notably the incomparable *porcino*. An important feature of the cuisine is the unrestrained use of vegetables and fruit.

LAZIO

If anything, the cooking of Lazio is Etruscan in character: simple and earthy. The singular gastronomical legacy of ancient Rome is not what is eaten but how. Romans still love lavish displays of food and conviviality at the table. To enter a local *trattoria* today is to witness in modern-day form the legendary Roman penchant for the table as the locals eat their food with unrestrained gusto. The air is filled with voices, all speaking at once, and the aromas of multitudinous dishes. If the approach is unrestrained, so are the flavours. Lazio is partial to herbs and aromatics, including mint, rosemary, sage, tarragon (otherwise used infrequently in Italy, except in Siena), pepper, cloves and cinnamon. The Romans likewise favour uncomplicated popular dishes (an old Roman saying goes, "the more you spend, the worse you eat"). Olive oil and lard are the preferred cooking fats. Characteristic dishes include a *fritto misto* of offal; pasta, bean and rice dishes; stews and roasted meats, notably *abbacchio* (roasted milk-fed baby lamb flavoured with rosemary); and artichokes cooked in superb ways.

ABRUZZO

Abruzzo is rugged mountain country, though three of the provinces have access to a short strip of coastline. Consequently, there are three styles of cooking: that of the sea, the mountains and the hinterland. Among the coastal region's favourite dishes are *scapece*, fried fish subsequently marinated in vinegar, and *fritto misto*, mixed fish fry. The cuisine of the mountains is founded on products derived from sheep, lamb and pecorino cheese. The famous local pasta speciality is *maccheroni alla chitarra*, "guitar macaroni", named for the guitar-like instrument on which it is formed, served with *ragù*. The inland region produces high-quality crops. Superior cherries, pears, apples, peaches and table grapes are exported all over Europe. The land is conducive to raising cattle, pigs, goats and fowl, and the region's pork products are well-known. One common feature of Abruzzese cooking is its use of cheese and hot red pepper.

MOLISE

Molise is the youngest region, having separated from Abruzzo in 1968, and relies primarily on agriculture and tourism. Wheat and olive oil are produced in relatively small amounts, though they are the staple ingredients, and excellent dried pasta is manufactured here. Having been tied to Abruzzo, the region has food traditions that are largely similar, with mountain, sea and inland cuisines. Molise borders on Apulia to the south, and like its neighbour, produces vegetables of remarkable flavour. There are superb cured pork products and local cheeses. The countryside is more serene and wooded than that of Abruzzo, a fact that contributes to the excellence of Molisan honey. Unique dishes include handmade *fusilli*, served with fiery tomato sauce, and *caragnoli*, ribbon-like fried pastries glazed with honey.

CAMPANIA

The exodus of emigrants from Naples has made many of this region's dishes famous all over the world, especially pizza and pasta. The tomato, which thrives in the region's long, hot summers and friable, volcanic soil, is also emblematic of Campanian cooking. There is an inordinate appetite for cheese. Silky mozzarella from buffalo milk, creamy scamorza and a host of other cheeses are familiar components in the region's prolific pizza and pasta dishes. They are also eaten as table cheeses. Neapolitans have been called *mangiamaccheroni* ("macaroni eaters") by their compatriots since the turn of the century, when the pasta industry took hold and *maccheroni* became a cheap source of nourishment for the masses. The name was superimposed on another more ancient one, *mangiafoglie* ("leaf eaters"), for the fertile soil produces vegetables of legendary quality. It is here in the 1950s that the scientist Ancel Keys found the lowest rate of heart disease in the western world. Notwithstanding, the Neapolitans have created a wonderful profusion of artful desserts and *gelati* (ice-creams).

Pizza Napoletana (see page 68)

BASILICATA

Peperonata con Carne di Maiale (see page 112)

Basilicata, which includes Lucania, derives its name from a Byzantine governor. Much of the region is barren, steep mountain land and there are three agricultural zones that correspond to three different altitudes. Feudalism and oppressive taxation in the past have had their impact on the population, and if there is a Lucanian style of cooking, it is one of making the most of humble ingredients. This is accomplished with the help of hot peppers of various kinds, especially *peperoncini* (chilli peppers) and even with ginger (a legacy of the Saracens), which is used with great enthusiasm. The pig and lard are of utmost importance in the diet and Basilicata's pork products have been famous since ancient times when the Roman Apicius recorded the following recipe for the Lucanian sausage: "Chop pepper, cumin, peverella, rue, parsley, sweet spices, bay berries and mix with ground pork, pounding all together with Apicius's salt, fat and fennel seeds; encase it in a long skin and hang it and smoke it".

PUGLIE (APULIA)

Ciceri e Tria
(see page 86)

The Greek presence is felt more in Apulia than anywhere else. Taranto, a city on its western coast, was once the capital of Magna Graecia. Other cities, including Gallipoli, Bari and Otranto, are also of Greek origin. The region is divided into three distinct provinces, each of which has its own pronounced culinary style. Whatever the differences, these styles are profoundly Mediterranean, founded on olive oil and dependent on vegetables, grains, fruit and seafood. Apulia is well known for its abundant produce, which supplies the region's large food industry. Olive oil, table grapes, figs and almonds are of particularly high quality and meet the demands of the most capricious tastes. Being nearly surrounded by coastline, the region has an astonishing variety and quantity of fish and shellfish, which are found in the many seafood dishes of the provinces. There is little meat in the diet, but a variety of excellent sausage products and fine cheeses of both cow's and sheep's milk compensate for this. Bread is made in many different ways and shapes. Apulia is also serious pasta country. Locally manufactured dried pasta has found markets all over the world. Handmade specialities also abound throughout the provinces, including *orecchiette* ("little ears"), *strascenate* ("dragged ones") and *cavatelli*. The popularity of pasta is proven by a saying: *"Criste mì, fa chiove le maccarrune, e le chianghe de le logge fatta ragù",* translatable as "Jesus, make it rain macaroni and fill the porticos of [our] balconies with meat sauce".

CALABRIA

Calabria is a land of remarkable natural beauty, of pristine beaches and panoramic mountain views. At the toe of the geographical boot, it is a stone's throw from Sicily over the Strait of Messina. This region has the closest historical ties to Greece. Having been extensively colonized in the 8th century BC, Greek Calabria at its zenith was a state of legendary wealth and power whose cities surpassed any others in Magna Graecia – even Athens – in splendour and luxury. In the course of its long and turbulent political history, it has been taken in turn by the Byzantines, the Saracens, the Normans, the Bourbons, and others in-between. Today, Calabria is isolated, having suffered from centuries of feudal rule, and along with other poor regions of the Italian south, it saw a mass exodus of emigrants to North America and other countries in the late nineteenth century and early twentieth century. Despite the difficulties of farming the land, there is a congenial environment for vegetables and fruit. Citrus fruit are grown and widely exported. The aubergine finds Calabrian soil particularly hospitable, and there is a veritable aubergine cuisine as a result. Other noteworthy products are tomatoes, onions and peppers. Seafood is abundant in the coastal areas, especially swordfish and tuna. Lamb and cheeses made from sheep's milk are significant local industries. There are occasional Sicilo-Arab touches in the cooking, but overall the cuisine is simple peasant food based on olive oil, pasta and an abundant variety of vegetables.

EMILIA-ROMAGNA

Cappelletti (see page 80)

Emilia-Romagna is comprised of two parts, Emilia to the west, and Romagna to the east. Its population is known for its formidable eating. The Italian love of good food finds its quintessence here, for this is the land of *parmigiano* cheese (Parmesan), Parma prosciutto, balsamic vinegar from Modena, tortellini and the tribe of stuffed pastas and other handmade egg pasta dishes, including *tagliatelle alla bolognese*. The variety and high quality of food in Emilia is the result of the rich soil of its extensive alluvial plain. This ideal agricultural land has placed Emilia ahead of all the other Italian regions in the production of wheat, tomatoes and fruit, and enabled it to become a major exporter of other food products, including rice and dried porcini. The lush, verdant landscape also makes it ideal for dairy cattle, which provide the milk, cream and butter that are at the foundation of many of the region's dishes. The pig is pampered here, as it is destined for the many exquisite sausages and hams. The east coast of the region faces the Adriatic, so there is also a seafood cuisine. Sturgeon, a valuable eating fish and the source of the even more precious black caviar, is caught in the Po River. What was said of Bologna by one Giovanni Schedel in the 15th century in his *Cronache* can be said of all of Emilia-Romagna to this day, "[it] is called the fat and the rich for the reason that it produces abundantly wheat, wine and everything necessary to life".

LIGURIA

Condiggion (see page 133)

A narrow and mountainous arch of coastline hinged to the French Riviera, Liguria is, above all, connected to the sea. That is not to say that its cuisine is predominantly one of fish. Rather, the cooking compensates for the life of the sailor who has spent months at sea without fresh home-grown foods. The Ligurians have been mushroom lovers since antiquity, and wild porcini and *ovoli* mushrooms thrive here. They are the most inventive vegetable cooks in all of Italy and make tarts of chard, spinach and borage. Another influence on the cooking has been its Muslim past, which has endowed it with an affinity for elaboration. Thus, the *cappon magro,* fast-day salad, is a towering, intricately designed pyramid of layer-upon-layer of boiled cauliflower, carrots, celery, green beans, artichokes, beetroot, potatoes, eggs, salt cod, bass, lobster and prawns. This is all arranged artfully on a bed of ship's biscuits anointed with olive oil, and decorated with capers, anchovies, preserved mushrooms, pickles, olives, mullet roe, possibly oysters and more prawns; then dressed with *salsa verde*. Ravioli, filled with everything from ricotta to pumpkin, fish or sweetbreads, are another speciality. While the spices that were trafficked through Genoa for centuries are ignored (a case of familiarity breeding contempt), the herbs that grow wild on the Ligurian slopes are used lavishly. Most famous of all the local dishes is *pesto*, a heady basil sauce served with noodles and in *minestrone*, which the Genoese claim to have invented. None of these dishes could exist without Ligurian olive oil, which is considered to be among the best in Italy.

PIEMONTE (PIEDMONT)

*Risotto alle Verdure
(see page 48)*

Piedmont is the land of butter, cheese and milk. It is also considered to make the best wine in Italy, Barolo, derived from the Nebbiolo grape. The terrain is suited to cattle-raising and the Piedmontese produce great cheeses, including tome and robiola. Fontina, which originated in Val d'Aosta, is also found here. It is the foundation of the region's famous *fonduta*, a cheese sauce flavoured with truffles (Piedmont is the only region where the precious white truffle is found in abundance). Pasta is confined to two forms, *agnolotti* and *cannelloni*. *Agnolotti* are stuffed with truffles, rice and meat, or sometimes with game (pheasant, hare or quail). *Cannelloni* are thin crêpes filled with veal, ham and cheese, then topped with béchamel sauce. Rice, grown locally, appears in everything from appetizers to desserts, though it is best represented in risotto. The Piedmontese love garlic and believe in its healing qualities, as the local proverb "garlic is the pharmacist of the peasant" demonstrates. *Bollito misto* (mixed boiled meats) is the most famous meat dish, which at its most streamlined consists of capon, chicken, beef, veal tongue and *cotechino* (a pork sausage), served with no less than three and up to five different sauces. Other unique local specialities include *bagna caôda*, vegetables dipped in an anchovy sauce, and *grissini*, crisp breadsticks stretched to an arm's length. Desserts are great in Piedmont, and each city has its own specialities. For example, Turin, the capital city, is famous for chocolates and caramels, Ovada for its *biscotti*.

VALLE D'AOSTA (VAL D'AOSTA)

This region is nestled between the French and Swiss Alps, which accounts for the fact that both French and German are spoken. Like the population, the cooking of the region is multinational at its roots. It ignores pasta, except for gnocchi made of cornmeal or potato and served with the splendid local cow's milk cheese, fontina. Like Piedmont, its southern neighbour, Val d'Aosta is a mountain culture. Butter and cheeses (tome, robiola and, above all, fontina) are produced in the Alps. No olive oil is used. The mountains provide wild goat and boar, chamois deer– unseen in most other Italian regions – hare, marmot and many species of game birds. The Alpine lakes have trout and the forests are full of chestnuts, raspberries and *mirtilli*, a type of blueberry. Here, polenta in a porridge form is enriched with milk and fontina. Alternatively, it is cut into pieces after cooling and setting, then sent to the oven smothered with freshly made sweet butter and cheese. Meat broth, a highly important part of the cuisine, is the foundation of all manner of thick soups that are often fortified with rice or black bread. The Teutonic influence is perhaps most obvious in the consumption of *speck*, a type of smoked ham that is also very popular in Trentino-Alto Adige. With such hefty eating, there is good reason for the dearth of desserts.

LOMBARDIA (LOMBARDY)

Ossobuco (see page 54)

There are nine mostly agricultural provinces in Lombardy, with Milan being the only industrial one. Although it has been said that a unified Lombard cuisine does not exist, this is not quite true. French and German tastes and cooking techniques have influenced the local cuisine since the time of Austrian domination. Certain dishes have gained international repute. Take as an example *ossobuco* with *risotto alla milanese* (braised veal with saffron risotto), *costolette alla milanese* (breaded fried veal rib chops), or *panettone* (the light, sweet bread riddled with raisins and candied fruit). Gourmets all over the world love Lombardy's *bresaola*, delicate air-cured beef fillet; and its famous cheeses, grana, mascarpone, stracchino, Gorgonzola and taleggio among them. Rice is king here, especially the variety grown locally for risotto. And who in Lombardy would make risotto without butter, the primary cooking fat since Roman times?

FRIULI-VENEZIA GIULIA

Friuli-Venezia Giulia is one of the least inhabited regions of Italy. During the course of its rocky history, waves of invading peoples, including the Romans, Venetians and Hapsburg Austrians, have swept over it. Venetian tastes predominate here, but there are two influential culinary traditions, that of Friuli, and that of Trieste. The food is mostly rough and hearty, though Venice superimposes some of its refinements in the first course with risotto, as does Austria in the pastry kitchen. Thick vegetable soups to which beans, rice or barley are added are typical Friuli fare. Pork stew with cabbage and goulash are of the Trieste cuisine, which is a melting pot of Venetian, Hungarian, Greek, Austrian, Slavic and Hebrew traditions. Polenta is the usual accompaniment to the sturdy game dishes typical of this mountain kitchen. Other foods of note are the sweet, lean ham of San Daniele, and Liptauer cheese, a combination of Gorgonzola and mascarpone, flavoured with spices, leek, anchovies and capers.

TRENTINO-ALTO ADIGE

Italian-speaking Trentino and German-speaking Alto Adige are distinct provinces with separate cuisines. The cooking of Trentino is a blend of Lombard and Venetian styles. Alto Adige, once the Austrian South Tyrol, is boldly Teutonic with a smattering of Slavic. Trentino cooking relies on polenta, meat and game, and on *stoccafisso* (unsalted dried cod). There is an extraordinary variety of local mushrooms: 250 wild species from this region alone can be found in the Trentino market. Pork is central to the cuisine of Alto Adige and *speck*, a smoked ham flavoured with juniper, garlic, bay and pepper, is made from it, as are numerous sausages. Bread is baked with rye or barley and seasoned with caraway in the Slavic style. This is all heavy stuff, but the abundance of freshwater fish from the Adige River lightens the fare. The wine and beer is also German in style, and it is interesting to note that there are at least five provincial colloquial words to describe various degrees of drunkenness, which is also atypical of the rest of the country.

VENETO

The cuisine of Venice and the Veneto is refined, with a touch of the exotic. Here we find sweet and sour, for example, a taste confined to those areas where there was strong Eastern influence. Venice was once a powerful city that supplied Europe with salt, spices and goods from the Orient. Its markets are still spectacular and its cooking is an unidentifiable amalgam of its worldly and extravagant past. The most important foods are rice, polenta, beans and *baccalà* (salt cod). No other region uses rice with such creativity and finesse. Pasta is not used much, except for *gnocchi*, to which the Veronese show homage with a yearly festival. The love of seafood does not overshadow a taste for meat, of which there is a great deal, often prepared in unusual ways — turkey with pomegranate comes to mind. It is not surprising that a land that traded in sugar should produce great sweets, and the Veneto does, in profusion. It is also noted for splendid wines, hence the saying that Venice is first a culture of water, then of wine.

SICILIA (SICILY)

Pesce Spada (see page 106)

Although the Greeks preceded the Saracens in Sicily, it was the latter who put a lasting mark on Sicilian cuisine. The island was under Arab rule for some two hundred years, and even after Norman occupation, the highly developed culture of Muslim Sicily continued to influence the life of the island. Unlike the culinary traditions of other regions, those of Sicily cannot be identified solely with either the peasant kitchen or that of the aristocracy. It is rather a case of a great cuisine arising from old traditions. Rare in Italian cooking, sweet and savoury flavours are brought together in one dish, such as in *pasta con le sarde,* a macaroni pie in which sardines and salted anchovies are juxtaposed with fennel, pine nuts and raisins. Also a legacy from the Arabs is a penchant for macaroni, which was introduced to the island in 1154 in the form of *itriyah*, hollowed out pasta "strings", and a gift for pastry-making.

SARDEGNA (SARDINIA)

Sardinian cooking is tied to pastoral traditions. It is one of utter simplicity and bold flavours. The primary elements are olive oil, lamb, bread and sheep's cheese, which is exported worldwide. Despite the torrid summer climate, there is a great variety of vegetables; artichokes and tomatoes are especially sought after. Dates, figs, citrus fruit, pomegranates, cherries, plums and nuts grow well and appear in a seemingly endless array of desserts and confections. Wild sage, rosemary, myrtle, bay and mint perfume the honey of the island. Saffron, a legacy of the Catalan settlements of the 13th century, is used extensively. The quality of Sardinian breads is exceptional. The most famous bread is *pane carasau* in dialect, or *carta da musica* in Italian, so named for its incredible thinness and the crunchy sound it makes when being eaten. Sardinians like pasta, too. Unique to the island are two varieties made from semolina: *fregula*, crumb-like soup pasta, and *malloreddus*, tiny saffron-tinted shells.

THE ITALIAN PANTRY

To achieve the flavour and goodness of authentic Italian cooking, every recipe should be approached with two principles in mind. The first is that you should begin with impeccably fresh ingredients. Secondly, these raw ingredients should be combined with genuine Italian products, such as aromatic extra-virgin olive oil, imported cheeses or speciality cured meats. These pages will introduce you to just some of the ingredients that are used to create the flavours of true Italian cuisine.

VEGETABLES

Italian vegetables are characterized by their flavour. This exceptional quality is the result of long growing seasons and the cultivators' skill. Vegetables are not grown for size or shape, but for flavour. They are allowed to reach full maturity in their natural surroundings and are picked ripe, when their flavours are fully formed and most acute.

OTHER TYPICAL VEGETABLES
Carrots, celery, onions, leeks, turnips, courgettes and courgette flowers, truffles and oyster mushrooms, cardoons, beetroot, pumpkin, cabbages, broccoli, broad beans, radishes, potatoes, cucumbers.

PEPPERS (Peperoni)
Sweet peppers may be green, yellow, red or orange, elongated or squat and round. Green peppers are not fully ripened and are less widely used than the others, which have matured to full colour, sweetness and depth of flavour. There are also varieties of hot peperoni.

AUBERGINES (Melanzane)
Introduced to Italy by the Saracens, aubergines are typically deep purple. Green aubergines are too bitter for use and have been picked when immature. Favour small or medium-sized specimens with smaller navels at the base (the male species) as these have fewer seeds. Indentations on the skin indicate overripeness.

PLUM TOMATOES (Pomodori San Marzano)
The San Marzano or plum tomato is the ideal variety for cooking. These tomatoes have thin skins, thick fleshy walls and relatively few seeds. To reach their peak of flavour, they must ripen on the vine under the sun. Well-ripened tomatoes make the best sauces.

Skin should look taut and polished

—Tips should be tight and closed

ASPARAGUS (Asparagi)
Asparagus, of which there are green, white and purple Genoese varieties, must be eaten soon after picking. The stalks should be very crisp and moist. Avoid those with tips that have begun to bud, a sure sign that the stalks have lost their sugar.

Fat white asparagus

SALAD LEAVES (Insalata)
Green salads are invariably eaten after the second course to refresh the palate. They are usually simple leafy salads, without croûtons, nuts or cheese, that include a variety of young, tender greens, both bitter and sweet for contrasting flavours. These might include radicchio, rucola (rocket), lollo rosso (red lettuce), young dandelion leaves and scarola (escarole). The leaves should be vibrant and crisp.

Lollo rosso

Rocket

Radicchio

ARTICHOKES (Carciofi)
Small artichokes are the most flavoursome. When allowed to grow too large, the hairy inner choke over-develops and the heart loses its tenderness and flavour. Avoid artichokes with leaves open like a dying rose, rather than lying sleek and tight against one another. Stems should be rigid and crisp.

MUSHROOMS (Funghi)
Intensely flavoured, fleshy and moist, porcini (ceps) are the king of mushrooms. They grow as large as dinner plates in Italy, where they are sometimes grilled over an open fire like a steak. Other varieties include the common white or brown-capped (chestnut) mushroom, egg-shaped ovoli and trompettes de mort.

Chestnut mushroom

Porcino
(Boletus edulus)

GREEN BEANS (Fagiolini)
If picked when still young, green beans are marvellously buttery and tender. If grown past their prime, the beans become starchy and hard, and the pods tough and stringy.

FENNEL (Finocchio)
The bulb of the fennel is anisey and sweet, while the feathery leaves have a strong flavour reminiscent of dill. Select the sweeter, rounder (female) bulbs and discard the tough stalk part. Wedges of bulb can be eaten raw or cooked.

Look for plump white bulbs without blemishes

Escarole

Red chicory

Spinach

CAULIFLOWER (Cavolfiore)
A member of the cabbage family, cauliflower has excellent nutritional properties. It is used cooked as a side dish, in pasta sauces and as a raw salad vegetable. There are also green (romanesco) and purple varieties. The crown should be spotless and the stalk crisp.

MIXED GREENS (Erbe)
Cooked greens are an important part of the Italian diet. Such vegetables as spinach, Swiss chard, chicory, escarole and cime di rapa (bitter broccoli) are typically blanched, then sautéed with olive oil and garlic, pancetta or beans. These greens are also used in pasta sauces, pies, soups, tarts, in stuffed pasta and on focaccia. As a general rule, select unblemished, unwrinkled and moist specimens.

FISH

The coastal regions of Italy have always relied on the daily catch from the sea to supplement the diet. Even in the northern and mountainous regions far from the sea, fish are procured from freshwater lakes and streams, and Italians always look forward to the fish course with exultant anticipation.

OTHER FISH AND SEAFOOD

Sole, grey mullet and mullet roe (bottarga), red snapper, salted herring, mackerel, cod, stoccafisso (saltless dried cod), grouper, turbot, dog-fish, scorpion fish, eel, carp, sturgeon, trout, perch, shad, and also frog.

ANCHOVIES (Alici)
As anchovies have no scales, they need only be boned before cooking. Fresh anchovies can be boiled, made into patties, breaded and deep-fried, or if very fresh, eaten raw with lemon.

Sea bass has gleaming silver scales with a darker back and white belly

SMALL FRY
No fish is too small to escape the Italian fisherman, even the tiny whitebait (bianchetti or pesciolini), which are infant sardines, and anchovies, and goby (rossetto or guatto). These tiny fish are deep-fried, made into fritters, cooked into frittate (omelettes) and soups, boiled or, if just caught, eaten raw.

SEA BASS
(Spigola or branzino)
The sea bass is a saltwater fish that migrates to rivers and lakes from spring until autumn. It is fished from both salt and fresh water. Its delicate white flesh is firm and relatively free of bone, which makes it eminently suitable for boiling or poaching, though it is also delicious grilled over charcoal or baked whole.

Whitebait

The red mullet has extraordinarily delicate white flesh

RED MULLET (Triglia)
There are several species of red mullet, ranging in colour from pink to true red; all are popular, eating fish. Their size is small, but the flesh is exceptionally tasty. Typical cooking methods include grilling, frying and baking in salt or parchment or with tomato.

SARDINES OR PILCHARDS (Sardine)

Fresh sardines have very delicate meat. They are a fatty fish so little oil or butter is required to cook them. Sardines are typically breaded and fried, grilled or baked. They may also be stuffed.

Sardines

SEA BREAM (Pagro)

There are many varieties of sea bream, with dentex and porgy being the largest members of the family. Sea bream has fine, sweet, firm flesh and is excellent grilled, roasted, cooked in parchment with herbs, stuffed and baked. It may be divided into fillets or used whole. Smaller fish are delicious simply fried.

Dentex

SALT COD (Baccalà)

The best salt cod is white and fleshy, not brownish and meagre-looking. It must be soaked in cold water overnight then rinsed before cooking. Once, it was difficult to find outside ethnic markets, but it is now more readily available and may be sold boneless and skinless, which eliminates some preparation work (see page 163). It has always been an important staple food for many Mediterranean countries and is an enormously versatile ingredient.

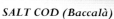

FISH STEAKS

Swordfish (pesce spada), *tuna* (tonno) *and monkfish* (rana pescatrice *or* coda di rospo) *are prized for their meaty, firm flesh, which makes them excellent for the grill. They are also suitable for breading, boiling, frying and baking. Swordfish tends towards dryness so is often marinated before cooking to improve its texture. The sweetest part of the tuna is the belly* (ventresca). *Monkfish is a far smaller fish and can be cooked whole (minus the head). It also appears in fish soups.*

Swordfish   **Tuna**   **Monkfish**

SHELLFISH

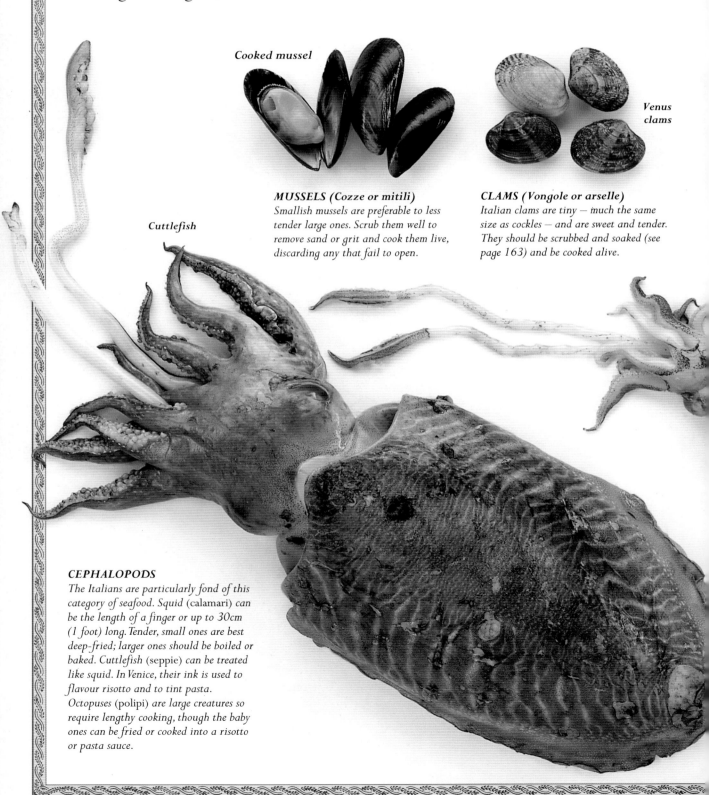

All manner of shellfish and cephalopods are prized for their briny flavour. As with other seafood, it is critical that they are impeccably fresh; molluscs and lobster should be bought and cooked live. The names of shellfish vary from region to region, which sometimes causes confusion.

OTHER TYPICAL SHELLFISH
Oysters, scallops, spiny lobsters, sea urchins, sea dates, razor clams, snails.

Cooked mussel

Cuttlefish

Venus clams

MUSSELS (Cozze or mitili)
Smallish mussels are preferable to less tender large ones. Scrub them well to remove sand or grit and cook them live, discarding any that fail to open.

CLAMS (Vongole or arselle)
Italian clams are tiny — much the same size as cockles — and are sweet and tender. They should be scrubbed and soaked (see page 163) and be cooked alive.

CEPHALOPODS
The Italians are particularly fond of this category of seafood. Squid (calamari) can be the length of a finger or up to 30cm (1 foot) long. Tender, small ones are best deep-fried; larger ones should be boiled or baked. Cuttlefish (seppie) can be treated like squid. In Venice, their ink is used to flavour risotto and to tint pasta. Octopuses (polipi) are large creatures so require lengthy cooking, though the baby ones can be fried or cooked into a risotto or pasta sauce.

Spider crab

CRAB (Granchio)
*Of all the types of crab found in
Mediterranean and Adriatic waters,
the spider crab (granseola) is the most
prized. The favourite Venetian way to
eat crab is to boil it, then remove and
shred the meat, combine it with lemon
juice, olive oil, salt and pepper, then
return to the shell for serving.*

Squid

Cooked langoustine

PRAWNS (Gamberi)
*Many types of prawns are valued for their
delicate meat. More of their briny flavour
remains intact if they are cooked unpeeled.
The dark intestinal vein must be removed
before eating; the underside vein, the nervous
system, is harmless. Langoustines (scampi) or
Dublin Bay prawns are a type of lobster. They
may be up to 30cm (1 foot) long and have
very sweet flesh. Treat them like a prawn or
lobster in cooking, according to size.*

Raw large prawns

MEAT

Although there is relatively little meat in the course of an Italian meal, a great variety of it is used, including game and domesticated meat. All parts of the animal that are good to eat are used. Pork is especially valued for fresh and cured sausages, and for speciality cured meats *(salumi)*, such as prosciutto.

OTHER RAW AND CURED MEATS

Capon, turkey, chicken, goose, pheasant, wild boar, hare, kid, rigatino (lean smoked pancetta), culatello and speck (smoked hams), sweet and hot fresh sausages, luganega (smoked pork sausage), salt pork.

GAME

Quail

Guinea fowl

GAME BIRDS

Guinea fowl and small game birds, such as quail, thrush, partridge, sparrow, pigeon, woodcock and snipe, are prized for their succulent, uniquely flavourful meat.

DUCK (Anatra)

There are two basic categories of duck: the large domesticated variety (shown here) and small wild birds, usually mallards. Look for young ducks, particularly for roasting, as they are much more tender.

RABBIT (Coniglio)

Domesticated rabbit has a mild flavour, similar to chicken, though it is more bony. Leaving the fur on until just before cooking keeps the flesh fresh and moist.

SALUMI (CURED MEATS)

MORTADELLA

A Bolognese speciality, mortadella is made from finely ground pork and is riddled with peppercorns and pistachios. It is encased in a skin to form a huge sausage, then cooked.

BRESAOLA

This salted, air-dried beef fillet dries out rapidly so should be eaten within 24 hours of slicing. It should be cut paper-thin and dressed with oil, lemon juice and pepper.

PANCETTA

Pancetta, *unsmoked bacon, is used in cooking. It is formed from the belly section of the pig, which is rolled with salt and spices, such as cloves, cinnamon and pepper. Unsmoked pancetta has a more subtle flavour than the smoked variety.*

Mortadella

Bresaola

Pancetta

MEAT CUTS

BEEF (Manzo)
Italian beef cuts are categorized as follows: "prime" cuts for quick grilling and sautéing, "choice" roasting cuts, and "select" cuts for long braising and stewing. Beef should be aged and nicely marbled with firm, white fat.

LAMB (Agnello)
For roasting, Italians prefer pale-fleshed, buttery, tender baby lamb (the Romans call it abbacchio), *or three-month-old, milk-fed lamb (*agnello di latte*). Older, red-fleshed lamb is typically stewed or braised.*

VEAL (Vitello)
This delicately flavoured, tender meat is highly prized in Italy. Veal calves are milk-fed and slaughtered from one month to one year of age while their flesh is still pale pink. Veal over six months, vitellone, *is a deeper red.*

PORK (Maiale)
Every part of this popular and versatile meat is eaten. For roasting, suckling pigs or prime cuts of older animals are used. Because of its natural sweetness, minced pork is often included in sauces and fillings.

VENISON (Cervo)
Venison and other meats from the roe-buck, fallow deer and chamois have a rich, gamy flavour. Young animals have more tender meat. Venison should be hung for a week and marinated before cooking.

OFFAL (Frattaglie)
Meat and fowl offal is cooked with great imagination. Kidneys, liver, brain, lungs, spleen, tongue, sweetbreads (thymus glands), tripe (stomach), and chicken gizzards, crests and wattles are all utilized.

COPPA (or Capocollo)
This cured pork product is made throughout Italy with various flavourings. The neck is boned, seasoned with salt, sugar, pepper, nutmeg or cloves, encased, then marinated in white wine. It is hung and aged for three months.

SALAMI
The three main types are fresh salami, including cotechino and zampone, dry-aged salami, which encompasses numerous local types such as Milano and soppressata, and cooked and preserved salami, such as mortadella. All are made of pork.

PROSCIUTTO
Prosciutto crudo, "raw ham", is a salted, air-dried, pork leg. The most renowned hams come from Parma and San Daniele. The best prosciutto crudo is fragrant, pale pink and tender to the bite. Prosciutto cotto, "cooked ham", comes in many varieties.

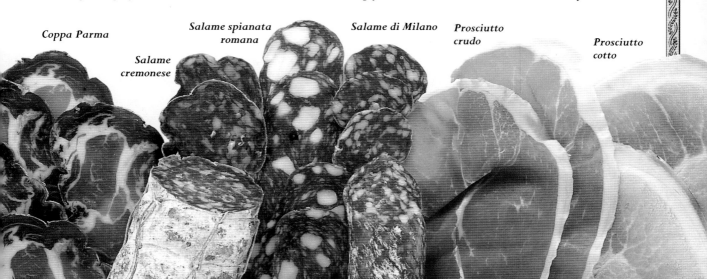

Coppa Parma

Salame cremonese

Salame spianata romana

Salame di Milano

Prosciutto crudo

Prosciutto cotto

CHEESES

The 450 cheeses produced in Italy are each a product of local geography, resources, history and tradition. Every region and province has its own cheeses which are made by hand by skilled cheese-makers whose craft has been passed down through the generations. Cheeses may be made from cow's, sheep's or goat's milk.

OTHER TYPICAL CHEESES

Fior di Sardegna, asiago, canestrato pugliese, robiola, montasio, murazzano, pecorino toscano, pressato, ragusano, casolet, monte veronese, silter, branzi.

FONTINA

The signature cow's milk cheese of Val d'Aosta, fontina is also eaten in neighbouring regions. It has a sweet, mild and nutty flavour and its excellent melting qualities make it suitable for fillings, toppings and sauces, such as the famous Piedmontese fonduta. Fontina is also a table cheese.

CACIOCAVALLO

This is a drawn-curd cheese from the south, like provolone. It is made from the milk of cows raised on a diet of wild grasses and plants, which gives the cheese a distinctive aroma and flavour.

Toma

Provolone

Fontina

Caciocavallo

TOMA

A flat round cheese usually made of cow's milk and produced in the Alpine region of Val d'Aosta. After the cheese is formed, it is covered with mountain grasses and left to ripen, which imbues it with a pleasant flavour and aroma.

PECORINO

This famous cheese is made from sheep's milk. There are young, soft tangy varieties suitable for use as table cheeses, and sharper aged, hard ones suitable for grating. Most pecorino exported abroad comes from Sardinia (pecorino sardo), Lazio (pecorino romano) and Tuscany.

PROVOLONE

A cow's milk cheese made all over Italy, provolone can be pear-shaped, spherical, oblong or pig-shaped, dolce (sweet) or piccante (sharp). It is a good melting cheese and table cheese.

Young pecorino

Aged pecorino

GORGONZOLA

This superb, fermented creamy cow's milk cheese, characterized by its blue veining and strong barnyard aroma, is a speciality of Lombardy. Young, runny Gorgonzola, dolce latte, is spread on bread, over hot polenta or made into a pasta sauce. Aged Gorgonzola is highly aromatic and pungent and is eaten as a table cheese.

Aged Gorgonzola

MOZZARELLA

A fresh, soft cheese made from buffalo milk (mozzarella di bufala), mozzarella can also be made from sheep's or cow's milk. It is meant to be eaten the same day as it is made; refrigerating arrests its flavour. It is the best melting cheese, suitable for topping southern-style baked dishes, and is sometimes smoked.

Markings of the basket in which it is left to drip dry

Ricotta

Mozzarella

RICOTTA

Ricotta *means "recooked", and is so named because it is made from whey released in the heating process of making other cheeses. It is a fresh, creamy cheese.* Ricotta salata *is lightly salted, solid but tender, and is grated or served as a table cheese. Ricotta forte is made from salted, hardened sheep's milk ricotta and is aged for one month.*

Scamorza

MASCARPONE

A thick, fresh, naturally sweet cream cheese, mascarpone is used in cooking and in baking, particularly in sauces and creams. It is also the basis of many uncooked desserts, such as tiramisù.

Mascarpone

SCAMORZA

This is a flask-shaped cow's milk cheese from the south with a fairly low fat content. Italians like to serve it grilled with ham and mushrooms.

Grana

GRANA OR GRANA PADANO

Young grana is an excellent table cheese, while mature grana is suitable for grating. It is a cow's milk cheese in the parmigiano family, but aged for less time and produced in larger quantities. Emilia-Romagna, Lombardy, Piedmont and the Veneto all produce this cheese.

Parmesan

TALEGGIO

A young, buttery cow's milk cheese from Bergamo in the mountains of Lombardy, taleggio can be eaten, with its distinctive orange crust, as a table cheese.

PARMIGIANO-REGGIANO

Parmigiano-reggiano *(Parmesan) has been made in Emilia-Romagna for 700 years. It is a cow's milk cheese that is aged for at least one year. It has a rich straw colour with an intense, complex flavour and moist, flaky texture. Only the authentic cheese has "parmigiano-reggiano" punched into the rind. This is an eating cheese as well as a grating/cooking cheese.*

BREADS, PASTA, GRAINS & PULSES

Grain and the products made from it have formed the bulk of the Mediterranean diet for 4,000 years. After the discovery of the "New World", beans, along with other vegetables, were adopted into the diet. Even now, these staple foods remain central to the cuisine.

OTHER STAPLE FOODS & BREADS
Farro (also called "spelt"; a type of wheat), barley, buckwheat, rye flour, fregula (large couscous), dried broad beans, peas, piadina, a flat griddle bread typical of Romagna.

GRAINS & BEANS

POLENTA
Fine cornmeal polenta and polenta taragna (buckwheat polenta) are essential staples, particularly in the northern region.

Carnaroli rice

Arborio rice

Vialone nano rice

RICE
Long-grain rice is used for boiling and in soups. Arborio, Vialone nano and Carnaroli rice are used for risotto because they are uniquely suited to slow cooking in a small quantity of liquid: the large core of the rice remains somewhat firm, while the exterior becomes creamy, absorbing all the flavours.

BORLOTTI BEANS
The colour of borlotti may vary from mottled red to brown or blue-grey. They are used fresh or dried, in baked dishes and soup.

CANNELLINI BEANS
These are the most common Italian beans. They have a creamy texture when cooked. Avoid the canned product.

LENTILS (Lenticchie)
Earthy brown lentils do not require pre-soaking. They are much used for soups, stews and baked dishes.

CHICK-PEAS (Ceci)
Dried, rehydrated chick-peas have a wonderful nutty flavour, far superior to the canned product.

BREADS

BREADS (Pane) AND FOCACCIA
Every Italian region has its own typical breads. They are made with refined wheat flour, wholemeal, semolina, cornmeal or rye, and may contain herbs, olives or cheese. Focacce, flat yeast breads, are eaten as antipasti or snacks.

Grissini sticks

Olive focaccia

Rye bread

Corn bread

Country loaf

PASTA

DRIED PASTA

There are 350 varieties of factory-made pasta produced from durum wheat semolina flour and water. The myriad shapes have been invented not only in the creative spirit, but also for particular uses.

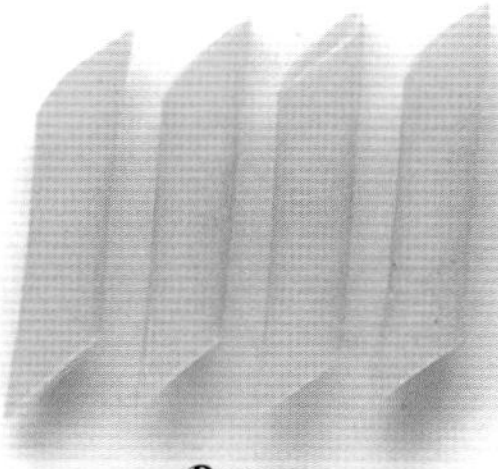

Penne

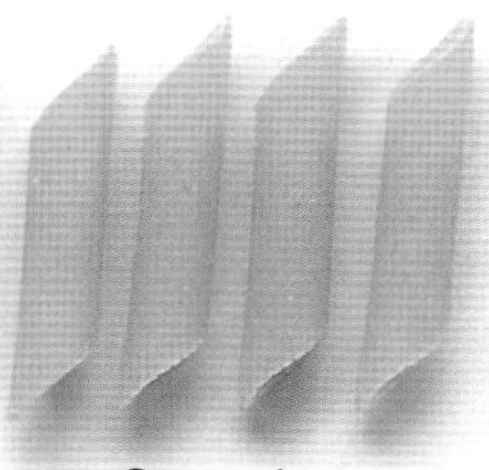

Penne rigate

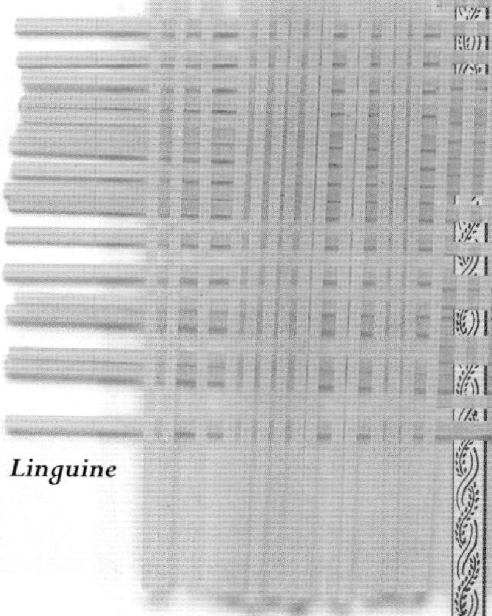

Linguine

Orecchiette

Farfalle

Conchiglie

Spaghetti

Orzo

Stelline

Anellini

DRIED PASTA FOR SOUP

Tiny pastina, such as orzo, come in many shapes. Slightly larger shapes, such as ditali, are meant for thicker soups. Capelli d'angelo ("angel's hair") pasta is used in clear broth.

FRESH PASTA

Fresh pasta means pasta that is made at home, not found in the refrigerator section of the supermarket. It is made with refined wheat flour and eggs, and is sometimes tinted and flavoured with spinach, tomato, beetroot or cocoa powder. It may also be made with buckwheat or semolina. It is used for all types of stuffed pasta shapes.

Fresh cappelletti

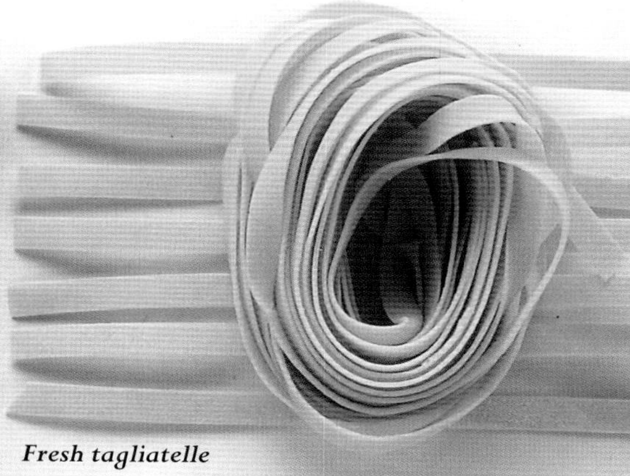

Fresh tagliatelle

SWEET BREADS

Sweet yeast breads studded with fruit, nuts and spices are an ancient tradition. The dough is usually enriched with eggs, butter or oil and may be flavoured with flower waters. Celebration breads contain fillings, chocolate or sweet wine.

Panettone

Pandoro flavoured with Marsala

Sweet bread rolls

AROMATICS

A wide variety of herbs and spices is used in Italian cooking, but usually in small quantities, adroitly matched to bring out, not mask, the main ingredients. Most herbs are best used fresh when their flavours and scents are at their peak.

OTHER AROMATICS

Mustard, mace, coriander, cumin, sesame seeds, chives, myrtle leaves (Sardinia), celery leaves, tarragon (Siena), horseradish.

Marjoram

BASIL (Basilico)

An annual tropical herb related to mint, basil is highly aromatic with a cloying, sweet flavour. There are many varieties, some more pungent than others. Because of its intensity, it should not be used indiscriminately. Avoid dried basil.

Basil

FENNEL

The fennel plant, which flourishes as a wild and domestic plant in hot climates, has a sweet aroma and a flavour reminiscent of liquorice. It provides seeds, bulb and feathery leaves.

Add young leaves to soups, salads and fish dishes

OREGANO (Origano)

The flavour and aroma of oregano are more bitter than those of marjoram. Its aggressive flavour limits its use in the kitchen, though it is found in certain southern dishes, such as pizza, and in zesty pasta sauces.

Both fresh and dried oregano work well

MARJORAM (Maggiorana)

Marjoram has a similar taste to oregano, but is more complex and mellow in comparison. This herb is very versatile and successful in both its fresh and dried forms.

Pepper is best used freshly ground from the whole corns

Look for plump, firm cloves

SEA SALT (Sale)

Sea salt is a natural product made by evaporating sea water. It has a concentrated, intense flavour. Coarse salt is also natural.

PEPPER (Pepe)

Black pepper is the dried, mature unhusked berry. White pepper is the inner centre of ripe pepper berries and has less of a bite.

GARLIC (Aglio)

A member of the onion family, garlic has extraordinary health-giving attributes. It is much used in southern Italian cooking. It should never be used in its bitter dried or powdered form. Avoid garlic that has begun to sprout.

JUNIPER (Ginepro)

The berries from an evergreen, juniper has a wild, musky scent and flavour, ideal for game. It should be crushed before use.

CHILLI PEPPER (Peperoncino)

Whole or crushed chillies are widely used either fresh or dried, particularly in the south, to give fire to sauces and pickles.

PARSLEY (Prezzemolo)
With its mild, agreeable grassy flavour, parsley is a ubiquitous Italian culinary herb. It is the foundation of many sauces and appears in a wide range of dishes. Use only the flavoursome flat-leaf variety for cooking. The curly-leaved variety can be used for garnishing.

Choose flat-leaf fresh parsley

SAGE (Salvia)
The musty, highly aromatic flavour of sage is well-matched with white meats such as pork or veal. Sage is also used to flavour butter as a dressing for gnocchi or stuffed pasta. Fresh sage leaves coated with batter and fried in olive oil make a delicious antipasto.

BAY (Alloro)
Bay leaves should be used sparingly. One dried leaf is enough to lend a hint of its powerful aroma to a soup or stew. Bay should always be kept whole and removed after cooking. It is almost always dried, but can be used fresh.

Cinnamon sticks

MINT (Menta)
There are numerous varieties of mint used fresh in Italian cooking, including wild mint (mentucia) and catmint. Mint is added judiciously to stuffings, vegetable dishes, sauces, salads and some fowl dishes.

ROSEMARY (Rosmarino)
Often found wild, rosemary is one of the most fragrant herbs. Its refreshing, pungent, pine-like aroma is retained even when dried. It is eminently suitable for flavouring roasted meats, particularly pork, lamb and veal, but it also gives a zing to tomato sauces and stewed dishes.

Ground cinnamon

CINNAMON (Canella)
This spice comes from the dried inner bark of an evergreen tree from the laurel family. Excepting in Sicily, it is used primarily for desserts, in stick or powdered form.

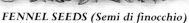

SAFFRON (Zafferano)
Fiery-coloured saffron comes from the stigmas of crocuses. As there are only three stigmas in each bloom, it is rare and costly.

CLOVES (Chiodi di garofano)
These nail-shaped cloves are the dried flower buds of an evergreen tree related to myrtle. They are used in baking and cooking.

NUTMEG (Noce moscata)
A small amount of this bitter, highly aromatic spice goes a long way so it should be used conservatively. To experience its flavour fully, grate it just before using.

FENNEL SEEDS (Semi di finocchio)
Sharp, aniseed-tasting fennel seeds are especially suited to pork. They are also used on roasts, in desserts and in sausages.

ANISE SEEDS (Anice)
Anise has a similar flavour to fennel, but is sweeter with less bite. It is typically found in sweet breads, biscotti and desserts.

THE PANTRY

Whether you are preparing a leisurely lunch or putting something together for a large family gathering or unexpected visitors, the foundation of the classic Italian kitchen is a well-stocked pantry that always contains high-quality, genuine products.

The best tuna meat taken from the belly of the fish

CANNED TUNA IN OLIVE OIL

Italian canned tuna, characterized by its excellent sweet flavour and rosy colour, is packed in olive oil, which imparts its fruity flavour to the meat.

OLIVES

There are many olive varieties, and they are usually named by their place of origin. All are green to begin with; the more they mature, the darker they become. Dry-cured olives have a wrinkled appearance and concentrated flavour.

Black Gaeta olives

ANCHOVIES IN OIL

Anchovies are preserved in olive oil or salt. The latter should be rinsed before use. They have a wide variety of uses, including as a flavouring for sauces and as a topping for pizza and focaccia.

DRIED PORCINI

These are the most tasty and sought-after wild mushrooms. In their dried form, the bosky, intense flavour is even more concentrated. Select fleshy, pale pieces, not dark, brittle fragments. Soak them in warm water for 30 minutes, then rinse and squeeze dry before use. The flavourful soaking liquid should be strained and used.

PINE NUTS (Pinoli)

The kernels of stone pine cones, these nuts are used in cooking and baking. They turn rancid quickly so should be refrigerated or frozen after purchase.

Salted capers

Olives marinated with herbs and olive oil

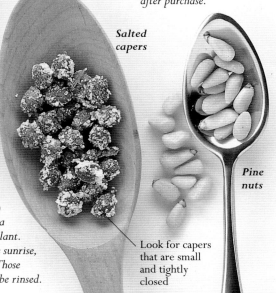

CAPERS (Capperi)

These are the buds of a wild Mediterranean plant. They are picked before sunrise, and pickled or salted. Those preserved in salt must be rinsed.

Look for capers that are small and tightly closed

Pine nuts

Dry-cured olives

Chianti vinegar

White wine vinegar

Olio santo

Extra-virgin olive oil

Balsamic vinegar

WINE (Vino)

Wine is a critical ingredient in many Italian dishes. Use the same good-quality red or white wine, or fortified wine such as vermouth, as you would for drinking. This sacred product is as much a part of the Italian meal as the food itself. It is the first thing to arrive, to calm the body, lift the spirit, arouse the appetite and aid digestion.

VINEGAR (Aceto)

The most flavourful vinegars are made from fermented wine, and are aged. The percentage of acidity — from 5% to 7% — indicates tartness. Balsamic vinegar, a product of Modena, is made from the boiled-down must of white grapes, and is aged for at least ten years in a series of casks made of aromatic woods. It has a sweet, mellow, rich flavour.

OLIVE OIL (Olio d'oliva)

Highly aromatic, fruity, cold-pressed extra-virgin olive oil, derived from the first pressing, is essential. Its colour varies from deep gold to grass green, and its flavour and aroma are affected by the olive variety, soil type and climate. It is best used young. Standard olive oil is lower grade, good for deep-frying. Olio santo is seasoned with hot red chillies.

PISTACHIOS (Pistacchi)

Pistachios are used in stuffings and in baking, most notably in sweet yeast breads. They should be natural (not red-dyed) and unsalted. Remove the shells and rub off the reddish membrane.

Canned peeled plum tomatoes

Sun-dried tomatoes

Tomato purée

TOMATO PRODUCTS

Whole canned tomatoes should not be too firm and there should be a high proportion of tomatoes to liquid (or purée). Concentrated tomato purée should be used judiciously as a thickener or for a touch of flavour or colour. Sun-dried tomatoes may be packed in salt, formed into blocks, stored dry, or preserved in olive oil. Those not packed in oil should be rehydrated by soaking in warm water for 15–30 minutes, then strained, squeezed dry and chopped. They are too leathery to eat whole, but can be added to sauces, stews and stuffings.

SWEET FLAVOURINGS & FRUIT

In contrast to the cooking traditions of many Arab and Asian countries, in Italian cooking sweet and savoury ingredients are kept apart, with sweet flavours generally reserved for the dessert course. Certain fruit and ingredients, such as lemon or fortified wine, span both tastes as they are either somewhat neutral or versatile.

OTHER SWEET FLAVOURINGS & FRUIT

Nectarines, raspberries, bilberries, cherries, plums, apples, melons, persimmons, loquats, pomegranates, quince, Vin Santo, brandy, rum, anisette, orange-flower water.

COFFEE (Caffè)
Italian coffee, espresso, is very dark, rich and strongly flavoured. In addition to its various beverage forms, it is used as an aromatic flavouring for granita *and* gelato *(ices and ice-creams), and in popular desserts such as* tiramisù.

CITRUS FRUIT
All fruit are consumed voraciously in Italy, no doubt because of their remarkable quality and flavour, but oranges, including blood and bitter varieties, tangerines, limes, lemons, citrons and grapefruit are used as much in cooking as for table fruit. The zest and juice are indispensable in many savoury dishes, breads, tarts and marmalades. They are left to mature on the trees, and the fragrant zest is never treated or waxed.

Blood orange

MARSALA
A sweet, fortified wine from Sicily, Marsala adds a distinctive, mellow flavour and depth to chicken and veal dishes. It is also used in desserts.

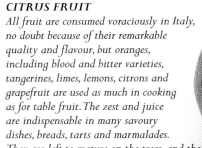

PEACHES (Pesche)
Italy shares a place with America for the highest peach production in the world, but Italian peaches are especially sweet and luscious. There are white and red varieties and they are eaten fresh, stuffed and baked, in pies, made into preserves or dried. They have a higher mineral and vitamin content than many other fruit.

APRICOTS (Albicocche)
The Arabs brought the apricot to the Mediterranean, where it still flourishes. It is a good source of copper and potassium and is rich in vitamin A when ripe. Select only fully mature, unblemished fruit.

HONEY (Miele)
Italian honeys are fragrant and assertive, made by bees feeding on wild herbs and flowers. Look for Tuscan chestnut honey, Alpine wild flower honey and orange blossom honey from Sicily.

CACTUS FRUIT (Fichi d'India)
These fruit, also called prickly pears in Italy, are prevalent wherever the climate is torrid, especially in Sicily and Sardinia where they grow wild. They must be fully ripe to eat. Cut the skin lengthways and pull it away from the succulent pulp. The seeds may be eaten or discarded.

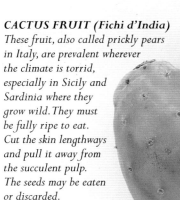

AMARETTI

These are delightful crisp little biscuits made from bitter almonds, egg whites and sugar. They are made for eating as they are, but are also widely used in desserts and for fruit stuffings, such as Piedmontese stuffed peaches.

CHOCOLATE (Cioccolata)

Dark chocolate, high in cocoa solids, is widely used, primarily for desserts. There are a few savoury dishes in which it appears in its unsweetened state, including Sicilian caponata and chocolate pasta, a legacy from the Renaissance kitchen.

GRAPES (Uva)

Different varieties of grapes are grown for wine and for the table, though all wine grapes are suitable for eating. Among the best table varieties are the white (green) and red muscatel, and miniature purple grapes called uva fragola. I have memories of walking down country lanes in Sardinia, Tuscany and Lazio and reaching up to pick grapes from the wild vines.

Unwaxed lemon

CANDIED FRUIT AND FLOWERS

All manner of fruit, even squash, is candied for use as a decoration on desserts and confections. This art is especially practised by the Sicilians. Parma and Venice are famous for their candied violet petals, and Liguria for its candied rose petals.

Candied fruit and peel

Crystallized violets

DRIED FRUIT

Fruit is often dried for winter use at the end of the harvest. Typical are raisins, sultanas, prunes and figs, which may be stuffed with chocolate, candied peel, fennel and almonds to make a wonderful sweetmeat.

Dates

Raisins

FIGS (Fichi)

The most common fig varieties are the black (purple) fig and the white (green) fig. These sugary-sweet fruit are delightful peeled and eaten as they are. Their natural sweetness is intensified when they are dried.

STRAWBERRIES (Fragoli)

Strawberries are eaten only in season, perhaps with a drop of balsamic vinegar or with sweet wine or mascarpone. Look for the tiny wild Italian species.

NUTS

All kinds of nuts, particularly hazelnuts, almonds, chestnuts and walnuts, are used in cooking, baking and in making liqueurs. Chestnuts must be cooked; other nuts can be toasted to bring out their flavours.

Almonds

Chestnuts

PEARS (Pere)

Pears have existed in Italy since Roman times, though their varieties have increased manifold since then. They are an ingredient of mostarda di Cremona, a condiment of candied fruit and mustard.

VANILLA (Vaniglia)

Available in extract or the more aromatic pod form, vanilla is used to flavour confections, custards and creams.

Vanilla pods

CLASSIC DISHES

This selection of dishes is designed to give you an impression of the flavours of classic Italian food. Selecting the recipes was not an easy task; there are so many recipes to choose from, unusual and familiar. My decision was to draw from every part of the geographical boot, north, south, central, east and west, to represent the taste of the sea, of the forests, of the mountains and the interior, and in so doing, to give a preview of Italy's enormously rich culinary tradition.

**All the dishes serve 4,
unless otherwise indicated.**

ANTIPASTI

In Italy, *antipasti* are not just perfunctory beginnings to dinner; rather, they can be among the most creative dishes in the Italian kitchen. Their variety is endless, the assortment delectable. Many antipasti are excellent served as main dishes, or as side dishes (*contorni*) or snacks.

CIPOLLINE IN AGRODOLCE

Sweet and sour onions

Italians are fond of pickling vegetables for antipasti. Unlike many pickles, these onions do not leave one's mouth puckered as the vinegar is tempered with sugar. They are excellent with cured meats, such as prosciutto, and the addition of cloves gives them a festive flavour, making them particularly suitable for serving with ham, duck, goose or turkey.

See page 63 for recipe.

ZUPPA DI MITILI ALLA PUGLIESE

Mussels in wine, Apulian style

This is not so much a soup as an appetite arouser. It is traditionally served over slices of bread that soak up the garlicky broth.

See page 65 for recipe.

POLPETTINE ALL' UMBRA

Little meatballs, Umbrian style

These savoury little delicacies can be sautéed, or cooked in a wine or tomato sauce or broth.

See page 67 for recipe.

FUNGHI FRITTI ALLA SARDA

Crispy fried mushrooms, Sardinian style

In Sardinia, wild mushrooms called cisti are prized for their intensely meaty flavour. This starkly simple dish was first made for me by my Sardinian aunt and uncle, and uses wild mushrooms to excellent effect. The subtly crunchy semolina coating hides a moist interior. They are also good with roasted meats.

See page 63 for recipe.

FRITTATA AGLI ASPARAGI

Asparagus and mushroom frittata

Frittatas are made with a wide variety of fillings, such as spring vegetables or even leftover sauced pasta. This version has a filling of asparagus and mushrooms, which is a particularly harmonious combination. It can be made on the stove in a frying pan, or it can be baked, whereupon it becomes a tortino.

See page 66 for recipe.

PEPERONI RIPIENI

Peppers stuffed with rice and Gorgonzola

Peppers are ideal for stuffing because their shape makes them a perfect receptacle. Fillings can be bread- or rice-based, and often incorporate ham, sausages, cheese and mushrooms. Here, the pungent but still delicate flavour of Gorgonzola cheese is set off by the natural sweetness of the peppers.

See page 64 for recipe.

MINESTRONE INVERNALE

Winter minestrone

Winter *minestroni* typically contain fewer vegetables than the summer versions. Only water (no stock) is used in making this hearty soup, and it is often ladled steaming hot over slices of stale bread that have been rubbed with garlic, toasted and then drizzled with fruity olive oil from the winter oil pressing. The favourite way of eating a minestrone such as this is to make it up to three days in advance, then reheat it with slices of stale bread. This is sometimes called *ribollita*, "reboiled", though the real *ribollita* of Tuscany is made with red cabbage and saltless bread. Serves 6.

INGREDIENTS

75ml (2½fl oz) extra-virgin olive oil, plus extra for toast
1 large onion, chopped
2 large potatoes, peeled and finely diced
1 small savoy cabbage (cavolo verza), shredded
500g (1lb) courgettes, finely diced
2 celery stalks with leaves, chopped
175g (6oz) string beans, trimmed and cut into
2.5cm (1in) pieces
500g (1lb) winter squash (such as butternut,
hubbard or acorn), peeled and diced
500g (1lb) fresh or canned drained tomatoes, skinned,
deseeded and chopped
½ a cauliflower, cut into slices and broken up
250g (8oz) dried haricot beans, rehydrated and cooked (see
page 161), or 500g (1lb) canned beans, rinsed and drained
2 litres (3½ pints) bean cooking liquid (if used) or water
2 bay leaves
30g (1oz) chopped fresh rosemary, oregano and thyme, or
1 tsp each dried
1 tbsp salt and ½ tsp freshly ground black pepper
12 slices stale robust Italian or peasant bread
4 large cloves garlic, chopped into quarters

PREPARATION

1 Warm the oil in a large saucepan and add the onion and potato. Sauté over a medium heat, stirring occasionally, until the onion is soft and the potato leaves a starchy film on the base of the pan, about 8 minutes.

2 Add all the vegetables, the beans, cooking liquid or water, herbs, salt and pepper. Simmer over a medium-low heat, partially covered, until the cabbage is tender and the other vegetables cooked through, about 1½ hours. Check the seasoning.

3 Rub the bread on both sides with the garlic then toast it lightly. Drizzle each slice with plenty of olive oil and place two slices in each soup plate. Pour the hot soup over the bread and serve.

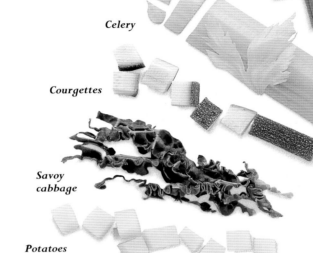

Celery

Courgettes

Savoy cabbage

Potatoes

Onion

Olive oil

Italian bread

Rosemary

Oregano

Bay
leaves

Thyme

Salt

Black
pepper

Garlic

Cauliflower

Beans and
liquid

Tomatoes

Winter squash

String beans

PIZZA AND FOCACCIA

Both pizza and focaccia have become standard dishes of the *cucina povera* (poor kitchen), being fast, economical and accessible. Their simplicity demands you use only the highest quality ingredients for the toppings.

PIZZETTA MARGHERITA

PIZZETTA MARGHERITA

Small pizza with a tomato, mozzarella and basil sauce

Little pizzas are excellent for snacks. One quantity of basic pizza dough (see page 170) will make eight of these little 15cm (6in) Neapolitan-style pizza bases. This classically simple topping uses sun-ripened tomatoes and aromatic fresh basil.

See page 68 for recipe.

PIZZA

Authentic Neapolitan pizza is baked in wood-fired brick ovens, giving the pizza dough a unique aroma. This method is obviously not practicable in home kitchens, but this recipe will produce an excellent crust in an ordinary home oven.

See page 68 for topping recipes.

PIZZA CON SCAROLA
Pizza with wilted escarole and olives

PIZZA CON RICOTTA
Pizza with ricotta and fennel seeds

PIZZA CON SALSICCIA
Pizza with sweet Italian sausage

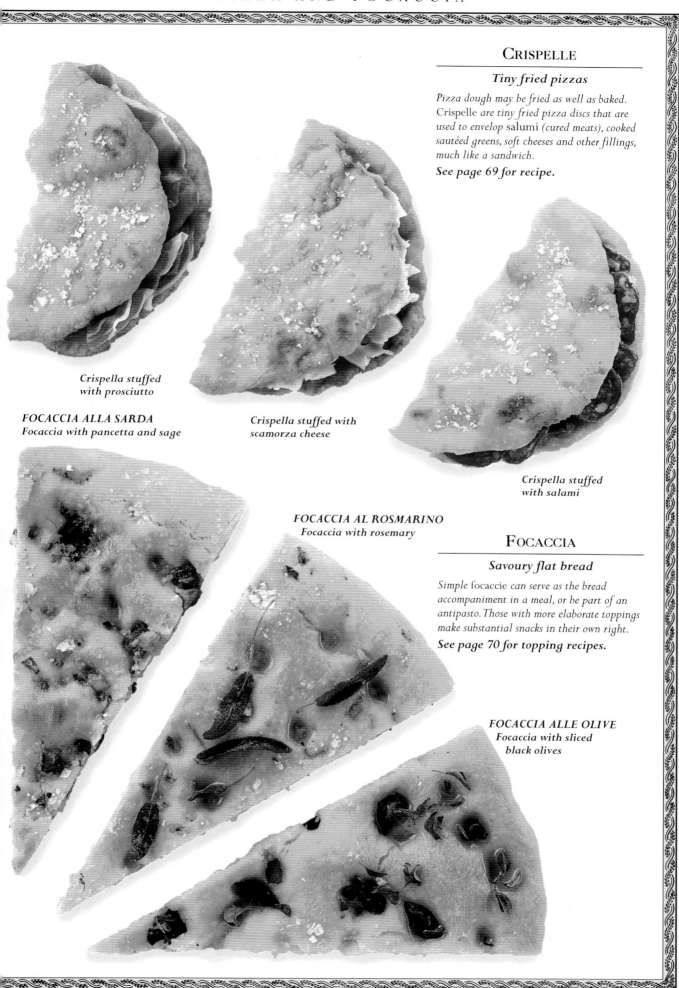

CRISPELLE

Tiny fried pizzas

Pizza dough may be fried as well as baked. Crispelle are tiny fried pizza discs that are used to envelop salumi *(cured meats), cooked sautéed greens, soft cheeses and other fillings, much like a sandwich.*

See page 69 for recipe.

Crispella stuffed with prosciutto

FOCACCIA ALLA SARDA
Focaccia with pancetta and sage

Crispella stuffed with scamorza cheese

Crispella stuffed with salami

FOCACCIA AL ROSMARINO
Focaccia with rosemary

FOCACCIA

Savoury flat bread

Simple focaccie *can serve as the bread accompaniment in a meal, or be part of an antipasto. Those with more elaborate toppings make substantial snacks in their own right.*

See page 70 for topping recipes.

FOCACCIA ALLE OLIVE
Focaccia with sliced black olives

LINGUINE ALLE VONGOLE

Linguine with clam sauce

This is one of the few Italian dishes that varies little from region to region or cook to cook. No doubt this is because the flavours of olive oil, clams, garlic, parsley and pepper are so adroitly matched that any other ingredient would simply be an imposition, although tomatoes may also be used, as here, to make the classic "red" clam sauce. Never add grated cheese to seafood sauces for pasta. Serves 4–6.

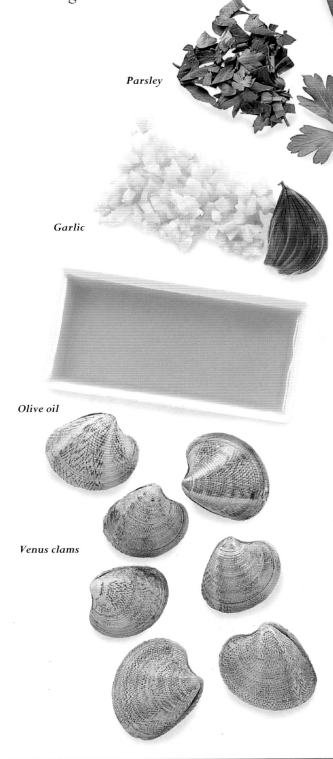

Parsley

Garlic

Olive oil

Venus clams

INGREDIENTS

2kg (4lb) small live venus clams or larger clams,
or cockles, soaked for at least 3 hours (see page 163)
125ml (4fl oz) extra-virgin olive oil
6 cloves garlic, finely chopped
6 tbsp chopped fresh flat-leaf parsley
375g (12oz) fresh or canned drained tomatoes, skinned,
deseeded and chopped
125ml (4fl oz) dry white wine
salt and freshly ground black pepper, to taste
500g (1lb) thin linguine or spaghetti

PREPARATION

1 Scrub the soaked clams with a stiff brush and rinse to remove any traces of grit (see page 163).
2 Combine the oil, garlic and half the parsley in a wide, deep frying pan large enough to hold the clams later. Turn the heat to medium-low and sauté gently until the garlic is soft but not coloured.
3 Add the tomatoes to the pan. Simmer over a medium-low heat, uncovered, until it forms a fairly thick sauce, about 10 minutes.
4 Pour in the wine and continue to sauté until the alcohol is evaporated, about 3 minutes.
5 Add ½ teaspoon of salt and the clams and cover immediately. Increase the heat to medium and leave the lid on until the clams open, 4–10 minutes, depending on the variety of clams used. Discard any unopened clams or empty shells. Stir in plenty of black pepper. The sauce will be very brothy and thin, but full of flavour.
6 Meanwhile, bring 5 litres (8 pints) of water to the boil. Add the linguine and 1½ tablespoons of salt and stir at once. Cook over a high heat, stirring occasionally with a wooden or plastic fork, until the pasta is almost *al dente*, about 7 minutes.
7 Drain the pasta and add it to the pan with the clam sauce. Return the pan to the heat and toss the pasta and the clam sauce together; some of the sauce will be absorbed by the pasta, but plenty will remain to keep the linguine very moist. Serve immediately, sprinkled with the remaining parsley.

Tomatoes

White wine

Salt

Black pepper

Linguine

RISOTTO ALLE VERDURE

Vegetable risotto

Here is a simple risotto that can be made year-round. Dried porcini or fresh wild mushrooms add a real boost of flavour, but cultivated mushrooms work well too. This dish should have a creamy, not mushy, consistency, and should be served with plenty of extra Parmesan cheese.

INGREDIENTS

15g (½oz) dried porcini mushrooms, or 125g (4oz) fresh wild mushrooms or cultivated mushrooms
1 litre (1¾ pints) Chicken Broth (see page 73) or good vegetable stock
45g (1½oz) unsalted butter
3 tbsp extra-virgin olive oil
2 large cloves garlic, finely chopped
1 onion, chopped
1 large celery stalk with leaves, chopped
1 small red or yellow pepper, or a combination, cored, deseeded and chopped
425g (14oz) Arborio rice
125ml (4fl oz) dry white wine
250g (8oz) tomatoes, skinned, deseeded, chopped and drained, or 90g (3oz) sun-dried tomatoes, chopped
salt, to taste
¼ tsp saffron strands, or 1 sachet (130mg) saffron powder
20g (¾oz) freshly grated Parmesan, plus extra to serve

PREPARATION

1 If using dried mushrooms, soak them in hot water for 30–40 minutes. Lift them out of the liquid (which can be used in another dish), rinse well then chop coarsely. Alternatively, clean and trim the fresh mushrooms, chop and set aside.
2 Warm the broth in a saucepan over a low heat.
3 Meanwhile, heat the butter and oil in a large frying pan. Add the garlic, onion, celery with leaves, pepper and chopped mushrooms. Sauté gently until softened but not browned. Transfer half the vegetable mixture to a plate and set aside.
4 Stir the rice into the remaining vegetable mixture in the pan. Sauté for 5 minutes, stirring constantly to make sure the grains are well coated.
5 Pour in the wine, and when it has been absorbed, stir in the tomatoes. Season, then add the saffron (if using strands, first crumble them into a little stock).
6 Add the hot broth to the rice a ladleful at a time, waiting until each addition is absorbed, and stirring constantly. After 20–25 minutes all the broth should be absorbed and the rice should be tender.
7 Remove the pan from the heat, check for salt then stir in the reserved vegetables and Parmesan. Serve immediately, offering additional cheese.

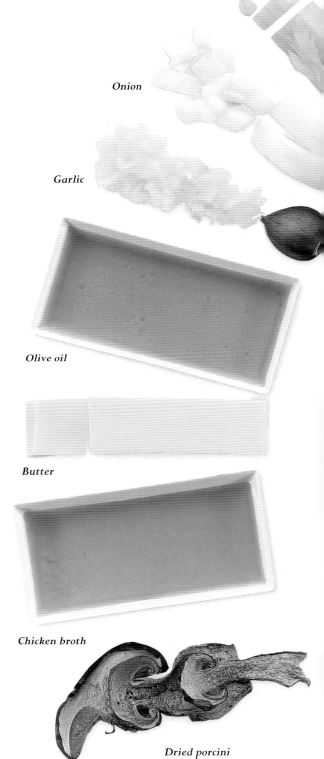

Onion

Garlic

Olive oil

Butter

Chicken broth

Dried porcini

Peppers

Arborio
rice

White wine

Tomatoes

Salt

Saffron

Parmesan

Celery
with leaves

PESCE LESSO CON DUE SALSE

Boiled fish with two sauces

The Italians often use a whole fish for this classically simple dish, which makes a very beautiful and dramatic presentation served with vibrant red and green sauces. Any fish, whole or filleted, can be cooked in this manner, although striped bass or salmon, whose flesh is more compact than sole and other such delicate fish, are better choices. White-fleshed fish is excellent with both a piquant Salsa Verde and a Salsetta Rossa Cruda made of sweet tomatoes, but the tomato sauce should not be served with salmon. Serves 6.

INGREDIENTS

1 tsp black peppercorns
1 large carrot, scraped
1 celery stalk with leaves
1 onion, quartered
1 clove garlic, unpeeled
3–4 sprigs fresh flat-leaf parsley
250ml (8fl oz) dry white wine
1 tbsp wine vinegar
1½ tbsp coarse salt
1 whole striped sea bass, approximately 2kg (4lb), gutted and scaled, or 2 x 375g (12oz) fillets, skin attached
extra-virgin olive oil to brush fish
escarole or curly endive, to serve
Salsa Verde and Salsetta Rossa Cruda
(see page 139), to serve

PREPARATION

1 Make the broth to poach the fish. Take a fish kettle or pan large enough to accommodate the fish without crowding and pour in 2 litres (3½ pints) of water if using a whole fish, 1.5 litres (2½ pints) if using fillets. Add the peppercorns, carrot, celery, onion, garlic, parsley, wine and vinegar. Bring the mixture to the boil then simmer over a medium heat for 15 minutes.

2 Season the broth with salt then lower in the fish, placing fillets skin-side down. Poach at a gentle simmer until the flesh is opaque, about 10 minutes per 2.5cm (1in), less 1 minute, measuring at the thickest part of the fish, or 9–10 minutes for fillets.

3 Using two fish slices, transfer the fish to a platter and neatly remove its skin while still warm. Leave the head and tail intact if using a whole fish. Brush with olive oil to keep the flesh moist and imbue it with extra flavour.

4 Garnish the platter with escarole leaves. Spoon half of each sauce over half of the fish and pass the remainder at the table. Serve warm or at room temperature (the fish can be kept covered with clingfilm at room temperature for up to 4 hours).

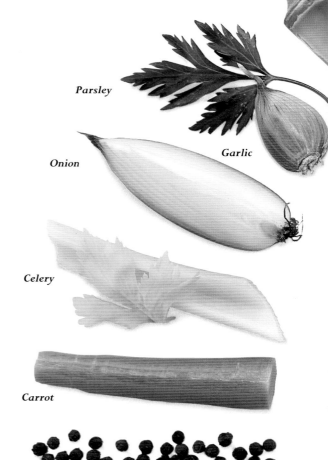

Parsley

Garlic

Onion

Celery

Carrot

Peppercorns

Sea bass

White wine

White wine
vinegar

Salt

Extra-virgin
olive oil

Escarole

Salsetta
Rossa Cruda

Salsa Verde

Gallinelle e Polenta

Poussin fricassee with polenta

Typical of the way game birds are cooked in Italy, this traditional country dish is also wonderful made with poussin. Its flavours evoke the northern woodlands with the earthy presence of wild mushrooms and the pungent scent of rosemary. Loose polenta is a perfect match for the stew. Serves 6.

INGREDIENTS

30g (1oz) dried porcini mushrooms
175g (6oz) fresh mushrooms (preferably wild)
3 poussins, each weighing 625g (1¼lb), quartered
45g (1½oz) unsalted butter
3 tbsp olive oil
¾ tsp salt, or to taste
freshly ground black pepper, to taste
1 tsp chopped fresh rosemary, or ½ tsp dried rosemary
175ml (6fl oz) dry white wine
125g (4oz) fresh or canned drained tomatoes,
skinned, deseeded and chopped
1 quantity Polenta (see page 169)
2 tsp plain flour, optional

PREPARATION

1 Soak the dried mushrooms in 175ml (6fl oz) of warm water for 30–40 minutes. Meanwhile slice the fresh mushrooms and set aside.
2 Drain the dried mushrooms, then rinse and chop them coarsely. Strain the liquid through a sieve lined with kitchen paper, and reserve it.
3 Heat the butter and oil in a large, deep pan, add the poussins and sauté until well browned all over.
4 Stir in the salt, pepper, rosemary and wine. Bring the mixture to the boil and cook over a medium heat for 5 minutes, to allow the alcohol to evaporate.
5 Add the dried and fresh mushrooms, the reserved soaking liquid and the tomatoes to the pan. Cook over a low heat, uncovered, for 30 minutes, turning the poussins occasionally.
6 Prepare the loose polenta (see page 169).
7 When the poussins are ready, the sauce will be quite thin. If a thicker sauce is desired, transfer the poussins and mushrooms to a warm platter and set aside. Mix 2–3 tablespoons of the sauce into the flour to make a smooth paste, stir this back into the pan and cook gently until a smooth sauce is formed. Return the poussins and mushrooms to the pan and cook for 2–3 minutes.
8 Spread the cooked polenta over a large, warm platter, make a well in the centre and spoon in the poussins and sauce. Pour any extra sauce into a jug and serve separately at the table.

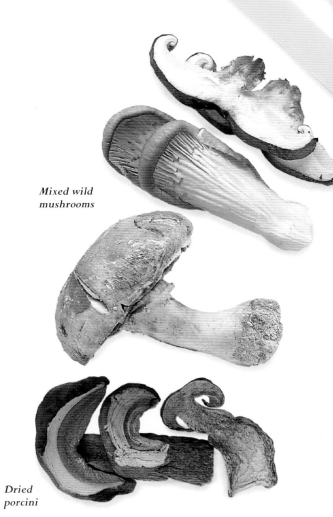

Mixed wild mushrooms

Dried porcini

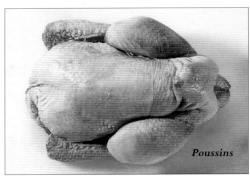

Poussins

Butter

Olive
oil

Salt

*Black
pepper*

Rosemary

White wine

Tomatoes

Polenta

OSSOBUCO ALLA MILANESE

Braised veal shins, Milanese style

This is one of the most delicate of meat dishes. It is served with *gremolata*, a mixture of garlic, herbs and lemon zest. To ensure tenderness, the veal pieces should be covered by the liquid in which they braise. The marrow, which is scooped out and eaten, is considered a great delicacy. Serve with Risotto alla Milanese (see page 92) or Purè di Patate (see page 129).

INGREDIENTS

4 tbsp olive oil
30g (1oz) unsalted butter
1 small onion, finely chopped
1 large clove garlic, bruised
1 small carrot, finely chopped
1 celery stalk with leaves, finely chopped
4 meaty veal hind shin bones, sawn into 3.5–5cm
(1½–2in) lengths and tied (see page 164)
30g (1oz) flour for dredging
salt and freshly ground white or black pepper, to taste
125ml (4fl oz) dry white wine
125g (4oz) fresh or canned drained tomatoes,
skinned, deseeded and finely chopped
1 tbsp chopped fresh flat-leaf parsley
½ tsp chopped fresh thyme, or ¼ tsp dried thyme
1 bay leaf
5cm (2in) strip lemon zest
250ml (8fl oz) Meat Broth (see page 72), plus extra

Gremolata
1 tbsp finely chopped lemon zest
1 small clove garlic, finely chopped
2 tbsp chopped fresh flat-leaf parsley
½ tsp chopped fresh thyme, or ¼ tsp dried thyme

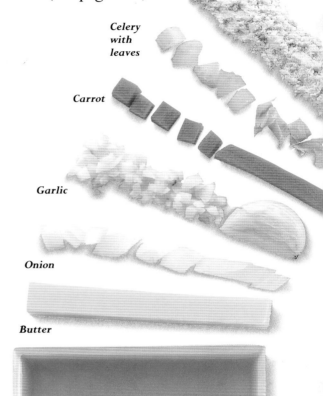

Celery with leaves

Carrot

Garlic

Onion

Butter

Olive oil

PREPARATION

1 Preheat the oven to 180°C/350°F/gas 4.
2 Heat half the oil with the butter in a casserole. Add the onion, garlic, carrot and celery and sauté gently until softened, about 10 minutes.
3 Warm the remaining oil in a wide heavy frying pan over a medium heat. Dredge the veal pieces in flour, place in the sizzling oil in a single layer and brown for 15–20 minutes. Season with ½ teaspoon of salt and plenty of pepper then place on top of the vegetables in the casserole.
4 Drain any oil from the pan and pour in the wine. Simmer for 3 minutes until the alcohol evaporates. Add the tomatoes, herbs, lemon zest and broth.
5 When the sauce is simmering, pour it into the casserole and bring to the boil. Transfer to the oven and cook, covered, for about 1¾ hours. Turn the meat regularly and add more broth if necessary.

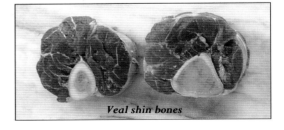

Veal shin bones

6 Transfer the veal, which should be meltingly tender but still on the bone, to a warm platter. Discard the zest and check the sauce's seasoning.
7 Combine all the ingredients for the gremolata, stir the mixture into the casserole sauce, warm it through then spoon it over the veal.

Black
pepper

Salt

Flour

White wine

Tomatoes

Parsley

Thyme

Bay leaf

Lemon zest

Meat broth

VEGETABLE DISHES

There is a universal Italian approach common to all regional styles. Ingredients should be exquisitely fresh and cooked in such a way as to preserve their natural flavours. Vegetable dishes in particular illustrate this ideal.

CONDIGGION

Summer vegetable salad

On the Italian table, foods are consumed when they are in season. Consequently, salads of fresh tomatoes and herbs are strictly summer fare. This is such a salad, made when tomatoes are in their luscious summer glory. The peppers are usually used raw, but I prefer to roast them first.

See page 133 for recipe.

PATATE AL FORNO

Scalloped potatoes baked in milk

Potatoes, which are essentially bland, are given a great boost by the rich, complex flavours of Parmesan cheese. This is a family recipe that never fails to delight.

See page 128 for recipe.

FAGIOLINI AL POMODORO

Green beans with tomato and garlic

Here is a dish that is as good — or better — at room temperature as it is hot. The beans should be young, buttery and tender.

See page 129 for recipe.

FRIARELLI

Sautéed escarole with beans and ham

This dish of sautéed escarole with creamy cannellini beans and pancetta is the Campanian variation of a popular hearty northern Italian dish.

See page 130 for recipe.

ASPARAGI ALLA PARMIGIANA

Asparagus, Parma style

The glorious cheese of Parma is well matched with the unique flavours and buttery textures of cooked asparagus in this traditional recipe. Be sure to start with perfectly fresh, crisp asparagus and genuine parmigiano-reggiano cheese.

See page 131 for recipe.

FINOCCHI GRATINATI

Baked fennel

Fresh fennel is a very popular vegetable in Italy and is superb eaten cooked or raw. This dish is a splendid accompaniment to pork, fowl and game dishes.

See page 130 for recipe.

TIRAMISÙ

Chocolate and mascarpone "pick me up"

There are many Italian recipes that transform leftover cake or biscuits, alcohol and a cream filling into a pudding-like dessert. *Tiramisù*, literally "pick me up", is probably the most popular of these, having caught on in restaurant circuits in and outside Italy. It is by its very nature an improvisational dessert and has many interpretations. However, to my mind, tiramisù is not tiramisù without the liqueur, or without the Italian cream cheese, mascarpone. I prefer orange liqueur for soaking the cake, but others, such as amaretto, can be substituted. Serves 12.

INGREDIENTS

500ml (16fl oz) strong espresso coffee, cooled
125ml (4fl oz) dark rum
375g (12oz) savoiardi biscuits, or stale sponge cake, cut into strips
6 eggs, separated
125g (4oz) granulated or caster sugar
1kg (2lb) mascarpone
250ml (8fl oz) orange or almond liqueur
125g (4oz) bitter chocolate, chopped
3 tbsp unsweetened cocoa powder

PREPARATION

1 Take a large oval or rectangular serving dish, 7–10cm (3–4in) deep, that will accommodate half the biscuits or sponge cake in a single layer. Pour the coffee and rum into a shallow bowl and dip half of the biscuits or cake in the coffee-rum mixture, soaking both sides. Take care not to let them disintegrate (the firmer savoiardi biscuits will take a little longer to soak up enough liquid).
2 Cover the base of the dish with the soaked biscuits or cake. Set aside the coffee-rum mixture.
3 Place the egg yolks in a bowl and beat until pale yellow. Add all but 1 tablespoon of the sugar, the mascarpone and liqueur and beat until well blended.
4 In another bowl, whisk the egg whites until fluffy but not stiff. Add the remaining sugar and whisk until stiff but not dry (if egg whites are overbeaten, they will start to liquefy at the bottom of the bowl). Fold the whites into the egg-mascarpone mixture.
5 Pour half of the mascarpone mixture over the biscuit or cake layer. Top with the chopped chocolate. Soak the remaining biscuits or cake and place them on top of the chocolate.
6 Blend any leftover coffee-rum mixture with the remaining mascarpone mixture and spread it over the biscuits. Sprinkle the top with cocoa, cover and refrigerate for 8 hours or overnight, or freeze for 2–3 hours before serving.

Egg yolks

Savoiardi biscuits

Dark rum

Espresso coffee

Sugar

Mascarpone

Orange liqueur

Egg white

Bitter
chocolate

Cocoa powder

RECIPES

The recipes in this chapter have survived decades and even centuries, and are still very much used in Italian cooking today. All reflect the rich history and regional traditions of Italy, as well as its culinary diversity. There is a fish soup from Gallipoli, which the locals claim dates back to 1000BC, duck with orange sauce, a creation of Caterina de' Medici's cooks in the fifteenth century, pasta dishes that are relative newcomers on the Italian scene, and delectable confections of modern popular fame.

**All the dishes serve 4,
unless otherwise indicated.**

ANTIPASTI

The *antipasto*, literally "before the meal" course, is composed of zesty little dishes offered individually or in assortment. Their variety is endless and this is as it should be, for what is the purpose of the starter but to create anticipation and excitement about the meal to follow? Many are excellent served as main dishes or as side dishes. An essential ingredient is often high-quality extra-virgin olive oil. This aromatic, handmade oil imparts irresistible flavour and transforms even the simplest food into a finished dish.

SCARPASSA
Ligurian aubergine fritters

The flavour and creamy texture of aubergine is enhanced superbly by deep-frying, as these fritters show.

INGREDIENTS

500g (1lb) aubergines, peeled and cut into
1cm (½ in) slices
salt
olive oil for brushing and frying
1 small egg, beaten
4 tbsp freshly grated Parmesan
6 tbsp fresh breadcrumbs, toasted, plus extra for dredging
1 tsp chopped fresh marjoram, or ½ tsp dried marjoram

PREPARATION

1 Sprinkle the aubergine slices with salt and leave in a colander to drain for at least 40 minutes.
2 Preheat the oven to 230°C/450°F/gas 8.
3 Line a baking sheet with foil. Wipe the aubergine slices with kitchen paper, then brush both sides with oil. Bake until tender, about 20 minutes. Remove from the oven and leave to cool slightly.
4 Finely chop the aubergine then combine it with the egg, Parmesan, 6 tablespoons of breadcrumbs and the marjoram. The mixture will be fairly moist. Add another tablespoon of breadcrumbs to firm up the texture if necessary. Shape the mixture into walnut-sized dumplings. Chill for at least 3 hours.
5 Pour oil to a depth of 2.5cm (1in) into a frying pan and heat. Spread the remaining breadcrumbs on waxed paper or a plate.
6 When the oil is hot enough to make the mixture sizzle, drop each fritter in the crumbs and then lower into the oil. Fry until golden, 45 seconds.
7 Transfer the fritters to a platter lined with kitchen paper and allow to drain. Serve hot.

FRITTELLE DI ZUCCHINI
Courgette fritters

A recipe from Udine in the northern region of Friuli given to me by my friends Valerie and Elio Serra. These fritters can be served as an antipasto, or as a side dish with fish or meat. They are easy to make and utterly irresistible if made with young, tender courgettes.

INGREDIENTS

500g (1lb) fresh, young courgettes, no more
than 175–250g (6–8oz) each
60g (2oz) flour, plus 2 tbsp as necessary
60g (2oz) freshly grated Parmesan
1 extra-large egg, beaten
pinch of freshly grated nutmeg
salt and freshly ground black or white pepper, to taste
olive oil for deep-frying

PREPARATION

1 Wash the courgettes and trim both ends. Slice them in half, and if they are very seedy, cut out and discard the seeds and soft centre.
2 Grate the courgettes on the large holes of a grater. Place the grated flesh in a bowl with the flour, Parmesan, egg, nutmeg, a small pinch of salt and pepper. Stir all the ingredients thoroughly until a fairly thick batter is formed. If it seems thin, add up to 2 tablespoons of extra flour.
3 Pour olive oil into a frying pan to a depth of 1cm (½in) and heat until hot enough to make the batter sizzle. Slip spoonfuls of the batter into the oil and push down lightly with the back of a spoon to flatten them slightly. Fry until golden-brown, about 2 minutes on each side. Do not allow them to burn but make sure the centre is cooked.
4 Drain the fritters on kitchen paper, transfer to a warm plate, sprinkle with salt, if desired, and serve.

FUNGHI FRITTI ALLA SARDA

Crispy fried mushrooms, Sardinian style

Illustrated on page 41.

INGREDIENTS

*375g (12oz) large fresh wild mushrooms such as porcini
or portobello, or large field mushrooms
150g (5oz) finely ground semolina
olive oil for frying
freshly ground fine sea salt and black pepper, to taste
1 tbsp chopped fresh flat-leaf parsley, optional*

PREPARATION

1 Clean and trim the mushrooms (do not wash them). Cut the stems lengthways into slices. If the caps are very large, slice them in half across.
2 Spread the semolina flour on a piece of waxed paper or in a wide shallow dish. Pour olive oil to a depth of 5mm (¼in) into a frying pan and heat.
3 When the oil is hot enough to make the mushrooms sizzle, dredge the first batch in the semolina, pressing down to coat them.
4 Slip the first batch of mushrooms into the oil and fry them over a medium-high heat until crispy on both sides and cooked through, approximately 8 minutes, according to size. Drain them on kitchen paper then dredge and fry the remaining caps and stems.
5 Sprinkle the mushrooms with salt and pepper. Scatter over the parsley and serve hot.

CIPOLLINE IN AGRODOLCE

Sweet and sour onions

Illustrated on page 40.

INGREDIENTS

*750g (1½lb) small (walnut-sized) white onions
2 tbsp olive oil
2 large cloves garlic, crushed
6 whole cloves
60ml (2fl oz) white wine vinegar
1 tbsp white sugar
¼ tsp salt
1 small dried hot red chilli, or 6 black peppercorns*

PREPARATION

1 Peel the onions and cook them in boiling water for 3 minutes. Drain and plunge them in cold water to arrest cooking.
2 Warm the oil in a heavy-bottomed saucepan. Add the onions and garlic and sauté gently for 5 minutes – do not allow them to colour.

3 Meanwhile, combine 60ml (2fl oz) of water, the cloves, vinegar, sugar, salt and chilli in a bowl. Add this mixture to the onions and garlic.
4 Partially cover the saucepan and simmer the onions for 10 minutes, stirring occasionally.
5 Allow the onions to cool – they are best left for at least 24 hours before serving. They can be stored for up to 2 weeks in the refrigerator and their flavour will strengthen as they keep.

CASTELLANA DI PEPERONI

Stuffed roasted pepper "sandwiches"

In this Piedmontese dish, roasted red peppers are skinned and deseeded then given a simple stuffing of fontina cheese and prosciutto. The resulting "sandwiches" are then briefly returned to the oven in order to melt the cheese. The procedure is straightforward, but the result excellent. For extra flavour, try grilling the peppers over charcoal. Serves 6.

INGREDIENTS

*6 large red or yellow peppers
6 thin slices prosciutto
6 thin slices fontina
olive oil for brushing*

PREPARATION

1 Preheat the oven to 200°C/400°F/gas 6.
2 Roast the whole peppers in the oven or under the grill until the skins are charred and the insides tender (see page 160). Remove from the heat.
3 Line a baking sheet with foil. When the peppers are cool enough to handle, cut them in half vertically. Remove the stem and lift off the skin, then scrape out the seeds.
4 Place a slice each of prosciutto and fontina on the inside of one half of each pepper. Cover with the other half of the pepper. Brush with olive oil and place on a baking sheet in the middle of the oven. Cook until the cheese is melted and the peppers warmed through. Serve hot or warm.

PEPERONI RIPIENI

Peppers stuffed with rice and Gorgonzola

Illustrated on page 41. Serves 8.

INGREDIENTS

90ml (3fl oz) olive oil
8 medium red or yellow peppers, or a mixture
1 onion, finely chopped
2 large cloves garlic, finely chopped
150g (5oz) long-grain white rice
1 tsp salt
2 sweet Italian pork sausages, about 250g (8oz),
casings removed and meat crumbled
125g (4oz) Gorgonzola, crumbled
2 tbsp freshly grated Parmesan
1 tsp fennel seeds
½ tsp freshly ground black pepper

PREPARATION

1 Preheat the oven to 200°C/400°F/gas 6.
2 Warm the oil in a frying pan over a medium heat. Add the peppers and sauté until coloured on all sides, but still firm to the touch, 5–7 minutes. Cook them in batches, if necessary.
3 Allow the peppers to cool then slice off the tops and reserve them. Scoop out and discard the seeds and ribs, being careful not to pierce the flesh. Set the peppers aside.
4 Drain off and reserve all but 2 tablespoons of the oil in the pan and set over a medium heat. Add the onion and garlic and cook until soft.
5 Stir in the rice and sauté until translucent, about 5 minutes. Add 350ml (12fl oz) of water and the salt and bring to the boil. Immediately reduce the heat to a gentle simmer, cover the pan and cook until all the liquid is absorbed, approximately 10 minutes. Taste for salt.
6 Pour a little of the reserved oil into a second frying pan and cook the sausage until it colours but does not harden, 4–5 minutes. Stir in the cooked rice, cheeses and fennel seeds. Check for salt and add the pepper. Remove the mixture from the heat and allow to cool slightly.
7 Stuff the peppers and replace their tops.
8 Select a baking dish that is large enough to hold the peppers without crowding them. Arrange the peppers, setting them upright. Add 3 tablespoons of water to the dish. Cover tightly with a lid or with foil, dull side out.
9 Bake the peppers for about 30 minutes, until they are tender but still hold their shape. Check the rice – it should be tender, but not mushy. Allow the peppers to settle for 10–15 minutes before serving. Serve hot or warm.

MELANZANE RIPIENE

Stuffed aubergine

So extraordinary is the Ligurian propensity for stuffing vegetables that one Genoese restaurant, now sadly gone, served nothing but stuffed vegetables. However, for some reason, aubergines grown outside Italy are excessively seedy, particularly as they mature. Look for small aubergines, no larger than 375g (12oz) each. This typically Ligurian dish can be prepared a day in advance, up to the point of baking, or it can be made up to 3 days in advance, refrigerated and reheated. Serves 6.

INGREDIENTS

3 medium or 4 small aubergines
salt, to taste
250g (8oz) mushrooms, trimmed
2 tbsp olive oil
1 large onion, chopped
1 large clove garlic, finely chopped
125g (4oz) prosciutto, chopped
2 eggs, beaten
¼ tsp freshly ground black pepper
1 tbsp breadcrumbs
2 tbsp freshly grated Parmesan or pecorino
1 tsp chopped fresh marjoram, or ½ tsp dried marjoram

PREPARATION

1 Cut the aubergines in half lengthways and scoop out the pulp, leaving about 1cm (½in) intact. Chop the pulp coarsely, discarding excess seeds, sprinkle with salt and weight down in a colander to drain.
2 Clean the mushrooms with a soft brush or cloth; do not wash them. Cut them in halves, or quarters if large, then slice.
3 Rinse the aubergine pulp, squeeze out the water and dry on kitchen paper.
4 Preheat the oven to 180°C/350°F/gas 4.
5 Heat the oil in a large frying pan, add the onion and garlic and sauté over medium-low heat until softened, about 5 minutes.
6 Add the mushrooms and prosciutto and continue to cook until the mushrooms are tender, about 2 minutes. Add the aubergine and toss for 1 minute. Allow the mixture to cool slightly.
7 Combine the eggs, ½ teaspoon of salt, pepper and breadcrumbs in a bowl. Add the cooled aubergine and mushroom mixture, Parmesan and marjoram. Mix well, then spoon the stuffing into the aubergine shells; the stuffing should not be heaped.
8 Arrange the aubergines in a baking dish. Pour 125ml (4fl oz) of water into the dish and cover with foil. Cook for 45 minutes, or until the aubergine shells are tender but not collapsed. Serve warm or at room temperature.

ZUPPA DI MITILI ALLA PUGLIESE

Mussels in white wine, Apulian style

Serves 8 as a starter or 4 as a main course.

INGREDIENTS

3kg (6lb) mussels, scrubbed and debearded (see page 163)
4 tbsp olive oil
1 onion, chopped
3 large cloves garlic, chopped
50g (1¾oz) chopped fresh flat-leaf parsley
2 tsp chopped fresh thyme, or 1 tsp dried thyme
1 bay leaf, crumbled
350ml (12fl oz) good dry white wine
freshly ground black pepper, to taste

PREPARATION

1 Wash the mussels then place them in a bowl of cold water and leave to soak (see page 163). Discard any that have opened.
2 Rinse the mussels again. Take a large heavy casserole pot and heat the oil and onion until the onion softens. Scatter in the garlic and parsley and sauté for a few minutes until golden.
3 Stir the mussels into the onion and parsley mixture. Add the thyme, bay leaf, wine and pepper, then cover and bring to the boil.
4 Turn the heat to low and simmer gently for 2–3 minutes, or until the mussels are open. Discard any mussels that remain closed.
5 Serve the mussels in shallow bowls, ladling over some of the broth, and accompany with plenty of fresh hot Italian bread.

COZZE ARRACANATI
Baked mussels, Apulian style

Baked mussels are one of Apulia's specialities as the region has abundant seafood and shellfish. In Pugliese cooking, arracanate, or arraganati, refers to anything baked with a breadcrumb topping. I've often wondered if the popular American hybrid of this dish, "clams oreganata", isn't a mispronunciation of the name. The quantities here are for 2 people.

INGREDIENTS

12 fresh large mussels or littleneck clams, debearded and scrubbed (see page 163)
1 lemon, cut into wedges, to serve
Topping
3 tbsp extra-virgin olive oil, plus extra for drizzling
4 tbsp fresh white breadcrumbs
pinch of hot red chilli flakes
1 tbsp chopped fresh flat-leaf parsley
½ tsp chopped fresh oregano, or ¼ tsp dried oregano
1 clove garlic, finely chopped

PREPARATION

1 Soak the mussels or clams in salted cold water (see page 163). Leave in the refrigerator for at least 3 hours to disgorge any grit or sand.
2 Scrub the shellfish and immerse them in hot water for 5–10 minutes to help open them. Working over a bowl to catch any juices, insert a small knife between the two halves of the shell and cut the shellfish in half, working towards the muscle on the base of the shell. Carefully detach the flesh then place it in one of the shell halves, discarding the other half.
3 Preheat the grill. Combine the topping ingredients and spoon some over each mussel or clam. Sprinkle with a little of the reserved juice to keep the flesh from burning, then drizzle with oil.
4 Place the mussels or clams in a dish and set it under the grill, 30cm (12in) from the heat, or as far away as possible. Grill them for about 6 minutes, making sure that the topping doesn't burn. Baste with more juice if necessary. Serve hot with lemon wedges.

FRITTATA AGLI ASPARAGI
Asparagus and mushroom frittata

Illustrated on page 41. Serves 6.

INGREDIENTS

500g (1lb) asparagus, tough ends removed
salt, to taste
125g (4oz) small mushrooms, trimmed
15g (½oz) butter
1 tbsp extra-virgin olive oil, plus oil for frying
6 spring onions, including 2.5cm (1in) green tops, sliced
5 eggs
3 tbsp freshly grated Parmesan
pinch of freshly ground white or black pepper

PREPARATION

1 Pare the thick skin at the base of each asparagus stalk to reveal the tender inside (see page 161). Steam or boil in salted water until just tender, 5–6 minutes. Plunge into cold water, drain and cut diagonally into 5mm (¼in) slices.
2 Clean the mushrooms using a soft brush or cloth; do not wash them. Slice them across.
3 Heat the butter and 1 tablespoon of oil in a 25cm (10in) omelette pan. When hot, add the mushrooms and spring onions and sauté for about 2 minutes, stirring frequently, until tender. Remove from the pan and set aside to cool.
4 Beat the eggs with the cheese, ½ teaspoon of salt and the pepper. Add the asparagus, mushrooms and onions, and combine thoroughly.
5 Heat a little oil in the omelette pan and when hot add the egg mixture, using a wooden spoon to distribute the vegetables evenly. Cook over a medium heat for 10 minutes, rotating the pan to allow the mixture to cook evenly. Preheat the grill.
6 Place the frittata under the grill and cook for 5–9 minutes, until lightly golden and set inside. Do not allow it to overcook. If the frittata is already browned but runny inside, finish cooking it on the top shelf of the oven at 230°C/450°F/gas 8.
7 Let the frittata rest for 5–10 minutes, then turn out on to a serving dish and cut into wedges. Serve warm or at room temperature.

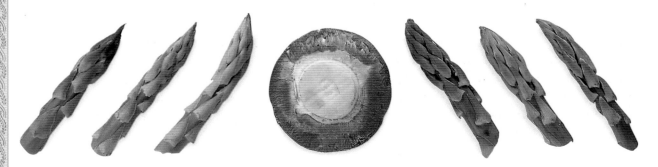

POLPETTINE ALL' UMBRA

Little meatballs, Umbrian style, cooked four ways

Outside Italy, meatballs are often served atop a pile of spaghetti, but in Italy, they are presented quite differently. They make an excellent antipasti for 8 cooked in a tomato or wine sauce, or coated in breadcrumbs and served plain. Alternatively, they can be poached in broth for a primo, or first course, for 4. Illustrated on page 40.

INGREDIENTS

60g (2oz) stale white bread, crusts removed, cubed
125ml (4fl oz) milk or stock for soaking bread
750g (1½lb) minced beef, or a mixture of beef and pork
60g (2oz) thinly sliced prosciutto, coarsely chopped
1 small onion, coarsely grated
2 tsp chopped fresh marjoram, or 1 tsp dried marjoram
zest of 1 lemon
2 tsp salt
freshly ground black pepper, to taste
1 egg, beaten

PREPARATION

1 Soak the bread in the milk or stock. When soft, squeeze out and discard the liquid. Use your hands to mix the bread with the remaining ingredients.
2 Take 2 teaspoons of the mixture at a time and form it into little round balls (if serving them as a main course, make the meatballs larger). Cook in any of the following ways:

METHOD 1 *FRIED IN A CRISPY COATING*
1 Pour oil to a depth of 2.5cm (1in) into a frying pan and heat. Dredge the first batch of meatballs in flour then roll in lightly toasted breadcrumbs.
2 When the oil is hot enough to make the meatballs sizzle, slip them into the pan one at a time. Fry over a medium heat until browned all over then drain on kitchen paper. Serve hot.

METHOD 2 *COOKED IN TOMATO SAUCE*
1 Dredge the meatballs in flour. Heat 4 tablespoons of olive oil in a frying pan over a medium heat. When the oil is hot, sauté the first batch until lightly browned but still pinkish inside, about 10 minutes. Drain on kitchen paper and set aside.
2 Add 1 large grated carrot, 1 finely chopped large celery stalk with leaves and 1 finely chopped onion to the frying pan with the meatball drippings. Sauté over a medium-low heat until the vegetables are softened, about 7 minutes.
3 Stir in 1.25kg (2½lb) of fresh or canned and drained plum tomatoes that have been skinned, deseeded and chopped (see page 160). Season well then simmer for 10 minutes.
4 Transfer the browned meatballs to the sauce and simmer over a medium-low heat, uncovered, until

the sauce has thickened and the meatballs are heated through, about 12 minutes. Serve hot.

METHOD 3 *COOKED IN WINE*
1 Heat 4 tablespoons of olive oil in a frying pan. Dredge the meatballs lightly in flour, and when the oil is hot enough to make them sizzle, sauté the first batch over a medium heat until lightly browned. Drain on kitchen paper.
2 Add 125ml (4fl oz) of dry white wine to the drippings in the pan and stir with a wooden spoon. Allow the alcohol to evaporate, about 2 minutes.
3 Reduce the heat to medium-low and return the meatballs to the pan. Simmer for 8 minutes until the meatballs are heated through. Serve hot.

METHOD 4 *COOKED IN BROTH*
1 Bring 2.5 litres (4 pints) of seasoned chicken broth (see page 73) or meat broth (see page 72) to the boil. Drop in a few meatballs at a time. When they float to the surface, they are cooked.
2 As the meatballs rise to the surface of the broth, transfer them to a platter and keep them warm. Serve in bowls with a little of the broth.

VARIATION

To make **Polpettine alla Toscana**, omit the marjoram and lemon zest and replace with 5g (¼oz) of freshly grated Parmesan and a pinch of freshly grated nutmeg.

PIZZA NAPOLETANA

Pizza, the simple flat bread of Naples, is fundamentally poor food. What makes Neapolitan pizza so good is the high-quality wheat used for the dough, the superb local tomatoes and olive oil, and also the aroma imparted by wood-fired ovens. Here is the classic Napoletana topping of fruity olive oil, tomatoes, oregano and garlic — no cheese; Roman-style pizza adds mozzarella. For the basic Pizza Dough recipe and baking times, see page 170. Makes two 30cm (12in) bases. Serves 8–16.

INGREDIENTS

1 quantity Pizza Dough (see pages 170–171)
Napoletana topping
750g (1½lb) fresh or canned drained tomatoes, skinned, deseeded and chopped
3 large cloves garlic, chopped
2 tbsp chopped fresh oregano, or 1 tbsp dried oregano
salt, to taste
4 tbsp extra-virgin olive oil
125g (4oz) mozzarella, shredded (for Roman-style)

PREPARATION

1 Preheat the oven to 200°C/400°F/gas 6.
2 Meanwhile, make the pizza bases as shown on page 170. Brush with oil then combine the tomato, garlic, oregano and salt. Spread this mixture over the bases and drizzle with oil, adding more to taste.
3 Bake until golden (see chart on page 170). If using cheese, take the pizzas from the oven 5 minutes before the end of cooking and top with mozzarella. Return to the oven and bake until the cheese is just melted. Leave to cool slightly before serving.

PIZZA TOPPINGS

Outside Italy, tomatoes have become associated with pizza almost exclusively. But in Italy, toppings include almost every conceivable food, including sautéed greens, seafood, local cheeses, chestnuts, olives, salumi, "cured meats", and fresh herbs. The quantities given here are for two 35cm (14in) bases (see page 170 for recipe), but you can choose any other size of pizza base and adjust the amount of topping accordingly. Illustrated on page 44.

CON RICOTTA

1kg (2lb) ricotta (drained weight)
250g (8oz) Provolone, shredded
1 tsp fennel seeds, crushed
salt and freshly ground black pepper, to taste
30g (1oz) freshly grated pecorino

Combine all the ingredients except the pecorino and spread the mixture on the bases. Season with salt and pepper to taste. Sprinkle the pecorino evenly over the top. Bake until golden (see baking time chart on page 170).

MARGHERITA

750g (1½lb) fresh or canned drained tomatoes, skinned, deseeded and chopped
4 tbsp extra-virgin olive oil
125g (4oz) mozzarella, shredded
large handful of fresh basil leaves, torn

Spread the tomato on the bases and drizzle with oil. Five minutes before the end of cooking, remove the pizza from the oven and sprinkle over the mozzarella and basil. Return to the oven and bake until the cheese is just melted (see baking time chart on page 170).

CON SCAROLA

4 tbsp extra-virgin olive oil, plus more to taste
8 large cloves garlic, chopped
1kg (2lb) escarole, shredded
salt and freshly ground black pepper, to taste
2 tsp chopped fresh oregano, or 1 tsp dried oregano
90g (3oz) strongly flavoured black olives, pitted and sliced

Pour the oil into a large frying pan and sauté the garlic until softened. Add the escarole and cook until wilted, tossing it frequently. Season to taste with salt and pepper, then add the oregano. Leave to cool. Spread it over the bases. Sprinkle with sliced olives and more oil. Bake until golden (see baking time chart on page 170).

CON SALSICCIA

750g (1½lb) fresh or canned drained tomatoes, skinned, deseeded and chopped
2 large cloves garlic, chopped
1 tsp fennel seeds, crushed
salt, to taste
500g (1lb) sweet Italian pork sausage meat, crumbled
4 tbsp freshly grated pecorino or Parmesan
extra-virgin olive oil for drizzling

Mix the tomatoes with the garlic, fennel and salt. Place the sausage meat in a cold frying pan with 60ml (2fl oz) of water. Sauté until the liquid has evaporated and the sausage is browned, then drain. Spread the tomato over the bases and top with sausage. Sprinkle with cheese and oil. Bake until golden (see baking time chart on page 170).

CRISPELLE
Tiny fried pizzas

Illustrated on page 45. Serves 8.

INGREDIENTS

1 quantity Pizza Dough (see page 170)
olive oil, for frying
coarse sea salt, to taste
salami, prosciutto or a soft or semi-soft Italian cheese,
such as mozzarella, toma, taleggio or stracchino, to serve

PREPARATION

1 Make the dough as directed on pages 170–71, up to step 4. Divide the dough into pieces the size of a small peach. Stretch each piece out to make a thin 15cm (6in) disc.
2 Pour oil to a depth of 2.5cm (1in) into a frying pan. When the oil is hot enough to make the dough sizzle, slip the discs into the pan and fry until golden-brown on both sides, about 5 minutes. Remove and drain on kitchen paper.

3 Sprinkle the outside of the crispelle with a little salt, then fold them around the chosen filling to make a sandwich and serve at once.

VARIATION

In Liguria, chopped fresh sage is added to the dough, which is then formed into finger-shaped fritters called *scabei*. The dough should be somewhat sticky for this.

Follow the basic Pizza Dough recipe (see pages 170–71), reducing the flour by 15g (½oz). Add 6 tablespoons of chopped fresh sage or 3 tablespoons of dried crumbled sage to the flour and salt in step 2 of the recipe. If using a food processor, work the dough for only 15 seconds.

Allow the dough to rise as for pizza, then knock it back with your knuckles to expel the air and divide it into 8 parts. Form each section into 1cm (½in) ropes and cut each rope into 15cm (6in) lengths. Cover with a damp tea towel and allow to rise for 30 minutes. Fry the scabei in hot olive oil, drain well and serve hot, sprinkled with sea salt.

FOCACCIA

The basic difference between focaccia and pizza is the thickness — focaccia is much thicker than pizza. Some are elaborate but many are simple flat breads sprinkled with olive oil, herbs or sea salt. The dough can be dimpled, trapping little pools of fragrant oil. Serves 6–8 as an accompaniment or as part of an antipasto. Makes one 35cm x 45cm (14 x 18in) base. Illustrated on page 45.

INGREDIENTS

1 quantity Pizza Dough (see page 170)
Alle Olive Topping
90g (3oz) pitted and sliced black olives, such as Niçoise, Gaeta or Ligurian
2 tsp chopped fresh marjoram, or 1 tsp dried marjoram
extra-virgin olive oil, for brushing

PREPARATION

1 To form the focaccia, follow the steps for making pizza dough shown on page 171, up to step 3.
2 When the dough is elastic, use the palms of your hands to stretch it to a thickness of 1cm (½in) and form the dough into a circle or rectangle.
3 Transfer the focaccia to an oiled baking sheet, cover with a clean tea towel and leave to rise again for 30 minutes.
4 Mark the focaccia as shown on page 171, cover and leave to rise until doubled in size, about 1 hour.
5 Preheat the oven to 200°C/400°F/gas 6.
6 Push the sliced olives into the dough. Brush the base with oil. Sprinkle the marjoram and oil on top.
7 Bake in the preheated oven until the edges are golden, 10–11 minutes. Allow to cool for 5 minutes before cutting. Serve hot or warm.

FOCACCIA TOPPINGS

AGLIO E OLIO

4 large cloves garlic, finely sliced or coarsely chopped
2½ tbsp extra-virgin olive oil

Combine the garlic and olive oil and sprinkle over the focaccia base. Bake as described in main recipe.

CON GORGONZOLA

375g (12oz) mild Gorgonzola, crumbled
2 large cloves garlic, roughly chopped
extra-virgin olive oil, for brushing

Combine the Gorgonzola and garlic in a bowl. Scatter over the focaccia and drizzle with olive oil, then bake as described in main recipe.

AL ROSMARINO

3 tbsp chopped fresh rosemary, or 1½ tbsp dried rosemary, added to the flour in step 2 of the recipe
olive oil, for brushing
fresh sage leaves, to garnish, optional
coarse sea salt

Add the rosemary to the flour in step 2 of the dough recipe on page 170. If using a food processor, work the dough for 15 seconds. Brush with oil, garnish with sage and salt, then bake as described in main recipe.

ALLA SARDA

125g (4oz) pancetta or bacon, diced
4 tbsp fresh chopped sage, or 2 tbsp dried crumbled sage, added to the flour and salt in step 2 of the recipe
olive oil, for brushing
coarse sea salt

Sauté the pancetta, then drain and add to the dough mixture in step 2 of the dough recipe on page 170. If using a food processor, work the dough for 15 seconds. Brush with oil, sprinkle with salt, then bake as described in main recipe.

CROSTINI CON FEGATINI DI POLLO ALLA SALVIA

Sautéed chicken livers with sage on crostini toasts

One always comes across variations of this lovely antipasto in Tuscany. Try this recipe when you can find the typically plump and immensely savoury livers of free-range chickens.

INGREDIENTS

250g (8oz) very fresh plump chicken livers
30g (1oz) unsalted butter
6 fresh sage leaves, or ½ tsp dried crumbled sage
12 thinly sliced rounds Italian or French bread, toasted
extra-virgin olive oil or butter, optional
2 tbsp dry white wine
salt and freshly ground black pepper, to taste

PREPARATION

1 Trim any fat, connecting tissue or discoloured flesh from the livers then quarter each one.
2 Heat the butter in a frying pan and add the livers and sage. Sauté for 4–5 minutes until browned on the outside but pinkish inside. Transfer to a plate.
3 Brush the bread with oil or butter if desired.
4 Add the wine to the juices left in the pan, stirring to incorporate any residue, and add seasoning.
5 Return the livers to the pan for up to 1 minute, mashing them coarsely. Serve on the crostini.

PANZEROTTI ALLA PUGLIESE

Apulian potato bread turnovers stuffed with pork

*There are many names for this genre of turnovers — such
as* calzoni *and* pizzelle. *The name* panzerotti *derives
from the Italian for belly, which is what the crescent-
shaped parcels look like when they swell up in the hot
oil. Fillings can be as simple as a few anchovies,
or a mixture of salami and mozzarella that melts
into a pleasing ooziness. Makes 24.*

INGREDIENTS

Dough

250g (8oz) whole boiling potatoes, unpeeled
10g (½oz) fresh yeast, or 1 sachet active dry yeast
125ml (4fl oz) warm water 100–110°F (38–43°C)
650g (1lb 5oz) strong bread flour
2¼ tsp salt
250ml (8fl oz) cold water
olive oil for brushing

Filling

2 tbsp extra-virgin olive oil
1 onion, chopped
750g (1½lb) minced pork
125g (4oz) stale bread, crusts removed
125ml (4fl oz) stock
2 tbsp chopped fresh flat-leaf parsley
30g (1oz) freshly grated pecorino
2 egg yolks
¾ tsp salt
freshly ground pepper, to taste
1 tbsp chopped fresh rosemary or sage, or
½ tsp dried rosemary or crumbled sage

To finish

2 egg whites, lightly beaten
olive oil for frying
sea salt, to taste

PREPARATION

1 To make the dough, boil the potatoes until
tender, about 20 minutes. Drain, leave until cool
enough to handle, then peel off the skins. Pass them
through a potato ricer or mash while still warm.
2 In a small bowl, combine the yeast with 60ml
(2fl oz) of warm water. Let the mixture rest in a
warm place for about 10 minutes, or until foamy.

3 In a large bowl, sift together 125g (4oz) of the
flour and the salt. Sprinkle over the potato and mix
together lightly with your hands. Make a well in
the centre of the flour-potato mixture.
4 Add the remaining warm water and the cold
water to the yeast mixture and pour into the well.
5 Gradually stir the flour-potato mixture into the
liquid until absorbed. Work in another 250g (8oz)
of flour, sifting each addition. When the dough
becomes stiff, use your hands to form it into a ball.
6 Lightly flour a pastry board. Knead the dough
for 8–10 minutes while gradually sifting over as
much of the remaining flour as is needed to form a
a dough that is silky and elastic.
7 Place the dough in a lightly oiled bowl and brush
its surface with oil. Cover the bowl with a clean
tea towel. Leave to rise at room temperature until
doubled in size, 1–2 hours. (The longer the rising,
the lighter the dough. If it rises too quickly, knock
it back with your knuckles and let it rise again.)

FILLING

1 Meanwhile, make the filling. Heat the oil in a
frying pan, add the onion and sauté over a medium
heat until soft, 3–4 minutes. Add the pork, reduce
the heat and sauté gently until the meat is browned
but still rosy. Drain and transfer to a bowl.
2 Soak the bread in the stock until soft. Squeeze
the bread dry and crumble it, discarding the stock.
Add the bread to the pork mixture with the parsley,
pecorino, egg yolks, seasoning and herbs. Mix well.
3 Knock back the dough and divide into 24 pieces.
Sprinkle a pastry board with flour and roll out
each piece to make a thin 10cm (4in) disc. Sprinkle
one side with pepper.
4 Place a heaped tablespoon of filling in the centre
of each disc. Brush the edges of the disc with egg
white. Fold the disc over and press round the edges
to seal. Transfer the parcels to baking tins lined
with kitchen paper and cover with clean tea towels
until ready to fry.
5 Pour olive oil to a depth of 2.5cm (1in) into a
frying pan. When the oil is hot enough to make the
dough sizzle, slip the panzerotti into the pan and
fry until golden on both sides, about 5 minutes.
Remove and drain on kitchen paper.
6 Sprinkle with a little salt and eat hot.

SOUPS

I am always amazed that many people will not go to the trouble of making soups at home though they are among the most satisfying of dishes. Italian soups are especially appealing as they are so varied, being made from everything to hand, from pulses to seafood or even bread. *Brodi* are clear broths in which soup pasta or *tortellini* may be cooked. *Minestre* are fairly light, while *minestroni*, "big soups", are packed with vegetables, beans and perhaps pasta or rice. To complicate matters further, *minestrine* are light soups of puréed vegetables, and *zuppe* are thick, hearty soups of anything from vegetables to fish.

BRODO DI CARNE
Meat broth

A good meat broth can provide a starting point for more complex soups. It can also enrich sauces and stews. For maximum flavour, the meat and supporting vegetables should begin cooking in cold water. In this way, the meat juices are released into the broth rather than being sealed in by immediate intense heat. The best broth is made with a combination of meats and fowl. Serves 8.

INGREDIENTS

1 kg (2lb) chicken backs or wings
1 kg (2lb) beef chuck, shin, short ribs or other economy cut
750g (1½lb) mixed fresh uncooked veal and
beef shin and marrow bones
1 fresh or canned tomato
1 onion, unpeeled and quartered
1 large carrot, scraped and quartered
1 large celery stalk with leaves
handful fresh flat-leaf parsley leaves and a bunch of stems
3 whole peppercorns
2–3 whole cloves
2–3 tsp salt

PREPARATION

1 Wash the chicken, removing any excess fat but keeping the skin on, and trim excess fat from the beef. Select a pan into which the meat will fit comfortably. Put in all the ingredients, except the salt. Add a maximum of 3 litres (5 pints) of cold water, to cover the meat by 5cm (2in). Cover the pot and bring to the boil.
2 Reduce the heat to low or medium-low and keep the broth at a gentle simmer. Leave the pan partially covered and skim the surface whenever scum forms to produce a clear broth. Cook at a steady, gentle simmer until the broth is full-bodied and tasty, about 3 hours. Check it from time to time and do not allow it to return to the boil.
3 Skim off any fat that has risen to the surface and remove the meat and bones. You can eat the meat separately: beef can be sliced, dressed with extra-virgin olive oil, lemon juice and parsley, or with Salsa Verde (see page 139) and served as a salad.
4 Strain the broth through cheesecloth or a very fine sieve into a bowl. Add salt to taste only if using immediately. Otherwise, cover and refrigerate for up to 4 days, or freeze for up to 6 months.

PASTINA IN BRODO DI POLLO

Chicken broth with pastina

In the Italian version of the proverbial chicken soup, the rich broth is served clear except for a little pastina (soup pasta). The chicken is served as a second course with some of the sauces described on pages 138–39 or Maionese Verde (see page 140). Although the vegetables are strained out, it is essential to use flavourful parsley and celery leaves. Follow this recipe, omitting pastina, to make a chicken broth for use in other recipes. Serves 6.

INGREDIENTS

*1 free-range chicken, about 1.75kg (3½lb),
including neck, heart and giblets
1 bay leaf
1 onion, unpeeled and quartered
1 carrot, scraped and roughly chopped
1 large celery stalk with leaves
1 fresh or canned tomato
1 small bunch fresh flat-leaf parsley
2 tsp salt, or to taste
¼ tsp whole black or white peppercorns
175g (6oz) pastina, such as stelline, "little stars",
orzo, "barley", acini di pepe, "peppercorns"
freshly grated Parmesan, to serve*

PREPARATION

1 Wash the chicken, removing any excess fat.
2 Place the bird in a pan into which it just fits comfortably (the aim is to cover the chicken without diluting the broth with too much water). Put in all the ingredients, except the pastina and Parmesan, reserving a little parsley. Add up to 2 litres (3½ pints) of cold water, to cover the chicken by about 2.5cm (1in). Cover and bring to the boil.
3 Reduce the heat and cook the broth at a gentle simmer. Leave the pot partially covered and check the broth occasionally, skimming the surface whenever scum forms. Cook until the chicken meat is tender but not falling from the bones, about 1 hour. Do not allow it to return to the boil.
4 Skim off any fat and take the pan from the heat. Transfer the chicken to a serving dish and cover.
5 Strain the broth through cheesecloth or a fine sieve. Check the seasoning, return to a pan and bring the broth to the boil. Stir in the pastina. Cook over a medium heat until the pastina is tender, about 5 minutes, according to shape.
6 Garnish each serving with a pinch of chopped parsley and a tablespoon of grated Parmesan.

MINESTRA DI MANZO E VERDURA CON ORZO

Beef soup with barley and vegetables

This exuberant minestra is one of the standbys of the home kitchen. With its collection of cold-weather vegetables and barley, it is an unbeatable first course in winter, and fortifying enough to be a one-pot meal for lunch or a light supper. Various cuts of beef can be used, including rump and hind shank (shin), but I find short ribs from the corner of the breast particularly succulent and meaty. Part of the joy of eating this comforting soup is to gnaw on the rib bones, so don't remove them before serving. Serves 6.

INGREDIENTS

*1.5kg (3lb) beef short ribs
2 bay leaves
1 onion, unpeeled and cut in half
1 large celery stalk with leaves
75g (2½oz) barley
1 tbsp plus ½ tsp salt
375g (12oz) cabbage, finely shredded
1 large potato, peeled and diced
2 small carrots, finely diced
250g (8oz) swede, finely diced
½ tsp freshly ground black pepper
freshly grated pecorino or Parmesan, to serve*

PREPARATION

1 In a large pan, combine the meat, 2.5 litres (4 pints) of water, the bay leaves, onion and celery. Bring to the boil, then reduce to a steady simmer. Cook until the meat is tender, about 1½ hours. Check occasionally and skim off any scum that forms on the surface.
2 Meanwhile, bring 750ml (1¼ pints) of water to the boil in a saucepan and add the barley and ½ teaspoon of salt. Cook over a medium heat until tender, about 30 minutes. Drain and set aside.
3 After the meat has been cooking for about 1 hour, add the cabbage, potato, carrots, swede and 1 tablespoon of salt.
4 Five minutes before the end of cooking, add the cooked barley and pepper.
5 When the soup is cooked, remove the onion and bay leaves. Transfer the beef ribs to a cutting board, trim off any excess fat and divide the ribs so that they can be evenly distributed when serving. Return them to the soup and check the seasoning. Serve hot, passing the grated cheese at the table.

MINESTRA DI GAMBERETTI E BIETOLA

Swiss chard and prawn soup with rice

Here is a variation of a recipe I learned from Lidia Bastianich, the chef-owner of Felidia, one of New York City's best Italian restaurants. While on a trip to Apulia, Lidia and I toured the local markets. I couldn't resist the beautiful scampi at the Gallipoli fish markets, and brought some back to our hotel. Lidia charmed our way into the hotel's kitchen, where she cooked them up into a lovely soup. Serves 8.

INGREDIENTS

500g (1lb) whole raw prawns
1kg (2lb) fish bone stock mixture, including 1 or 2 fish heads (gills removed) from lean white fish such as cod, haddock, halibut, red snapper, bass and whiting
2 small onions, 1 unpeeled
2 large carrots, 1 cut in half and 1 coarsely grated
1 celery stalk
3 whole white peppercorns
1½ tbsp salt
4 tbsp extra-virgin olive oil
250g (8oz) boiling or baking potatoes, peeled and diced
2 tsp tomato purée
100g (3½oz) Arborio rice
1kg (2lb) Swiss chard tops, finely shredded then chopped
freshly ground black pepper, to taste

PREPARATION

1 Devein and shell the prawns (see page 163), reserving the shells for the stock. Chop each prawn into four pieces, halving them lengthways, then cutting them across. Cover and refrigerate.
2 Put the fish bones in a large stock pot with the prawn shells and 3 litres (5 pints) of water. Halve the unpeeled onion and add it to the pot with the halved carrot, celery, peppercorns and salt. Cover, leaving a small gap, and bring the stock to the boil. Reduce the heat and simmer for 30 minutes. Allow to cool. Strain the stock through a fine sieve; discard the solids.
3 In a large pan, warm the olive oil and sauté the potato over a medium heat until it begins to colour. Finely chop the remaining onion and add to the pan. Add the grated carrot and cook until soft.
4 Stir in the tomato purée then add the fish stock. Bring to the boil and add the rice. Simmer, partially covered, until the rice is three-quarters cooked, about 10 minutes.
5 Add the Swiss chard and cook until tender, a further 10 minutes. Remove the soup from the heat and stir in the prawns. Add pepper, adjust the seasoning and serve hot.

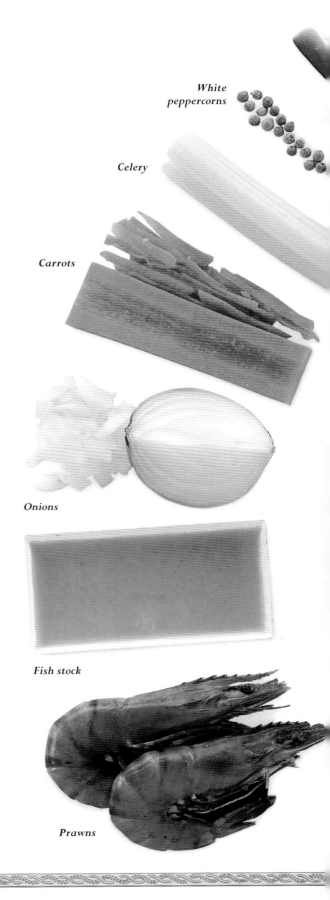

White peppercorns

Celery

Carrots

Onions

Fish stock

Prawns

Salt

Olive oil

Potatoes

Tomato
purée

Arborio
rice

Swiss
chard

Black pepper

Knödl alla Tirolese in Brod

Bread dumplings in broth

Stale bread is never thrown away in Italian kitchens and bread dumplings are a Tyrolean speciality. Use sturdy, sugar-free peasant-style bread. Serves 6–8.

INGREDIENTS

1 quantity Meat Broth or Chicken Broth (see pages 72–3)
Dumplings
250g (8oz) stale bread, crusts removed, sliced
60g (2oz) unsalted butter
1 large onion, coarsely grated
4 tbsp chopped fresh flat-leaf parsley
2 extra-large eggs, lightly beaten
1 tsp salt
¼ tsp freshly ground white or black pepper
125ml (4fl oz) milk
½ tsp baking powder
30g (1oz) flour

PREPARATION

1 Shred the bread into tiny pieces and set aside.
2 Melt the butter in a frying pan and add the onion and parsley. Sauté gently until the onion is soft, then add the bread and toss everything together. Sauté for about 7 minutes, tossing occasionally.
3 Meanwhile, mix together the eggs, salt, pepper and milk. Sift in the baking powder and flour and mix well. Allow the bread mixture to cool slightly then add it to the egg mixture. Mix the ingredients by hand, cover and allow to rest for 1–3 hours.
4 Bring the broth to the boil in a large pan. Shape the bread mixture into dumplings the size of large olives and drop into the broth. Cook them in batches if necessary, making sure they do not touch each other as they cook. Cover the pot and cook very gently for 5 minutes. Serve hot.

Zuppa di Scarola

Escarole soup

Either escarole or curly endive may be used for this light, appealing soup. I grew up with this dish. The aroma of croûtons frying in fruity olive oil, and their beguiling sizzle as my mother transferred them into our bowls of steaming soup, still lingers when I think of it. Serves 6.

INGREDIENTS

1 quantity Chicken Broth (see page 73)
500g (1lb) escarole or curly endive, washed thoroughly
250g (8oz) stale peasant-style bread, crusts removed
90ml (3fl oz) extra-virgin olive oil, for frying bread
freshly grated Parmesan, to serve

PREPARATION

1 Warm the chicken broth in a large pan.
2 Cut the escarole across into very fine shreds, then cut the shreds into 5cm (2in) pieces.
3 Bring the broth to the boil. Stir in the greens, cover partially and allow to cook for about 8 minutes, until tender but not disintegrated.
4 Meanwhile, cut the bread into cubes. Warm the oil in a frying pan, add the bread cubes and fry until golden, about 5 minutes. Drain on kitchen paper.
5 Pour the soup into bowls. Toss in the hot croûtons and pass the Parmesan at the table.

Minestrina di Zucchine

Courgette soup

One of the many soup fantasias from my mother's kitchen. The natural sweetness of courgette is intensified in this soup, where it is combined with onion, butter and milk. It is perfect as a first course when fish is on the menu.

INGREDIENTS

1kg (2lb) small courgettes, topped and tailed
60g (2oz) unsalted butter
1 tbsp sunflower oil
1 onion, chopped
1 large celery stalk with leaves, chopped
2 bay leaves
1 tsp chopped fresh marjoram, or ½ tsp dried marjoram
2 tbsp flour
250ml (8fl oz) scalded (hot) milk
750ml (1¼ pints) Chicken Broth (see page 73) or stock
1 tsp salt
¼ tsp freshly ground black pepper

PREPARATION

1 Finely chop or coarsely grate the courgettes.
2 Heat half the butter with the oil in a large pan. Add the onion and sauté until soft, about 4 minutes. Add the celery and leaves, courgette, bay leaves and marjoram and sweat over a medium-low heat for 7–8 minutes, stirring to coat them in the oil.
3 Cover the pan and continue to cook over a low heat until completely softened, about 15 minutes.
4 Meanwhile, make a béchamel sauce. Melt the remaining butter and gradually stir in the flour until absorbed. Add the milk a little at a time, stirring constantly to prevent lumps from forming. Stir in the broth. Remove the bay leaves from the vegetable mixture.
5 Pour the béchamel-broth mixture into a blender with the vegetables and liquefy. Return the soup to the pan and heat through gently. Stir in the salt and pepper. Serve hot or at room temperature.

MINESTRA DI ZUCCA
Pumpkin soup

*Zucca, a type of pumpkin whose flesh is very like
butternut squash in its colour, compact texture and
sweetness, is used very imaginatively in the Italian
kitchen. It finds its way into gnocchi, pasta stuffings,
risotto, all manner of vegetable dishes, fritters and
desserts. This pumpkin soup recipe, however, is as much
a testimony to my mother's resourcefulness and
imagination as it is to the Italian way with squash.
Serve it hot or at room temperature.*

INGREDIENTS

*1kg (2lb) small pumpkins or butternut squash
45g (1½oz) unsalted butter
1 small onion, grated or finely chopped
500ml (16fl oz) Chicken Broth (see page 73)
125ml (4fl oz) milk
good pinch of freshly grated nutmeg
zest of half an orange
1 tsp salt
pinch of white pepper*

PREPARATION

1 Preheat the oven to 200°C/400°F/gas 6.
2 Cut the pumpkins in half lengthways and place
them flesh side down on baking sheets. Bake until
tender, about 40 minutes. When cool enough to
handle, remove the seeds and rind. Reserve about
250g (8oz) of the flesh and dice the rest.
3 Melt the butter in a pan. Add the onion and
sauté gently until softened. Stir in the pumpkin
and sauté for 5 minutes to marry the flavours.
4 Add the broth, milk, nutmeg, orange zest and
salt, and simmer for 2 minutes. Remove the pan
from the heat and leave to cool slightly.
5 Purée the mixture in a blender then return it to
the pan to heat through. Cut the reserved pumpkin
into bite-sized slices and add to the soup with the
pepper. Serve hot or warm.

VARIATION

Add 2 chopped fennel stalks and 2 tablespoons of
tender fennel fronds to the pan with the onion.
Reserve a few additional fronds; chop them and
sprinkle over the soup before serving.

PASTA

This chapter includes delectable recipes for both fresh, homemade pasta and the myriad types of dried, factory-produced pasta. In the first category fall light potato *gnocchi*, *crespelle* (akin to French crêpes), noodles and little pasta parcels with savoury fillings. Most of the 350 or more varieties of dried pasta are made solely from durum wheat and water. They range from tiny *pastine* for soups to string shapes that are perfect with robust sauces, and large pasta for stuffing. The various shapes also absorb and combine with sauces differently. Dried pasta requires different treatment to its more delicate fresh counterpart.

GNOCCHI DI PATATE

Potato gnocchi with tomato sauce and cheese

Gnocchi are simple to make and can be the most satisfying of pasta dishes. It is impossible to give an exact recipe as the amount of flour needed depends on the moisture content of the potatoes. Gnocchi are best made with floury-textured, older potatoes that have a lower water content. The less flour used, the lighter the gnocchi. If possible, use a potato ricer (see page 161) to mash the potatoes; a hand-masher is the next best option. Makes enough for 6 as a main course or 8 as a first course. Illustrated on page 83.

INGREDIENTS

1kg (2lb) white floury boiling or baking potatoes of uniform size, washed and dried
175g (6oz) plain flour, plus more as needed
1 tsp coarse sea salt
¼ tsp freshly ground white pepper
Sauce
1 quantity Sugo di Pomodoro (see page 138) or Pesto (see page 141)
45g (1½oz) shredded soft cheese such as scamorza or mozzarella
freshly grated Parmesan, optional

PREPARATION

1 Preheat the oven to 200°C/400°F/gas 6.
2 Bake the potatoes until tender, ¾–1 hour, depending on their size. Meanwhile, line three baking sheets with kitchen paper. Pour the flour on to a work surface and make a well in its centre.
3 Smear a large shallow serving dish with a little of the sauce, and keep warm.
4 When the potatoes are just cool enough to handle, peel off their skins (they must be warm when mixed with the flour). Pass them through a ricer into the centre of the well of the flour (see page 161), or mash them and add to the well of the flour. Sprinkle with salt and pepper.
5 Incorporate the flour into the potatoes with a spoon, drawing it in to form a uniform, tender dough. It should be quite soft without being sticky.
6 Knead the dough lightly for 5 minutes. Cut it into quarters and work with one piece at a time. Keep the remainder refrigerated until ready to use (it can be refrigerated for up to 30 minutes).
7 Using your hands, roll the dough into a rope 1.5cm (¾in) thick. Cut this into 1.5cm (¾in) pieces. Take each piece and drag it along the side of a cheese grater to make a concave dumpling (see page 161). If the dough becomes a little sticky,

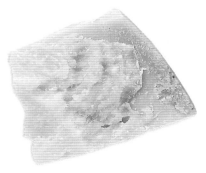

sprinkle it and the grater with flour; if the dough becomes very sticky, knead in more flour.

8 Transfer the gnocchi to the baking sheets, arranging them in a single layer so they are not touching. Meanwhile, fill a pan three-quarters full of water, cover and bring to a rapid boil.

9 Slide the first batch of gnocchi into the water. Add 2 tablespoons of salt and stir with a wooden spoon. As soon as the gnocchi float to the surface, scoop them out and transfer to a colander. Repeat with the remaining gnocchi then place them in the serving dish. Spoon over the sauce and scatter over the soft cheese, if using. Bake in an oven preheated to 220°C/425°F/gas 7 for 5 minutes, or until the cheese melts. Serve immediately with Parmesan.

VARIATION

• Make a Gorgonzola sauce. Melt 60g (2oz) of unsalted butter in a pan. Crumble in 175g (6oz) of Gorgonzola and stir until melted. Pour in 250ml (8fl oz) of double cream and heat through. Remove from the heat, stir in freshly ground white pepper and 2 tablespoons of freshly grated Parmesan.

• Make a sage butter sauce. Melt 90g (3oz) of unsalted butter in a pan. Add a handful of fresh sage leaves and sauté them for 3 minutes, pressing down on them with a wooden spoon. Pour the sage butter over the gnocchi and sprinkle with Parmesan.

GNOCCHI ALLA FONTINA VALDOSTANA

Baked potato gnocchi with fontina

Fontina from the Valle d'Aosta is one of Italy's great cheeses. Its sweet creaminess combines with butter and Parmesan to make an appealing topping for gnocchi. Serves 6.

INGREDIENTS

1 quantity Gnocchi di Patate (see page 78)
60g (2oz) unsalted butter, melted, plus butter to grease
pinch of freshly grated nutmeg
60g (2oz) shredded fontina
2 tbsp freshly grated Parmesan

PREPARATION

1 Make the gnocchi dumplings as directed. Grease a shallow baking dish with butter and arrange the drained gnocchi in a single layer.

2 Preheat the oven to 230°C/450°F/gas 8.

3 Drizzle the butter over the gnocchi, sprinkle with nutmeg then scatter over the fontina and Parmesan. Bake at the top of the oven until the fontina has melted, about 5 minutes. Serve at once.

RAVIOLI ALLA POTENTINA

Ravioli with ricotta, prosciutto and pecorino

In this particular recipe from Potentina in the southern region of Basilicata, prosciutto is added to the traditional local filling of creamy ricotta and sharp pecorino. The result is an appealingly tangy mixture. The classic northern Emilian filling of ricotta, Parmesan, Swiss chard or spinach and nutmeg is also delicious. Serve with Sugo di Pomodoro (see page 138) and a sprinkling of ricotta salata, or simply with butter and grated pecorino cheese. Makes about 90 ravioli; enough for 4–6 as a main course.

INGREDIENTS

1 quantity Pasta Fresca (see page 166), made with an equal mixture of semolina flour and plain flour
1 egg white
Sugo di Pomodoro (see page 138) and/or freshly grated ricotta salata or pecorino, to serve
Filling
1kg (2lb) ricotta
2 egg yolks
90g (3oz) freshly grated pecorino
60g (2oz) thinly sliced prosciutto crudo, finely chopped
½ tsp salt
¼ tsp freshly ground white pepper
2 tbsp finely chopped fresh flat-leaf parsley

PREPARATION

1 To make the filling, place the ricotta in a sieve or cheesecloth over a bowl and leave to drain in the refrigerator for 3–4 hours, until firm. Mix it thoroughly with the remaining ingredients.

2 Roll out the pasta (see page 168). Work with only two strips of dough at a time; keep the rest covered until ready to use. Set the strips side by side, as described for Making Ravioli, step 1.

3 Distribute the filling and paint criss-cross lines of egg white between the mounds of filling, as described in step 2.

4 Place the second strip of pasta over the filled one, then seal and cut into squares, as described in step 3.

5 Place the ravioli, without overlapping them, on trays lined with tea towels sprinkled with cornmeal. Leave to dry for up to 4 hours, turning occasionally.

6 Bring a large pan of salted water to the boil. Add the ravioli, cover until the water boils again, then cook gently for 3–5 minutes, uncovered, stirring occasionally. Transfer them to a warm serving bowl.

7 Spoon the sauce over the ravioli, if desired, and pass the grated ricotta or pecorino at the table.

CAPPELLETTI

Little pasta dumplings with meat and cheese

Pasta dumplings are a speciality of Emilia-Romagna. The dough is always made purely of white flour and eggs, but the fillings vary considerably throughout the region. This is the recipe for the traditional stuffing of Bologna and Modena, and it is a fragrant, subtly seasoned mixture of pork, cured meats, turkey breast and Parmesan. Cappelletti are usually cooked in broth, as here; they can also be served with a cream sauce, or simply with butter and fresh Parmesan. Makes enough for 10–12 as a soup dish or 4–5 as a sauced pasta dish.

INGREDIENTS

Pasta

1 quantity Pasta Fresca (see page 166), made with 300g (10oz) flour and 3 large eggs (no oil and salt)
milk or beaten egg to seal dumplings, optional
flour, to dust

Filling

30g (1oz) unsalted butter
125g (4oz) boneless turkey or chicken breast, diced
125g (4oz) boneless pork loin, finely diced
60g (2oz) prosciutto crudo, thinly sliced
90g (3oz) mortadella or high-quality salami, such as soppressata (see page 27), thinly sliced
30g (1oz) freshly grated Parmesan
¼ tsp freshly grated nutmeg
½ tsp salt
freshly ground white pepper, to taste
1 egg

For cooking in broth (in brodo)

1 quantity Meat Broth (see page 72) or Chicken Broth (see page 73)

PREPARATION

1 To make the filling, melt the butter in a frying pan over a medium heat. Add the turkey and sauté for no more than 2 minutes over a medium-low heat until it loses its pinkness – do not allow it to brown and get hard. Transfer the turkey to a bowl.

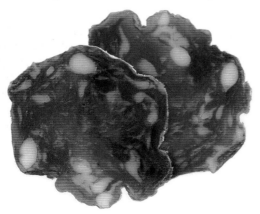

2 Reduce the heat slightly, add the pork to the butter in the pan and sauté for 2–3 minutes. Mix the pork with the turkey and chill until cooled, about 10 minutes.

3 Combine the prosciutto and mortadella on a board and chop them finely. Alternatively, cut them into dice and then mince them in a food processor for no more than a few seconds at a time, taking care not to grind them to a paste.

4 When the turkey and pork have cooled, chop them very finely, as described above. Thoroughly combine the meats, cheese, nutmeg, salt, pepper and egg with a wooden spoon, but do not beat them. Set the mixture aside.

TO FORM THE CAPPELLETTI

1 Roll the dough out as thinly as possible, either by hand or with a pasta machine (see page 167). Work with a quarter of the dough at a time. Keep the strips covered with a slightly damp tea towel until ready to use.

2 Using a pastry wheel or knife, cut each strip of pasta into 5cm (2in) strips, then cut each of these into 5cm (2in) squares. Stuff and shape the cappelletti as shown opposite.

3 Line a baking tray with a tea towel sprinkled with flour and leave the cappelletti to dry. Do not allow them to overlap, and turn them occasionally so they dry evenly. Leave for up to 4 hours before cooking, refrigerating or freezing them.

TO COOK THE CAPPELLETTI

1 Bring the broth to the boil in a large pan.

2 Slide the cappelletti into the broth. Stir, then cover the pan and bring back to the boil. Simmer gently to prevent the cappelletti from breaking. After 3–5 minutes, taste the pasta for doneness. Remove from the heat and serve immediately.

VARIATIONS

• For cappelletti with butter and cheese, fill a pan three-quarters full of water and bring to the boil. Slide the cappelletti into the water. Stir, then cover and bring back to the boil. Simmer for 3–5 minutes, then taste for doneness. Transfer the cappelletti to a warm serving bowl and scatter with 90–125g (3–4oz) of unsalted butter and 60g (2oz) of Parmesan. Serve at once with extra Parmesan.

• For cappelletti in a cream sauce (*alla panna*), gently melt 60g (2oz) of butter in a frying pan. Add 175ml (6fl oz) of double cream and simmer over a medium-low heat until the sauce thickens, about 10 minutes. Meanwhile, cook the cappelletti as described above. Remove the sauce from the heat, drain the cappelletti and add to the pan with 60g (2oz) of freshly grated Parmesan. Check the seasoning and serve immediately.

MAKING CAPPELLETTI

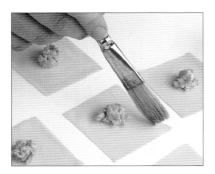  

1 Spoon a ¼ teaspoonful of mixture on to the centre of each square of pasta. Dip a pastry brush or your finger into a little water, milk or beaten egg and run it along the inside edges.

2 Fold the square in half to make a triangle, bringing up the edges of one side to just below the other. Press together. The dumpling should resemble a small stuffed kerchief.

3 Wrap the dumpling around your finger, holding the peaked end up, with the stuffed side away from you. Overlap the two bottom corners of the triangle and pinch together.

*TAGLIATELLE CON
SALSA BOLOGNESE*
*Tagliatelle with
bolognese sauce
(page 88)*

GNOCCHI DI PATATE
*Potato gnocchi with tomato
sauce and cheese
(page 78)*

CONCHIGLIE ALLA PUTTANESCA
*Pasta shells with harlot's sauce,
Tuscan style
(page 85)*

LASAGNE IMBOTTITE
Lasagne stuffed in the style of Naples

This elaborate festive dish is usually reserved for giovedi grasso, *"fat Thursday", at the end of Carnival. Meatballs and sausages are typically included, and sometimes sliced hard-boiled eggs. Omit the meatballs for a quicker version. Serves 8 as a main course.*

INGREDIENTS

½ quantity Polpettine meatballs (see page 67), optional
olive oil for frying
500g (1lb) dried lasagne or other wide noodles
Sauce
875g (1¾lb) canned tomatoes in juice
75ml (2½fl oz) extra-virgin olive oil
60g (2oz) pancetta or prosciutto crudo, sliced approximately 1mm (¹⁄₁₆in) thick, finely chopped
2 tbsp chopped fresh flat-leaf parsley
1 carrot, finely chopped
1 celery stalk with leaves, finely chopped
2 large cloves garlic, finely chopped
1 small onion, finely chopped
500g (1lb) sweet Italian sausages
375g (12oz) minced lean beef or pork, or a mixture
1¼ tsp salt
4 tbsp tomato purée
175ml (6fl oz) good-quality dry red wine
freshly ground black pepper, to taste
750g (1½lb) ricotta
125g (4oz) freshly grated pecorino or Parmesan
625g (1¼lb) mozzarella, shredded

PREPARATION

1 Sauté the meatballs in oil, if using, then set aside.
2 Drain the tomatoes, reserving their juice. Strain the juice and deseed the tomatoes. Chop the tomatoes and set aside with their juice.
3 Warm the oil in a pan. Add the pancetta and fry until golden. Stir in the parsley, carrot, celery, garlic and onion, and sauté until softened, 10–12 minutes.
4 Remove the casings of three sausages and mix the meat with the minced meat. Add to the pan with the vegetables and sprinkle in the salt. Sauté until the meat is lightly coloured, about 8 minutes.
5 Stir in the tomato purée and wine. Simmer for 3 minutes then add the tomatoes and juice. Cover partially and simmer until a thick sauce forms, about 1 hour. Check the seasoning and set aside.
6 Meanwhile, cook the remaining sausages until lightly browned (see page 164). Cover and refrigerate until ready to use.
7 Bring 5 litres (8 pints) of salted water to the boil. Add the lasagne and cook until almost done, about 9 minutes, stirring occasionally. Drain, reserving

90ml (3fl oz) of water. Rinse the lasagne under cold water then lay on waxed paper. (If using ready-to-use lasagne, follow the package instructions.)
8 Blend the ricotta, reserved pasta water, or a little fresh water if using ready-to-use lasagne, and half the pecorino in a bowl. Cut the fried sausages into long thin slices. Halve the meatballs, if using.
9 Preheat the oven to 220°C/425°F/gas 7.

TO ASSEMBLE

1 Smear a little meat sauce on the base of a 25 x 35cm (10 x 14in) baking dish. Cover with a layer of lasagne noodles. Spread some of the ricotta mixture over the pasta, then sprinkle with pecorino.
2 Follow with a layer of sauce, some of the sliced sausages and meatballs, then a layer of mozzarella.
3 Repeat the process, layering all the ingredients in the same order until they are used up. You should have three layers of pasta. Top the final layer with meat sauce scattered with sliced sausages, meatballs, mozzarella and pecorino.
4 Bake the lasagne at the top of the oven until it is bubbly and golden, about 25 minutes. Allow to settle for 15 minutes before serving.

ORECCHIETTE CON SALSICCIA E CIME DI RAPA
Orecchiette with sausage and bitter broccoli

Cime di rapa *is the authentic green to use in this Apulian dish, but kale makes a good substitute. Serves 6.*

INGREDIENTS

75ml (2½fl oz) extra-virgin olive oil
375g (12oz) sweet Italian sausages, casings removed
4 cloves garlic, finely chopped
¼ tsp crushed dried red chillies, or to taste
1kg (2lb) cime di rapa (bitter broccoli) or kale, stems peeled and trimmed, chopped into 2.5cm (1in) pieces
salt, to taste
500g (1lb) orecchiette

PREPARATION

1 Warm 2 tablespoons of oil in a deep frying pan. Add the sausage meat and brown over a medium-low heat for 10 minutes. Stir in the garlic and chilli and cook until softened, about 3 minutes.
2 Add the greens and 125ml (4fl oz) of water to the sausage. Toss thoroughly then cook, covered, over a medium-low heat, until the greens are tender, about 10 minutes, stirring occasionally.
3 Meanwhile, bring 5 litres (8 pints) of salted water to the boil, add the pasta and cook until *al dente*. Drain the pasta, toss thoroughly with the sauce and remaining oil and season well before serving.

BUCATINI ALL' AMATRICIANA
Bucatini with tomato and bacon sauce

INGREDIENTS

750g (1½lb) canned tomatoes in juice, or 1.25kg (2½lb)
fresh tomatoes, skinned, deseeded and chopped
30g (1oz) unsalted butter, or 2 tbsp extra-virgin olive oil
1 small onion, chopped
2 large cloves garlic, bruised
60g (2oz) chunk pancetta or thickly sliced lean bacon
strips, blanched in boiling water for 1 minute
pinch of crushed dried red chillies
salt, to taste
500g (1lb) bucatini or spaghetti
freshly grated Parmesan or pecorino or a mixture, to serve

PREPARATION

1 If using canned tomatoes, drain them, reserving
the juice. Remove any seeds, chop the flesh and set
aside. If using fresh chopped tomatoes, place them
in a colander and leave to drain for 5 minutes.
2 Warm the butter or oil in a frying pan over a
medium-low heat. Add the onion and garlic and fry
until golden, about 6 minutes. Chop the pancetta
into julienne strips and sauté lightly for 5 minutes.
3 Stir in the chilli, tomato and juice and ½ teaspoon
of salt. Simmer gently until thickened, about
35 minutes, stirring occasionally. Discard the garlic.
4 Meanwhile, bring 5 litres (8 pints) of salted water
to the boil, add the pasta and stir immediately. Cook
over a high heat, stirring occasionally, until *al dente*.
5 Drain the pasta and toss it with the sauce. Serve
hot, with plenty of grated cheese.

CONCHIGLIE ALLA PUTTANESCA
Pasta with harlot's sauce, Tuscan style

While the Neapolitans serve this dish hot, the puttanesca
sauce I've had in the homes of Tuscan friends has almost
always been uncooked and chilled. Try it when good, sun-
ripened tomatoes are available. Illustrated on page 82.

INGREDIENTS

625g (1¼lb) fresh tomatoes, skinned, deseeded and chopped
125ml (4fl oz) extra-virgin olive oil
2 large cloves garlic, chopped
8 large fresh basil leaves, torn into small pieces
1 tbsp chopped fresh flat-leaf parsley
45g (1½oz) black olives such as Gaeta or Niçoise, sliced
1 tbsp small capers, rinsed and drained
¼ tsp crushed dried red chillies, or to taste
½ tsp salt, or to taste
500g (1lb) conchiglie or spaghetti

PREPARATION

1 Mix the sauce ingredients together, stirring them
well. Leave to marinate for at least 1 hour at room
temperature, or cover and chill for up to 3 days.
2 Cook the pasta as described in step 4, left, and
drain and add it to the bowl with the sauce, tossing
everything together. Serve at room temperature.

SPAGHETTI ALLA CARBONARA
Spaghetti with eggs and bacon

Although this popular spaghetti dish is fairly modern,
it has become so widespread that it deserves a place
among the classics. Part of its success depends upon
using some of the pasta cooking water to moisturize
the egg-based sauce. Serves 4–6.

INGREDIENTS

150g (5oz) chunk pancetta or bacon, blanched in
boiling water for 1 minute, cut into very
thin slices and then finely diced
3 tbsp extra-virgin olive oil
5 large cloves garlic, bruised
90ml (3fl oz) dry white wine
4 extra-large eggs, beaten
2 tbsp single cream, optional
20g (¾oz) freshly grated Parmesan
2 tbsp freshly grated pecorino
salt, to taste
500g (1lb) spaghetti
plenty of freshly ground pepper

PREPARATION

1 Put the pancetta and 3 tablespoons of water in a
large non-stick frying pan over a medium heat.
When the water has evaporated and the pancetta
starts to colour, drain off all but 1 tablespoon of fat.
2 Add the oil and garlic to the frying pan. Sauté
over a medium-low heat until the pancetta is
browned and the garlic is golden, about 4 minutes.
3 Deglaze the pan by stirring in the wine. Discard
the garlic and take the pan off the heat.
4 Beat the eggs with the cream, if using, cheese
and ½ teaspoon of salt in a separate bowl.
5 Bring 5 litres (8 pints) of salted water to the boil
and add the pasta. Stir quickly, then cook over a
high heat, stirring occasionally, until *al dente*.
6 Drain the pasta, reserving 250ml (8fl oz) of the
cooking water. While the pasta is still wet and
piping hot, toss it thoroughly with the pancetta.
7 Quickly add the egg mixture to the frying pan,
tossing it thoroughly. Add enough cooking water
to create an abundant, creamy sauce. Sprinkle with
pepper and serve at once.

CICERI E TRIA

Salentine fettuccine with chick-peas and onions

*The Salento region extends to the very tip of the heel
of the Italian boot. Many of its unique dishes are based
on vegetables, pulses and seafood and are almost spartan
in their simplicity. My variation of this robust dish is a
pleasing combination of soft and crispy textures.*

INGREDIENTS

125ml (4fl oz) extra-virgin olive oil
1 onion, chopped
1 large celery stalk with leaves, chopped
1 carrot, coarsely grated
3 large cloves garlic, finely chopped
*200g (7oz) dried chick-peas, rehydrated and cooked (see
page 161), plus 400ml (14fl oz) of their cooking liquid,
or 475g (15oz) canned chick-peas, drained*
*1½ tsp chopped fresh rosemary, or ¾ tsp dried rosemary
salt, to taste*
*½ quantity Pasta Fresca (see page 166), made with
250g (8oz) semolina flour, 2 eggs and ½ tsp salt, cut into
fettuccine, or 375g (12oz) dried fettuccine or tagliatelle*
2 tbsp chopped fresh flat-leaf parsley
freshly ground black pepper, to taste

PREPARATION

1 Heat 90ml (3fl oz) of the oil in a large frying
pan. Add the onion, celery, carrot and garlic, and
sauté gently until softened, about 10 minutes.
2 Add the chick-peas, rosemary and ¾ teaspoon
of salt to the frying pan. Crush most of the
chick-peas with a potato masher or fork, leaving
only a handful whole.
3 Stir in the reserved chick-pea cooking liquid, if
using rehydrated chick-peas, or 400ml (14fl oz) of
fresh water. Simmer until the flavours blend and
a sauce is formed, about 8 minutes.
4 Meanwhile, bring 5 litres (8 pints) of salted
water to the boil for the pasta. Add 250g (8oz) of
the pasta and set the rest aside. Bring to the boil
again and cook over a high heat until tender, about
2 minutes from the second boil for fresh pasta and
6–8 minutes for dried. Drain, reserving 250ml
(8fl oz) of cooking water. Transfer the pasta to the
pan with the chick-peas while still dripping wet.
5 Add the parsley to the frying pan and toss
everything together. If necessary, add some of the
reserved cooking water to moisten the sauce.
Check the seasoning.
6 Heat the remaining oil in a frying pan. When it
is hot, toss in the remaining uncooked noodles.
When they are browned, add them with their oil
to the other noodles, scattering them on top.
Sprinkle with plenty of pepper and serve.

Garlic

Carrots

Celery

Onion

Olive oil

Chick-peas

Rosemary

Salt

Fettuccine

Flat-leaf
parsley

Black
pepper

TAGLIATELLE CON SALSA BOLOGNESE

Tagliatelle with bolognese sauce

Outside Italy, bolognese sauce has become synonymous with a nondescript meat and tomato mixture, but the authentic version is complex and fragrant. A variety of meats, and sometimes cured meats, are simmered with celery, tomatoes and onion, and a little milk and white wine, to form a delicate, creamy sauce. I include minced pork for its rich flavour and sweetness, and mortadella for its subtle spiciness. Serves 6–8. Illustrated on page 82.

INGREDIENTS

250g (8oz) fresh or canned drained tomatoes, skinned, deseeded and chopped and juice reserved
30g (1oz) unsalted butter
½ tbsp extra-virgin olive oil
30g (1oz) chunk pancetta, finely chopped
1 small onion, finely chopped
1 small celery stalk with leaves, finely chopped
1 small carrot, finely chopped
1 tbsp chopped fresh flat-leaf parsley
175g (6oz) lean minced beef
90g (3oz) minced pork
30g (1oz) mortadella, finely chopped, optional
⅓ tsp salt, or to taste
90ml (3fl oz) good-quality dry white wine
90ml (3fl oz) milk
good pinch of freshly grated nutmeg
2 tbsp tomato purée
175ml (6fl oz) Meat Broth (see page 72) or good stock
1 quantity Pasta Fresca (see page 166), cut into tagliatelle, or 750g (1½lb) dried pasta, such as fusilli or orecchiette
freshly ground white or black pepper, to taste
freshly grated Parmesan, to serve

PREPARATION

1 Strain the tomato juice and discard the seeds. Set aside the chopped tomatoes and their juice.
2 In a large heavy-based pan or deep frying pan, melt 1½ tablespoons of butter with the oil. Stir in the pancetta and sauté until lightly coloured.
3 Add the onion, celery, carrot and parsley and sauté until softened but not browned, about 12 minutes. Keeping the heat very low, add the minced meat, mortadella, if using, and the salt. Allow the meat to colour lightly, about 2 minutes, and use a wooden spoon to break up the chunks.
4 Pour in the wine. Simmer very gently until the alcohol evaporates and the liquid begins to be absorbed, about 3 minutes.
5 Add the milk and nutmeg and simmer for 10 minutes. Stir in the tomato purée dissolved in 60ml (2fl oz) of broth. Add the tomatoes and

juice. As soon as the sauce begins to simmer, turn the heat down as low as possible. Cover partially and cook for at least 4 hours, stirring occasionally. Add the remaining broth as the sauce cooks.
6 When the sauce is thick, creamy and fragrant, remove it from the heat and stir in the remaining butter and the pepper. Check the seasoning.
7 Bring 5 litres (8 pints) of salted water to the boil. When the water is boiling rapidly, stir in the fresh or dried pasta. Cover, and as soon as the water returns to the boil, remove the lid and stir again. Cook the fresh pasta for 10 seconds after the water has returned to the boil, then drain immediately, or cook the dried pasta until *al dente*, then drain.
8 Transfer the tagliatelle to a warm serving bowl, toss with the sauce and sprinkle with Parmesan.

MACCHERONI ALLA BARESE CON CAVOLFIORE

Penne with cauliflower and onions, Bari style

Apulian cuisine is known for its many imaginative vegetable dishes. I learnt this flavour-packed and nutritious recipe from Anna Amendolara Nurse, whose parents emigrated to New York from Bari. Serves 4–6.

INGREDIENTS

1 large cauliflower, about 1.25–1.5kg (2½–3lb), trimmed and cut into small florets
salt, to taste
125ml (4fl oz) extra-virgin olive oil
2 onions, cut lengthways into thick slices
500g (1lb) penne rigate or other ridged tubular pasta
1 tbsp chopped fresh flat-leaf parsley
pinch of crushed dried red chillies
freshly ground black pepper, to taste

PREPARATION

1 Bring 7.5 litres (12 pints) of water to the boil. Add the cauliflower and 2 tablespoons of salt, and boil until almost tender, 4–5 minutes. Transfer the florets to a bowl; do not discard the cooking water.
2 Gently heat the oil in a heavy pan. Add the onion and cook until golden.
3 When the onion is almost done, return the cauliflower water to the boil. Add the penne and cook until almost *al dente*, about 7 minutes. Add the cauliflower and cook until it is heated through, about 1 minute longer. Drain off all but 250ml (8fl oz) of the cooking water. Transfer the cauliflower, pasta and water to a warm bowl.
4 Quickly reheat the oil and onion and add to the penne. Season with the parsley, chilli, salt and black pepper, and serve at once.

CRESPELLE
Crêpes

Crespelle *are little pancakes that appear throughout the Italian regions, and have different names wherever they are found: in Tuscany, they are fazzoletti, "handkerchiefs"; in Calabria, manicotti, "little muffs". They may be filled with meat, seafood, vegetables or cheese, rolled up, then covered with tomato or béchamel sauce and baked. For light, delicate crêpes, the batter must be very thin, almost watery. Don't worry if the first one or two in the batch are imperfect; you'll soon get the hang of it and the rest will no doubt be flawless. Makes 20 crêpes.*

INGREDIENTS

4 large eggs (size 1)
600ml (1 pint) milk, or more if necessary
pinch of sugar
½ tsp salt
175g (6oz) unbleached white flour
sunflower oil for frying

PREPARATION

1 Whisk together the eggs, milk, sugar and salt. Add the flour, sifting it in gradually while beating with the whisk to break up any lumps. The batter should be extremely thin – almost watery. Cover and allow to rest for 30 minutes.
2 Over a medium-high heat, warm ½ teaspoon of oil in a cold, non-stick 20cm (8in) crêpe pan or shallow frying pan with curved sides, rotating it to coat the entire base of the pan. Test the heat of the oil by pouring in a teaspoon of batter.
3 Cook the crespelle one at a time, pouring about 3 tablespoons of batter into the hot pan for each one. The batter should spread until it makes a large, thin pancake, completely covering the pan. Tilt and rotate the pan to spread the mixture evenly.
4 When tiny holes begin to form in the crêpe, about 1 minute, flip it over and cook lightly on the reverse side for about 30 seconds.
5 Transfer the crespelle to a platter and cover with a plate or clingfilm until ready to use. Repeat with the remaining batter, adding more oil when needed.

MANICOTTI
Crêpes stuffed with ricotta, Calabrian style

Manicotti *are crêpes with a ricotta filling baked in a tomato sauce. This particular version is traditionally served at the Calabrian* cenone, *the meatless meal eaten on Christmas Eve, or on Sundays or holidays. Serves 6.*

INGREDIENTS

¼ quantity Sugo di Pomodoro (see page 138)
1 quantity Crespelle (see left)
Filling
500g (1lb) ricotta, drained in a sieve for 2 hours
2½ tbsp freshly grated pecorino or Parmesan
1 egg
1 tbsp chopped fresh flat-leaf parsley
¼ tsp salt
pinch of freshly ground white or black pepper
125g (4oz) mozzarella, cut into strips about 5cm (2in) long and 5mm (¼in) wide

PREPARATION

1 Make the crespelle as described left, and stack and set aside until ready to fill.
2 Combine the ricotta with two-thirds of the grated cheese, the egg, parsley, salt and pepper. Taste and adjust the seasoning if necessary.
3 Preheat the oven to 200°F/400°F/gas 6.
4 Smear a thin layer of tomato sauce on the base of two baking dishes. Place a tablespoon of filling at one end of each crêpe. Lay a strip of mozzarella on the filling and roll the crêpe up tightly.
5 Take a little of the filling on your finger and run it along the inside edge of the crêpe, then press down the edges to seal them. Place the crêpe rolls in the baking dish, leaving space around each one.
6 Spoon 3–4 tablespoons of the tomato sauce on top of the crespelle to moisten them; do not drench them. Sprinkle with the remaining grated cheese. If there is any mozzarella left, cut it into small dice and sprinkle over the top.
7 Bake the dish at the top of the oven until bubbly and golden, 10–15 minutes. Allow to cool for 10 minutes before serving.

BEANS, RICE AND POLENTA

Corn and beans, introduced to Europe from the New World, have become staples in the Italian diet. In its simplest guise polenta, made from ground corn, is served "loose" as a sort of porridge, but, as befits its versatility, it may appear in many other forms. Beans are used fresh and dried and include lentils, chick-peas, cannellini and borlotti. Risotto is impossible without Italian rice, which is uniquely suited to slow cooking in a small amount of liquid. Rice is always served as a first course, except for Risotto alla Milanese, the traditional accompaniment to Ossobuco (see page 54).

FAGIOLI IN STUFA
Beans stewed with garlic and herbs

The Tuscans are inordinately fond of eating beans and consequently they have many recipes for bean dishes. This aromatic stew of beans and herbs is typical of the region's cooking, being effectively simple. Serves 4–6.

INGREDIENTS

*375g (12oz) dried cannellini or haricot beans, or
1.5kg (3lb) drained canned beans
2 bay leaves
salt, to taste
4 tbsp extra-virgin olive oil
2 large cloves garlic, chopped
2 tbsp chopped fresh flat-leaf parsley
1½ tsp chopped fresh marjoram, or ¾ tsp dried marjoram
freshly ground white pepper, to taste*

PREPARATION

1 If using dried beans, rehydrate and cook them as described on page 161, adding 2 bay leaves to the cooking pot. Season the cooked beans with salt and allow to steep in their liquid until the salt is absorbed, at least 15 minutes. Drain, reserving 3 tablespoons of the cooking liquid.
2 Warm the oil and garlic together until the garlic is soft but not coloured, about 3 minutes. Stir in the parsley and marjoram, then add the beans and the reserved liquid or 3 tablespoons of fresh water.
3 Cover the pan and simmer for 10–15 minutes. Check the seasoning, add pepper and serve hot.

VARIATION

Add 125g (4oz) of skinned, deseeded and chopped fresh or canned tomatoes to the beans with the parsley and marjoram in step 2.

LENTICCHIE ALLA CASALINGA
Lentils with butter and parsley

While this dish is traditionally served alongside pork and game, it can satisfy as a vegetarian meal if accompanied by a salad or other side dish. The cooked lentils are also good served cold with a dressing of lemon juice, extra-virgin olive oil, parsley and chopped onion.

INGREDIENTS

*250g (8oz) brown lentils, rinsed and drained
2 tsp coarse salt
1 large bay leaf
small bunch parsley stems, tied together
3 large cloves garlic, cut in half
45g (1½oz) unsalted butter at room temperature
juice of ½ lemon, plus 1½ lemons,
cut into wedges, to serve
2 tbsp finely chopped fresh flat-leaf parsley
freshly ground black pepper, to taste*

PREPARATION

1 Place the lentils in a pan with 1 litre (1¾ pints) of water, the salt, bay leaf, parsley stems and garlic. Bring to the boil, then simmer over a medium-low heat until the lentils are tender but not falling apart, about 25 minutes.
2 Drain the lentils, discarding the bay leaf, parsley stems and garlic.
3 Meanwhile, beat the butter in a small bowl until it is creamy. Blend the lemon juice into the butter, then beat in 1 tablespoon of chopped parsley. Mix the parsley butter into the hot lentils, tossing them gently. Check the seasoning.
4 Sprinkle the remaining tablespoon of parsley over the lentils and grind some pepper over them. Serve the lentils hot or warm with lemon wedges.

CASSERUOLA DI LENTICCHIE CON SALSICCE

Lentil stew with sausages

Pork and lentils have a natural affinity for each other. My mother always served this hearty, fortifying stew in winter. It takes little effort to make and can be prepared hours or even days in advance. Serves 6.

INGREDIENTS

*500g (1lb) brown lentils, rinsed and drained
2 bay leaves
2 small celery stalks with leaves, 1 whole
and 1 finely chopped
1 tbsp salt
2 tbsp olive oil, plus extra if necessary
8 meaty pork sausages, preferably Italian
1 carrot, chopped
1 small onion, finely chopped
2 large cloves garlic, finely chopped
3 tbsp tomato purée*

PREPARATION

1 Place the lentils in a saucepan with 2 litres (3½ pints) of water, the bay leaf, whole celery stalk and salt. Bring to the boil, then simmer gently until the lentils are *al dente*, about 25 minutes. Drain, reserving 750ml (1¼ pints) of the cooking liquid. Discard the bay leaf and celery.

2 Warm the oil in a large pan or casserole over a medium-low heat. Add the sausages and pierce them with a fork to release some of the fat. Sauté until browned all over, about 12 minutes. Remove from the pan and drain off all but 2 tablespoons of the fat (if there is not enough fat, add more oil).

3 Add the chopped celery and leaves, the carrot, onion and garlic, and sauté gently until softened, about 8 minutes. Stir in the tomato purée and the lentil cooking liquid and slowly bring to the boil.

4 Return the lentils and sausages to the pan, cover and simmer gently until the sausages are cooked through, about 10 minutes. Check the seasoning, slice the sausages if desired, and serve hot.

RISOTTO ALLA MILANESE
Saffron risotto, Milanese style

*Risotto is a simple dish to make if the following
things are remembered: use authentic Italian Arborio,
Carnaroli or Vialone nano rice; make sure the broth is
kept hot (cold liquid will bring down the temperature)
and, as always in Italian cooking, use the best and
purest ingredients available. Serves 6.*

INGREDIENTS

*1.5 litres (2½ pints) Meat Broth (see page 72) or
Chicken Broth (see page 73)
90g (3oz) unsalted butter
2 tbsp beef marrow, chopped, or 30g (1oz) additional
butter, or 60g (2oz) finely chopped pancetta
1 onion, finely chopped
475g (15oz) Arborio, Carnaroli or Vialone nano rice
125ml (4fl oz) dry white wine
generous ½ tsp saffron strands
45g (1½oz) freshly grated Parmesan, plus extra
for serving
freshly ground white pepper, to taste*

PREPARATION

1 Gently heat the broth and keep it warm
over a low flame.
2 Heat half the butter with the beef marrow or
additional butter or pancetta in a pan. When the
marrow is melted, add the onion and sauté over a
low heat until softened, about 5 minutes.
3 Add the rice and sauté for 3–4 minutes, stirring
continually to coat the grains. Pour in the wine and
reduce the heat slightly. When all the wine has
been absorbed into the rice, add a ladleful of hot
broth and stir thoroughly.
4 Once the broth has been almost completely
absorbed, add another ladleful. Continue stirring
and adding the broth, a ladleful at a time, until the
rice is half-cooked, about 15 minutes. At this
point, dissolve the saffron in a ladleful of hot broth
and pour into the pan. Add the remainder of the
broth, waiting for each ladleful to be absorbed
before adding the next.
5 When the rice is tender but still slightly chewy,
remove it from the heat; it should be creamy, but
not mushy. Stir in the remaining butter and the
Parmesan. Check the seasoning and serve.

RISOTTO ALLA MARINARA
Seafood risotto

*There are infinite variations on the theme of seafood
risotto throughout the northern coastal regions.
Most contain squid and prawns of some kind. Fish, clams
and mussels may also be included. The finished texture
of a risotto should be what the Venetians call all' onda,
"with a wave", that is very moist, almost wet. Parmesan
cheese is never served with seafood dishes. Serves 4–6.*

INGREDIENTS

*500g (1lb) whole white-fleshed fish, such as sea bream,
snapper, mullet or bass, scaled and gutted
750g (1½ lb) small tender squid
250g (8oz) unpeeled raw small or medium prawns
1 onion, unpeeled and quartered, plus 1 onion, chopped
2 carrots, 1 whole and 1 chopped
2 celery stalks with leaves, 1 whole and 1 chopped
4 sprigs fresh flat-leaf parsley
1 whole fennel, plus 3 tbsp chopped tender fennel fronds,
if available, or 2 bay leaves
¼ tsp black or white peppercorns
salt
60g (2oz) unsalted butter
1 tbsp extra-virgin olive oil
1 large clove garlic, bruised
475g (15oz) Arborio, Carnaroli or Vialone nano rice
125ml (4fl oz) good dry white wine
2 sachets (260mg) saffron powder, or ¼ tsp saffron strands
freshly ground black pepper, to taste*

PREPARATION

1 Fillet the fish, reserving the head, tail and bones
for stock. Cut the fish fillets into 2.5cm (1in) dice.
Cover until ready to use.
2 Clean the squid (see page 99). Cut the body
into 5mm (¼in) rings and quarter or halve the
tentacles. Rinse and dry all the squid pieces.
3 Peel and devein the prawns (see page 163),
reserving the shells. Rinse the prawns, pat dry then
cut in half lengthways. Cover until ready to use.
4 Make a stock. Place the prawn shells and fish
trimmings in a pot with the whole onion and
carrot, the whole celery stalk, parsley sprigs,
whole piece of fennel and peppercorns. Add
1.75 litres (3 pints) of cold water and 1 tablespoon
of salt. Bring to the boil then simmer over a
medium-low heat for 35 minutes, skimming the
foam off the top as it forms. Strain the finished
stock into a pan and keep warm.
5 Heat 15g (½oz) of butter in a non-stick frying
pan. Add the prawns and diced fish and sauté until
lightly coloured on all sides, 4–5 minutes. Set aside.
6 Heat the remaining butter with the olive oil in a

wide, deep frying pan. Add the garlic, chopped onion, carrot and celery. Sauté gently until the vegetables soften, about 8 minutes, stirring occasionally. Add the squid, raise the heat to high and sauté until nicely coloured all over, about 6 minutes. Reduce the heat to medium-high and remove the garlic clove.

7 Stir in the rice and sauté for 3–4 minutes, stirring continually to coat the grains in the oil. Pour in the wine and reduce the heat slightly. When the wine has been fully absorbed, add a ladleful of hot fish stock, stirring well.

8 Once the stock has been almost completely absorbed, add a further ladleful. Continue adding the stock, a ladleful at a time, until the rice is half-done, approximately 15 minutes. At this point, dissolve the saffron in a little stock then stir it into the rice. Add all but a tablespoon of the remaining stock a ladleful at a time, waiting for each addition to be absorbed before adding the next. Stir in the fish and prawns just before adding the last ladleful.

9 Stir the final tablespoon of stock into the fish frying pan to deglaze it, then pour these pan juices into the risotto. When the rice is tender but still slightly chewy, remove the pan from the heat. The risotto should be creamy, but not mushy. Check for salt, add pepper and stir in the chopped fennel fronds, if using. Serve immediately.

RISOTTO CON POMODORO E BASILICO

Risotto with tomato and basil

Here is a good risotto to make in the summer when sweet, vine-ripened tomatoes and fresh basil are available.

INGREDIENTS

750–900ml (1¼–1½ pints) Meat Broth (see page 72)
2oz (60g) unsalted butter
2 large cloves garlic, bruised
1 onion, chopped
300g (10oz) fresh or canned drained tomatoes,
skinned, deseeded and chopped
325g (11oz) Arborio, Carnaroli or Vialone nano rice
20g (¾oz) freshly grated Parmesan, plus extra for serving
10 large fresh basil leaves, torn into very small pieces
freshly ground black pepper, to taste
salt, to taste

PREPARATION

1 Gently heat the broth and keep it warm over a low flame.
2 Meanwhile, melt half the butter in a saucepan, add the garlic and onion and sauté gently until softened, 4–5 minutes. Discard the garlic.
3 Stir in the tomatoes and simmer over a medium-low heat until the sauce is thickened and aromatic, about 20 minutes, stirring occasionally.
4 In a large frying pan over a medium heat, melt the remaining butter and add the rice. Sauté for 3–4 minutes, stirring continually to coat the grains.
5 Heat the tomato sauce through and stir it into the rice. Reduce the heat to medium and simmer until the sauce is absorbed, stirring continually.
6 Add a ladleful of the hot broth and stir frequently. When it has been almost completely absorbed, add another ladleful of hot broth and stir well. Continue adding the broth, a ladleful at a time, until the rice is tender but still slightly chewy, 20–25 minutes. It should be creamy, but not mushy.
7 Remove the pan from the heat. Stir in the grated Parmesan and the basil. Taste for salt and add pepper. Serve the finished risotto piping hot, passing additional Parmesan at the table.

VARIATION

Just before serving, finely dice 125g (4oz) of mozzarella and stir it into the hot risotto, allowing it to melt slightly.

RISO IN PEVERADA

Rice with chicken livers in the style of the Veneto

The description peverada *indicates that a dish includes* pepitella, *a peppery herb in the mint family used to flavour Venetian game and risotto dishes. Mint can be substituted for pepitella in this pleasant risotto, which successfully brings together several distinctive ingredients. Serves 6.*

INGREDIENTS

250g (8oz) chicken livers
1.5 litres (2½ pints) Meat Broth (see page 72)
30g (1oz) unsalted butter
2 tbsp olive oil
30g (1oz) beef marrow, chopped or 30g (1oz) additional
butter, or 60g (2oz) finely chopped pancetta
1 onion, chopped
5cm (2in) strip of lemon zest, blanched
2 tbsp chopped fresh mint or flat-leaf parsley
475g (15oz) Arborio, Carnaroli or Vialone nano rice
125ml (4fl oz) dry white wine
salt, to taste
30g (1oz) freshly grated Parmesan, plus extra to serve

PREPARATION

1 Wash the livers and trim off any connective tissue, fat or discoloured parts. Dice the livers.
2 Gently heat the broth and keep it warm over a low flame.
3 Meanwhile, combine half the butter, the oil and the beef marrow in a pan over a medium-low heat. When the butter is melted, add the onion, lemon zest and half the mint. Sauté gently until softened but not coloured, about 5 minutes.
4 Add the livers and sauté them with the onion mixture until they are browned on all sides, about 2 minutes. Add the rice and sauté for 3–4 minutes, stirring continually to coat the grains. Pour in the wine and reduce the heat slightly.
5 Add a ladleful of hot broth and stir thoroughly. When it has been almost completely absorbed, add another ladleful of hot broth and stir well. Continue adding the broth, a ladleful at a time, until the rice is tender but still slightly chewy, 20–25 minutes. It should be creamy, but not mushy. Taste for salt.
6 Remove the pan from the heat then stir in the remaining butter and mint and the grated Parmesan cheese. Serve piping hot, passing additional Parmesan at the table.

RISO ARROSTO

Roasted rice with sausage and artichokes

Unlike a risotto, this Ligurian rice dish can be made well in advance. Veal sweetbreads or other economical meat cuts are typically included. Italian rice produces excellent results, but other rice varieties can be used. Serves 6.

INGREDIENTS

4 artichokes, about 175–250g (6–8oz) each
salt, to taste
1 tbsp vegetable oil
500g (1lb) crumbled high quality pork sausage meat
45g (1½oz) unsalted butter
1 onion, chopped
2 tbsp chopped fresh flat-leaf parsley
325g (11oz) Arborio, Carnaroli or Vialone nano rice
30g (1oz) freshly grated Parmesan
350ml (12fl oz) Meat Broth (see page 72) or good stock

PREPARATION

1 Prepare the artichokes. Cut off and trim the stems then halve them lengthways. Using a paring knife, tear off the artichoke's tough outer leaves, leaving the tender inner leaves. Slice across the top of the artichoke with a serrated knife, leaving 3.5cm (1½in) of the base. Trim off any tough parts, cut each base into quarters lengthways and cut out the choke.
2 Place the hearts and stems in water acidulated with lemon juice.
3 Bring enough salted water to cover the artichokes to the boil and drop them in. Cook until half-done, 3–6 minutes. Drain and set aside.
4 Heat the oil in a frying pan and add the sausage. Brown for about 7 minutes, stirring occasionally. Drain off any excess oil and set aside.
5 Preheat the oven to 200°C/400°F/gas 6.
6 Heat 30g (1oz) of butter in another frying pan. Add the onion and parsley and sauté until the onion is translucent, about 3 minutes. Add the parboiled artichokes and the rice and sauté for 1–2 minutes, stirring continually. Remove from the heat. Combine the sausage meat, the artichoke and rice mixture and all but 2 tablespoons of the Parmesan. Transfer the mixture to a baking dish.
7 Stir ½ teaspoon of salt into the broth and stir the broth into the rice mixture. Cover the dish with foil and bake in the oven until the broth is absorbed and the rice tender, 20–25 minutes. Remove from the oven and preheat the grill.
8 Uncover the dish and dot the rice with the remaining butter and Parmesan. Set the dish about 15cm (6in) below the grill and leave to form a golden crust, 2–4 minutes. Allow to settle for 10 minutes before serving hot or warm.

POLENTA MARITATA

Baked polenta casserole

Maritata means "married", possibly signifying that the components of this pasticcio (literally a "mess" or "muddle", but meaning any kind of baked dish) are well suited to one another. Of the various types of polenta pasticcio found in Italian cooking, many of which include a meat sauce, this is the simplest and lightest. It is an excellent dish in the warm weather when basil and tomatoes are bountiful. Serves 8.

INGREDIENTS

1 quantity Polenta (see page 169)
1½ tbsp chopped fresh basil
300g (10oz) mozzarella, shredded
Sauce
3 tbsp extra-virgin olive oil
4 large cloves garlic, bruised
1.25kg (2½lb) fresh or canned drained tomatoes, skinned, deseeded and chopped
3 tbsp chopped fresh basil
salt and freshly ground black pepper, to taste

PREPARATION

1 To make the sauce, warm the oil in a saucepan over a medium heat. Add the garlic and sauté until golden, about 4 minutes.
2 Add the tomatoes and basil and stir. Bring to a simmer and continue to cook for 25 minutes.
3 Remove the sauce from the heat and allow it to cool slightly, then pass it through a food mill or sieve, pushing through as much pulp as possible. Add salt and pepper to taste and set aside.
4 Preheat the oven to 200°C/400°F/gas 6.
5 Make the polenta crostini as described on page 169, cutting the hardened polenta into 7cm (3in) squares (do not fry or grill them).
6 Layer half the polenta squares on the base of a prepared dish. Pour over half the sauce and scatter over half the basil and mozzarella.
7 Place the remaining polenta squares on top, then spoon over the remainder of the sauce. Sprinkle with the rest of the basil and cheese.
8 Bake in the middle of the oven until the cheese is melted and golden and the pasticcio is bubbling, 20–25 minutes. Remove from the oven and allow it to settle for 10 minutes before cutting it into squares. Serve hot.

FEGATINI DI POLLO CON FUNGHI E POLENTA

Chicken livers and mushrooms with polenta

This dish of chicken livers, with its earthy sauce of shallots, mushrooms, sage and red wine, is a perfect dish with which to serve polenta. The polenta can take any form — fried, grilled or loose. The only chicken livers that will do are springy plump ones.

INGREDIENTS

½ quantity Polenta (see page 169), prepared according to taste
Sauce
500g (1lb) very fresh chicken livers
150g (5oz) wild or cultivated mushrooms
2 tbsp extra-virgin olive oil
30g (1oz) unsalted butter
2 tbsp finely chopped shallots or spring onions
½ tsp crushed dried green peppercorns, or freshly ground black or white pepper, to taste
¼ tsp salt, or to taste
60ml (2fl oz) good red wine
1 tsp plain flour
90ml (3fl oz) Meat Broth (see page 72)
1 tbsp chopped fresh flat-leaf parsley

PREPARATION

1 If serving fried or grilled polenta crostini, make the polenta and leave it to set, as described on page 169. If serving loose polenta, prepare the chicken liver sauce before making the polenta.
2 Wash the livers and trim any connective tissue, fat or discoloured areas. Separate any pairs, but leave each liver whole.
3 Clean and trim the mushrooms; do not wash them. Slice them and set aside.
4 Heat half the oil with the butter in a frying pan. Add the shallots or spring onions and cook gently until softened, 4–5 minutes. Add the mushrooms and sauté, tossing occasionally, until lightly golden, 1–2 minutes. Remove the shallots and mushrooms from the pan and set aside.
5 Warm the second tablespoon of olive oil in the pan and when it is hot enough to make the livers sizzle, add them. Sear over a medium heat until golden all over, about 3 minutes. Do not allow the livers to overcook.
6 Return the shallots and mushrooms to the pan and add the crushed peppercorns and salt.
7 Pour in the wine and allow it to evaporate, 2–3 minutes, using a wooden spoon to turn the livers in the wine occasionally. Transfer the livers, shallots and mushrooms to a plate and set aside while you finish the sauce.

8 Stir the flour into 2–3 tablespoons of broth to form a smooth paste. Add the paste to the juices in the pan with the remaining broth. Simmer over a medium heat until the sauce thickens, about 4 minutes. Return the livers to the pan and stir in the parsley. Set aside until ready to serve (it will take 1–2 minutes to heat through).
9 Serve the chicken liver sauce with a platter of piping-hot loose polenta dotted with 30g (1oz) of unsalted butter, or with crisp, golden grilled or fried polenta crostini.

POLENTA PASTICCIATA DI MIA NONNA

My grandmother's baked polenta

There are many versions of polenta pasticciata — literally a "mess" of polenta baked into a casserole with sauce and, usually, cheese. I am particularly fond of this one, inherited from my maternal Sardinian grandmother, Giulia Esu. Typically a northern dish, polenta was probably introduced to Sardinia in the 19th century by the Piedmontese. Serves 8.

INGREDIENTS

1 quantity Polenta crostini (see page 169)
Sauce
5g (¼oz) dried porcini mushrooms
2 tbsp olive oil
30g (1oz) unsalted butter
1 small onion, chopped
1 carrot, chopped
1 celery stalk, chopped
2 tbsp chopped fresh flat-leaf parsley
375g (12oz) lean minced beef or mixture of beef and pork
2 tbsp tomato purée
125ml (4fl oz) red wine
625g (1¼lb) canned tomatoes in purée or juice, deseeded and chopped but purée or juice retained
½ tsp salt, or more to taste
freshly ground black pepper, to taste
250g (8oz) semi-soft pecorino, coarsely grated

PREPARATION

1 Make the polenta crostini as described on page 169, cutting the hardened polenta into 7cm (3in) squares (do nor fry or grill them).
2 To make the sauce, soak the dried mushrooms in 60ml (2fl oz) of warm water for about 30 minutes, then drain, reserving the liquid. Rinse the mushrooms under cold water then chop coarsely.
3 Heat the oil and butter together then add the onion, carrot, celery and parsley. Sauté gently until softened, approximately 10 minutes.
4 Add the meat and cook over a low heat until it is coloured but still slightly pink inside, 5 minutes. Do not overcook the meat or it will harden.
5 Stir in the mushrooms, tomato purée, the mushroom liquid and wine. Simmer gently for 3 minutes to evaporate the alcohol. Add the tomatoes and purée or juice, salt and pepper, and simmer over a medium-low heat, partially covered, for 30 minutes, stirring occasionally.
6 Preheat the oven to 230°C/450°F/gas 8.
7 Layer the polenta squares in the baking dish. Spoon a layer of sauce over the polenta. Scatter over a layer of cheese. Repeat the procedure, ending with a layer of cheese on top. You may have a little sauce left over that you can use in another dish.
8 Place the dish on the upper rack of the oven and bake for 15–20 minutes, or until the casserole is bubbling and the cheese is golden on top. Allow to settle for 10–15 minutes before serving.

VARIATION

If semi-soft pecorino is unavailable, use Spanish Manchego cheese (a sheep's cheese), or caciocavallo.

FISH AND SEAFOOD

The one characteristic that marks Italian seafood is its astonishing flavour; the very essence of the sea seems to be found in every bite. In general, Italians prefer to cook fish whole as a great deal of flavour permeates the fish from the head, bones and skin. Most seafood dishes are quite simple, except perhaps for the celebrated *zuppa di pesce*, fish soup, which typically contains all manner of local fish from the daily catch. *Baccalà*, salt cod, is in a category all of its own, enjoying immense popularity from north to south.

ZUPPA DI PESCE ALLA GALLIPOLINA

Seafood "soup" in the style of Gallipoli

In Italy there are seemingly endless versions of zuppa di pesce. *The Tuscans, for example, make their celebrated* cacciucco; *in Venice there is* brodetto; *in Genoa,* burrida. *Some are brothy soups; some are chowders thick with shellfish. All are poured over slices of sturdy bread rubbed with garlic and sprinkled with fruity olive oil. Gallipoli, an ancient seaport on the west coast of Apulia, is renowned for its fish soup, which the locals claim dates back to 1000 BC. The Gallipoli version is made largely of crustaceans cooked in their shells and locally caught fish, but this recipe, my own adaptation, is based on more readily available fish and shellfish. Serves 6.*

INGREDIENTS

500g (1lb) Venus clams or cockles, well-scrubbed
12 small mussels, debearded and scrubbed (see page 163)
500g (1lb) young, tender squid
250g (8oz) medium-sized prawns in their shells
175ml (6fl oz) extra-virgin olive oil
1 large onion, chopped
3 large cloves garlic, 2 finely chopped and 1 halved
6 tbsp chopped fresh flat-leaf parsley
pinch of crushed dried red chillies
125ml (4fl oz) dry white wine
750g (1½lb) fresh or canned drained tomatoes, skinned, deseeded and chopped
3 tbsp tomato purée
1 tsp sea salt
500g (1lb) whole white-fleshed fish such as sea bream, whiting, snapper or hake, scaled, gutted and cut into pieces, or 250g (8oz) fillets from any of the above or grouper, cod or bass
12 x 1cm (½in) thick slices coarse peasant-style bread, to serve

PREPARATION

1 Place the clams and mussels in a bowl of water to soak (see page 163). Partially cover them and refrigerate for several hours, or up to 2 days (if refrigerating longer than overnight, change the water). Drain, and scrub them well.

2 Clean the squid (see opposite). Cut the body into 5mm (¼in) rings and cut the tentacles into halves or quarters, depending upon their size.

3 Slit the prawns down the back through the shell to remove the dark intestinal vein. Rinse them in cold water, but leave the shells attached on the underside (they will add flavour to the broth).

4 Warm 60ml (2fl oz) of oil in a large deep frying pan. Add the onion and the finely chopped garlic, and sauté until softened, about 4 minutes. Add all but 2 tablespoons of parsley and the crushed chillies and sauté for another minute.

5 Stir in the wine and continue to cook over a medium heat until the alcohol evaporates, about 3 minutes. Add the tomatoes and tomato purée, the salt and 500ml (16fl oz) of water. Cover partially and continue to cook over a medium heat at a steady simmer until the sauce thickens, about 15 minutes, stirring occasionally.

6 Add the clams, mussels and squid. Stir, cover and cook for 3–4 minutes. Stir in the prawns and fish, cover, and cook over a medium heat for 6–7 minutes, removing the cover once or twice to turn the seafood so that it cooks evenly. Taste the broth for seasoning and add the remaining parsley to the pan. Remove the *zuppa* from the heat.

7 Meanwhile, use the remaining halved garlic clove to rub the slices of bread. Fry the bread in the remaining olive oil then drain it on kitchen paper. Place two slices of fried bread in each soup plate and ladle over hot broth. The seafood may be served on top or as a separate course.

CLEANING SQUID

1 *Separate the head and tentacles from the body by grasping the head below the eyes and pulling this top section away from the body cavity. Remove and discard the ink sac from the head.*

2 *Cut the head from the tentacles at the "waist" above the eyes. Remove the hard "beak" from the base of the tentacles. Under cold running water, peel off the speckled skin.*

3 *Remove the cellophane-like "spine" from the body and clean out any insides remaining in the cavity. Rinse well. Cut the body and tentacles as described, then rinse and dry the pieces.*

FRITTO MISTO DI MARE
Mixed fish fry

This is a dish that appears on tourist menus all along the Italian coastline. An Italian fish fry is exquisite eating when made properly with the freshest seafood. In the simplest method, the seafood is dredged in flour and then deep-fried in olive oil. I prefer to use a pastella, or "batter", and adding wine to the batter produces a particularly crispy coating. Deep-fried foods absorb less oil than sautéed foods, if made properly. It is essential that the fish is uncompromisingly fresh (frozen fish becomes waterlogged) and seafood must be dried thoroughly after washing to allow the batter to adhere. It may seem extravagant to use olive oil for deep-frying, but its fruity flavour is irreplaceable. Serves 4–6.

INGREDIENTS

1.5kg (3lb) fresh mixed seafood, including large prawns, small squid and fish fillets such as hake, whiting, snapper, grouper, sole, flounder, haddock or cod
1 tbsp coarse sea salt
olive oil for deep-frying
fine sea salt and 2 lemons, cut into wedges, to serve
Batter
100g (3½oz) plain flour
½ tsp fine sea salt
3 tbsp dry white wine
125ml (4fl oz) water
1½ tbsp olive oil
1 egg, separated

PREPARATION

1 Peel and devein the prawns (see page 163). Clean the squid (see page 99). Cut the body into 5mm (¼in) rings and chop the tentacles in half.
2 To make the batter, sift together the flour and salt into a bowl. Mix the wine and water and then add it to the flour, combining it thoroughly. Stir in the oil then the egg yolk. Cover the bowl and allow to stand at room temperature for 2 hours.
3 Meanwhile, cover the seafood with cold water and add the tablespoon of coarse sea salt. Cover and chill for approximately 1 hour. Drain then dry thoroughly with kitchen paper or clean tea towels.
4 Beat the egg white until it stands up in peaks, then fold it into the batter.
5 Pour enough olive oil into a deep-fryer or deep frying pan to reach 5cm (2in) up the sides of the pan. Heat to 190°C/375°F, or until a drop of batter sputters when dropped into the oil – it must be hot enough to produce a crispy coating. It is advisable to use a splatter shield over the pot because the squid tentacles cause the hot oil to spit.
6 Just before you are ready to fry, drop the first batch of seafood into the batter, saving the squid for the last batch. Turn it so that it is evenly coated. Carefully slip the first batch into the oil – do not crowd the pan as this causes the oil temperature to drop, making the fish absorb too much oil.
7 Fry the seafood until golden on all sides, about 4 minutes. Remove the seafood with a slotted spoon and drain on kitchen paper. Repeat with the remaining seafood. Serve immediately with fine sea salt and lemon wedges. (The olive oil can be filtered after frying and reused.)

SCAMPI ALLA GRIGLIA CON SALVIA
Grilled prawns with sage

Scampi, or gamberoni, are large, succulent prawns that make a terrific antipasto or main course when cooked on an open fire. Serves 2.

INGREDIENTS

500g (1lb) large prawns, peeled
2 tsp fine sea salt, plus salt to serve
125ml (4fl oz) extra-virgin olive oil
3 large cloves garlic, finely chopped
2 tsp finely chopped fresh sage, or
¾ tsp dried crumbled sage
freshly ground white or black pepper, to taste

PREPARATION

1 Peel and devein the prawns (see page 163), but do not cut so deeply as to butterfly them. Rinse them well under cold running water.
2 Place the prawns in a bowl of iced water. Add 2 tablespoons of sea salt and allow to stand for 15 minutes to bring out some of the prawns' briny flavour (removing their shells robs the prawns of some of their natural flavour). Drain, then dry thoroughly with kitchen paper.
3 In a bowl, combine the prawns with the oil, garlic and sage. Cover and leave to marinate in the refrigerator for up to 3 hours.
4 Meanwhile, prepare a charcoal grill or preheat an indoor grill. Position the rack close to the heat source so that it heats through.
5 Thread the prawns securely on to metal skewers and brush with the marinade.
6 Transfer the skewers to the grill and cook about 5cm (2in) from the heat source for 1½ minutes on the first side and 1 minute on the second, brushing them with any remaining marinade. The outside of each prawn should be crispy and charred, the inside moist and tender. Sprinkle to taste with sea salt and pepper, and serve immediately.

SCAMPI AL FORNO

Baked prawns with garlic and parsley

This way of cooking prawns is so obvious that I almost left it out. But it occurred to me that as there are various methods for cooking this classic dish, I should include the recipe here. In this method, the prawns are baked rather than cooked on top of the stove. Serve it with plenty of crusty bread to mop up the deliciously garlicky juices. Serves 2. Illustrated on page 105.

INGREDIENTS

500g (1lb) large prawns
1 tsp sea salt
125ml (4fl oz) extra-virgin olive oil
4 large cloves garlic, finely chopped
pinch of crushed dried red chillies, or 1–2 whole dried peperoncini (hot chillies)
2 tbsp chopped fresh flat-leaf parsley
60ml (2fl oz) freshly squeezed lemon juice

PREPARATION

1 Preheat the oven to 200°C/400°F/gas 6.
2 Peel, devein and butterfly the prawns (see page 163). Soak in iced salt water and allow to stand for 15 minutes to bring out their briny flavour (removing their shells robs the prawns of some of their natural flavour). Drain, then dry the prawns thoroughly with kitchen paper.
3 In a baking dish, combine the oil, garlic, chillies, half the parsley, half the lemon juice and the prawns.
4 Slide the dish on to the middle rack of the oven and bake until the prawns turn pink, about 10 minutes. Remove from the oven immediately.
5 Sprinkle with the remaining parsley and lemon juice and serve immediately.

VARIATION

To make a lovely crispy coating for the prawns, toss 2 tablespoons of fresh toasted breadcrumbs with the prawns just before baking.

CALAMARI IN ZIMINO ALLA LIVORNESE

Stewed squid with spinach, Leghorn style

Throughout Italy, squid is commonly paired with tomatoes when it is stewed, and it is very good indeed done in this style, but I like this uniquely Tuscan way of cooking squid with Swiss chard or spinach. Serves 4–6.

INGREDIENTS

750g (1½lb) Swiss chard, trimmed, or
500g (1lb) fresh spinach, stems removed
750g (1½lb) squid
3 tbsp extra-virgin olive oil
1 large clove garlic, chopped
1 small onion, chopped
1 small carrot, chopped
1 small celery stalk with leaves, chopped
2 tbsp chopped fresh flat-leaf parsley
90ml (3fl oz) dry white wine
½ tsp salt
1 tbsp tomato purée
2 tsp chopped fresh rosemary, or ½ tsp dried rosemary
pinch of crushed dried red chillies

PREPARATION

1 Place the washed Swiss chard or spinach in a pan with the drops of water still clinging to the leaves. Cover completely and cook over a medium heat until the leaves wilt and become tender, about 3 minutes. Remove from the heat and allow to cool. Squeeze out as much water as you can. Chop the leaves and set aside.
2 Clean the squid (see page 99). Cut the body into rings 5mm (¼in) wide and cut the tentacles into halves or quarters, depending upon their size. Rinse and dry the squid pieces thoroughly.
3 Pour the oil into a large frying pan and warm over a medium heat. Add the garlic, onion, carrot, celery and parsley. Sauté until the vegetables soften, about 7 minutes, stirring occasionally.
4 Add the squid pieces and immediately raise the heat to high. Sauté for 5 minutes, making sure the flesh is seared evenly.
5 Add the wine and continue to sauté, still over a high heat, until the alcohol is evaporated, about 3 minutes. Reduce the heat to medium and then stir in the salt, tomato purée, 2 tablespoons of water and the rosemary.
6 Partially cover the pan and simmer for an additional 20 minutes, stirring occasionally to cook evenly. Add the wilted Swiss chard or spinach and the chillies. Cook until the greens are warmed through, about 5 minutes more, then check for salt and pepper. Serve immediately.

SOGLIOLE AL CARTOCCIO
Sole in parchment

Cooking in parchment is an ancient practice, but the simplicity of the method is well suited to the needs of the modern cook. Parchment or foil, used dull-side out, are suitable. All the flavours and moisture are sealed in, making this method ideal for delicate foods. Keeping the fish whole allows the most savoury parts to permeate the flesh with their flavour, but fillets can be cooked this way (see variation). It is best to use fresh herbs as their aroma penetrates the delicate flesh without overpowering it. If rosemary and sage are not available, use parsley, basil or fennel fronds. Serve with Salsa Rossa alla Ligure (see page 138), or simply with slices of lemon.

INGREDIENTS

*4 whole sole or other white-fleshed fish such as flounder,
red snapper, pompano or sea bream,
about 375g (12oz) each, gutted and scaled
extra-virgin olive oil
fine sea salt and freshly ground white pepper
4 cloves garlic, thinly sliced
4 sprigs fresh rosemary
4 leaves fresh sage
1 quantity Salsa Rossa alla Ligure (see page 138)*

PREPARATION

1 Preheat the oven to 220°C/425°F/gas 7.
2 Wash the fish well inside and out then pat dry inside and out with kitchen paper.
3 Cut four pieces of parchment paper or foil, each large enough to wrap the fish completely.
4 Rub the inside and the exterior of the fish with oil and sprinkle with salt and pepper. Stuff the cavity of each fish with the garlic and herbs.
5 Place each fish in the centre of the parchment or foil, folding the edges in to seal well (use paper clips to secure the parchment). Place the parcels in a baking dish and cook for 20 minutes.
6 If using parchment, each person can be served a fish packet at the table. If using foil, open the packet and transfer the fish to a serving dish, or to individual plates. Pass the sauce at the table.

VARIATION

Replace the whole fish with four fillets from any firm-fleshed white fish, each weighing about 300g (10oz). Preheat the oven to 200°C/400°F/gas 6. Cut four pieces of parchment or foil. Finely slice one onion and divide it between the parcels. Drizzle the fillets with the oil and season. Scatter the herbs and garlic over the fish. Seal and cook as above.

TRIGLIE ALLA GRIGLIA

Grilled red mullet with garlic

Red and grey mullet are among the most popular fish, especially the red species. Because their flesh is so tasty, the simplest cooking methods are the best for bringing out their natural flavour. Smaller mullet can be fried or baked.

INGREDIENTS

8 red mullet, each about 250g (8oz), scaled and gutted
fine sea salt and freshly ground pepper, to taste
6 cloves garlic, thinly sliced lengthways
4 sprigs fresh rosemary
60g (2oz) flour for dredging
olive oil, to baste
2 fresh lemons, cut into wedges, to serve

PREPARATION

1 Preheat the grill and oil the grill pan.
2 Wash the mullet and dry thoroughly with kitchen paper. Sprinkle the insides of the fish with salt and pepper. Make two slits on each side of the fish and insert a sliver of garlic in each. Stuff the remaining garlic slices and the rosemary into the cavities.
3 Dredge the fish in flour and sprinkle both sides with plenty of oil. Place them side-by-side on the preheated grill pan. There should be some space around each of the mullet.
4 Place the pan 15–18cm (6–7in) from the grill flame and leave until the fish is cooked thoroughly and golden-brown on the surface, about 4 minutes. Turn the fish, sprinkle with a little more oil, and grill for an additional 3 minutes.
5 Serve immediately with lemon wedges.

SOGLIOLE ALL'ABRUZZESE

Sole with garlic, lemon and olives, Abruzzi style

Small Adriatic sole are cooked in this way in the Abruzzian province of Teramo. Flounder may be used, but they need longer cooking. Illustrated on page 104. Serves 2.

INGREDIENTS

2 whole sole, about 375–500g (¾lb–1lb) each, scaled and gutted, or 4 sole fillets, each about 125g (4oz)
approximately 45g (1½oz) flour for dredging
3–4 tbsp extra-virgin olive oil (only 3 tbsp for fillets)
2 large cloves garlic, bruised
2 tbsp freshly squeezed lemon juice
10 sharply flavoured black olives, pitted and chopped
small pinch crushed dried red chillies
¼ tsp salt, or to taste
2 tbsp chopped fresh flat-leaf parsley

PREPARATION

1 Rinse the whole fish or fillets, then dry them thoroughly on kitchen paper.
2 Spread the flour on to a plate. Warm the oil and garlic in a large non-stick frying pan. Sauté gently until the garlic is golden then discard it.
3 Dust the fish in flour then raise the heat and slip it into the hot oil. Sauté until lightly golden, about 4 minutes on each side for whole fish and 1 minute on each side for fillets, according to thickness. Transfer to a warm plate and reduce the heat.
4 Stir the lemon juice and 2 tablespoons of water into the pan. When the liquid begins to bubble, add the olives, chillies, salt and parsley. Allow to heat through briefly, then pour over the fish and serve.

TONNO ALLA STEMPERATA

Tuna with onion, olives and capers, Sicilian style

This popular way of cooking tuna and swordfish produces a pleasantly tart sauce. The fillets shouldn't be too thick as tuna tends to become dry if cooked for too long.

INGREDIENTS

4 x 1cm (½in) thick tuna fillets, each about 150g (5oz), skinned and trimmed
3 tbsp flour, for dusting
75ml (2½fl oz) extra-virgin olive oil
1 large onion, finely sliced then roughly chopped
4 tbsp white wine vinegar
pinch of salt
90g (3oz) pitted and sliced black olives
3 tbsp small capers, drained
freshly ground black pepper, to taste

PREPARATION

1 Rinse the fillets, then dry on kitchen paper.
2 Spread the flour on to a plate. Warm the oil in a large, preferably non-stick frying pan.
3 Dust the fillets in flour then slip them into the hot oil all at once. Brown them lightly on each side for 45 seconds–1 minute, then turn them quickly and brown on the other side for no more than 45 seconds. Transfer them to a warm plate.
4 Add the onion to the frying pan, reduce the heat slightly and cook them until soft and lightly coloured, about 6 minutes. Stir in the vinegar, salt, olives and capers then pour in 90ml (3fl oz) of water. Cook the mixture, stirring occasionally, for about 2 minutes.
5 Return the tuna to the pan, placing them over the bed of onions, cover and cook for another 45 seconds. Serve the tuna steaks, spooning the onion mixture on top, and grind over the pepper.

BACCALÀ AL FORNO
Baked salt cod with
potatoes and tomatoes
(page 109)

SOGLIOLE ALL'ABRUZZESE
Sole with garlic, lemon and
olives, Abruzzi style
(page 103)

SCAMPI AL FORNO
Baked prawns with
garlic and parsley
(page 101)

PESCE SPADA AL SALMORIGLIO
Swordfish with lemon sauce

In Sicily and Calabria, swordfish is typically grilled on the open fire and served with lemon sauce, which purists say should contain a splash of sea water. The quality of the oil used is very important, because it and the lemon juice are the dominating flavours. Fresh tuna can be substituted for swordfish with equally good results. It is delicious served with Patate Fritte, as here (see page 127).

INGREDIENTS

1kg (2lb) swordfish or tuna steaks,
2.5cm (1in) thick, skinned
freshly ground black pepper, to taste
Marinade
4 tbsp olive oil
90ml (3fl oz) dry white wine
2 large cloves garlic, cut lengthways into thin slivers
1 onion, halved and thinly sliced
1 bay leaf
Salmoriglio sauce
2 tbsp freshly squeezed lemon juice
4 tbsp extra-virgin olive oil
1 small clove garlic, finely chopped
¼ tsp chopped fresh oregano, or a pinch of dried oregano
1 tsp chopped fresh flat-leaf parsley
pinch of sea salt

PREPARATION

1 Prepare a charcoal grill or preheat an indoor grill. If oven-grilling, line a grill pan with foil and preheat the grill and the pan.
2 Combine the ingredients for the marinade. Place the fish in the marinade. Cover and chill for 30 minutes–1 hour, turning the pieces once.
3 To make the sauce, put the lemon juice in a bowl. Add the oil in a slow, steady stream, using a whisk or electric beater to emulsify it thoroughly. Add the garlic, continuing to beat, then stir in the oregano, parsley and salt.
4 Remove the fish from the marinade; reserve the marinade. If making kebabs, cut the fish into chunks and thread them on to skewers, leaving a little space between each piece. Alternatively, cut each steak in half.
5 Brush the fish with marinade. Place the kebabs or pieces on the grill pan or oiled barbecue rack and position 5cm (2in) away from the heat; leave the door open if using an electric oven. Grill until the fish colours, about 2 minutes. Turn and baste with marinade then cook for another 2 minutes.
6 Transfer the fish to a serving dish. Sprinkle with pepper, drizzle with the lemon sauce and serve immediately with Patate Fritte (see page 127).

Garlic

Dry white wine

Olive oil

Swordfish

Onion

Bay leaf

Lemon juice

Oregano

Flat-leaf
parsley

Sea salt

Black
pepper

MERLUZZO ALLE ERBE
Poached hake fillets with fresh herbs

Here is a light, simple way to cook fish fillets. The dish is best served at room temperature and can be made up to 2 hours in advance of serving. Our family often cooked hake or cod this way, but any white-fleshed fish fillets can be used. Cooking time should be somewhat less for very delicate fish fillets such as flounder or sole. Serves 2–3.

INGREDIENTS
1 bay leaf
1 small spring onion, including green tops, trimmed, sliced lengthways and cut into three pieces
2 sprigs fresh flat-leaf parsley
½ tsp sea salt
750g (1½lb) hake or cod fillets
Topping
1 small spring onion, including 5cm (2in) of green top, trimmed and very thinly sliced
1½ tbsp chopped fresh flat-leaf parsley
2 tsp chopped fresh thyme, or ½ tsp dried thyme
roughly grated zest of ½ a lemon
juice of 1 large lemon
4 tbsp extra-virgin olive oil
freshly ground white or black pepper, to taste

PREPARATION
1 Pour 1 litre (1¾ pints) of cold water into a large frying pan wide enough to accommodate the fillets without crowding. Add the bay leaf, spring onion and parsley sprigs. Bring to the boil and add the salt.
2 Slip the fillets into the frying pan, cover completely and lower the heat to medium so that the water boils gently. Cook for 5–7 minutes, depending on the thickness of the fillets. Use a wide spatula to transfer the fillets, one by one, to a serving plate without breaking them. Reserve one tablespoon of the fish cooking water.
3 In a small bowl, combine the topping ingredients and stir in the reserved tablespoon of cooking water. Spoon the topping over the fish, cover and allow to come to room temperature before serving.

TAIEDDA
Baked fish fillets with vegetables, potatoes and white wine

Taiedda, also called tiella, *is an Apulian dish with a Spanish history. Its name is thought to have derived from the Spanish "paella" and, in common with paella, it is a "one pot" dish. But the similarities stop there. Taiedda is a layered baked dish composed largely of vegetables (sometimes vegetables alone), and fish, shellfish or salt cod. Purists insist that the true version must include potatoes (of which the locals are inordinately fond), and grated cheese, but it is often made with rice instead. Like most Italian food, the dish has peasant roots. It was prepared before the family left for their day's work in the fields and left to cook slowly in the ashes of the hearth until they were reunited for dinner. Serves 6.*

INGREDIENTS
750g (1½lb) potatoes, cooked, peeled and thinly sliced
1 onion, quartered and very thinly sliced
2 large carrots, finely shredded or grated
1kg (2lb) white fish fillets such as flounder, sole or haddock
½ tsp salt
freshly ground white pepper, to taste
45g (1½oz) unsalted butter, melted, plus butter to grease
125ml (4fl oz) dry white wine
2 tbsp breadcrumbs

PREPARATION
1 Preheat the oven to 190°C / 375°F / gas 5.
2 Grease a baking dish approximately 23 x 30cm (9 x 12in). Place half of the potatoes in the dish, follow with half the onion, half the carrot and half the fish. Sprinkle with half of the salt, and only very lightly with pepper. Drizzle over half of the butter.
3 Make a second layer with the remaining potatoes, onion, carrots, fish and salt. Sprinkle lightly with additional pepper. Pour the wine over the top; when it has seeped through to the bottom of the dish, sprinkle the top with the crumbs and drizzle over the remaining butter.
4 Cover the dish with foil and bake it in the middle of the oven for 20–30 minutes (cooking time will be affected by the size of the dish), or until the fish is tender but not overcooked. Remove the foil during the last 5 minutes of baking.
5 If the dish contains an excessive amount of pan juices, pour them into a small saucepan. Simmer over a medium heat for 5–10 minutes, until reduced, and then pour the juices over the dish just before serving. Serve hot.

BACCALÀ STUFATO CON OLIVE E PATATE

Salt cod stewed with olives and potatoes

Baccalà, *salt cod, has been prominent in the cuisines of Mediterranean seafaring peoples since ancient times when dried foodstuffs were important staples. The Italians are especially fond of it, and use it in many imaginative ways. Once rehydrated and cooked, baccalà is enormously versatile, and is used in salads, croquettes and fritters, soups and stews. See page 163 for advice on choosing and preparing salt cod. Serves 6.*

INGREDIENTS

*750g (1½lb) baccalà (salt cod),
preferably skinned and boned
3 tbsp olive oil
1 onion, chopped
2 cloves garlic, finely chopped
2 tbsp chopped fresh flat-leaf parsley
12 sharply flavoured green olives
1 tbsp small capers, drained
1 tbsp freshly squeezed lemon juice
4 boiling potatoes, peeled and halved
freshly ground black or white pepper, to taste*

PREPARATION

1 To rehydrate the salt cod, soak it in cold water as described on page 163, keeping it covered in the refrigerator. Drain and rinse in fresh water, remove any skin and bones that remain and cut the flesh into 5cm (2in) chunks.

2 Place the oil, onion and garlic in a large frying pan and sauté until softened but not browned. Stir in the parsley, keeping the pan over a low heat. Add the salt cod and gently sauté on both sides for about 5 minutes.

3 Add the olives and capers, 175ml (6fl oz) of water and the lemon juice. Cover and leave to simmer until tender, about 18–20 minutes.

4 Meanwhile, cut the potatoes into 5mm (¼in) slices. Place them in a pan and cover with cold water. Boil until half-cooked, about 10 minutes, then drain. Add them to the frying pan 15 minutes before the salt cod has finished cooking. Cover and cook gently. Serve hot.

VARIATION

For a tomato version, replace the lemon juice with 1 tablespoon of wine vinegar blended with 2 tablespoons of tomato purée and increase the amount of water to 250ml (8fl oz).

BACCALÀ AL FORNO

Baked salt cod and potatoes with tomatoes

Anna Amendolara Nurse, a well-known teacher of Italian cooking, gave me this recipe for her favourite baccalà dish. Illustrated on page 104.

INGREDIENTS

*750g (1½lb) baccalà (salt cod),
preferably skinned and boned
625g (1¼lb) fresh or canned drained tomatoes,
skinned, deseeded and coarsely chopped
4 boiling potatoes, peeled and cut into sixths lengthways
1 large onion, cut into sixths lengthways
2 cloves garlic, halved
90g (3oz) oil-packed black olives, drained
30g (1oz) chopped fresh flat-leaf parsley
salt and freshly ground black pepper, to taste
60g (2oz) dry breadcrumbs
125ml (4fl oz) extra-virgin olive oil*

PREPARATION

1 To rehydrate the salt cod, soak it in cold water as described on page 163, keeping it covered in the refrigerator. Drain and rinse in fresh water, remove any skin and bones that remain and cut the flesh into 5cm (2in) chunks.

2 Preheat the oven to 190°C/375°F/gas 5.

3 Place half of the tomatoes in a 25 x 35cm (10 x 14 in) baking dish. Place the salt cod, potatoes and onion in a single layer over the tomatoes. Arrange the remaining tomatoes, garlic and olives on top.

4 Sprinkle over the parsley, salt and pepper then cover with breadcrumbs. Drizzle the top with the oil, distributing it evenly over the dish. Pour over 250ml (8fl oz) of water, being careful not to disturb the breadcrumbs.

5 Bake the dish in the preheated oven until the potatoes are tender and the breadcrumbs golden-brown, about 1½ hours.

MEAT DISHES

The meat course is not the focus of an Italian meal. Having been preceded by the substantial *primo*, meat usually follows in relatively small portions. The flavour of Italian meat is excellent as farmed animals are still raised naturally. Italians are also inordinately fond of game of any kind. Cooking methods are often simple. Wood-fired grills are used outdoors and in restaurants, while pot-roasting and boiling are the most common techniques in the home, producing succulent dishes with rich, concentrated sauces.

MANZO LESSO CON SALSE VARIE

Boiled beef with various sauces

Meat cooked in water has exceptional sweetness, and it remains juicy and succulent as it bathes in its own luscious broth. This is a splendid dish if the cut used is well-marbled and carves easily. Compatible sauces include Salsetta Rossa Cruda, Salsa Verde, in any of its variations, (see page 139) and Maionese Verde (see page 140).

INGREDIENTS

1.5kg (3lb) beef rump roast, brisket or tied chuck roast
1 carrot, scraped and quartered
1 celery stalk with leaves, halved
1 onion, unpeeled and quartered
1 small tomato, skinned, deseeded and quartered
handful of parsley sprigs
1 bay leaf
2 tbsp salt, or to taste
½ tsp whole black or white peppercorns
Salsa Verde and / or Salsetta Rossa Cruda (see page 139)
or Maionese Verde (see page 140), to serve

PREPARATION

1 Place the beef, vegetables, herbs, salt and peppercorns in a large pan with 5cm (2in) of water to cover and bring to the boil. Lower the heat and simmer gently, partially covered, for 3½ hours, turning the meat halfway through cooking. If necessary, add more water to keep the meat covered and skim off any foam as it forms.
2 Check the broth for salt, then transfer the meat to a cutting board. Strain the broth and set it aside then slice the meat thinly. Arrange it on a serving platter, spooning over a little broth. Serve the sliced beef with the chosen sauces, reserving the remaining broth for use as a soup.

POLPETTONE FARCITO

Meatloaf stuffed with ham and parsley frittatine

Do not confuse this lovely, moist meatloaf with the bouncy, grey, gravy-covered square meal variety. The Italian version is made with several kinds of meat, giving it a complex, delicate flavour, and there is often an omelette or hard-boiled eggs in the middle, which looks very pretty when the loaf is sliced. In this recipe, ham and frittatine, "omelettes", speckled with parsley are rolled into the middle of the loaf, producing a pink, yellow and green helix in the centre of every slice. It may be served hot or cold with the fortified pan juices or Salsetta Rossa Cruda. Serves 10–15. Illustrated on page 121.

INGREDIENTS

Polpettone mixture
125g (4oz) stale white bread, crusts removed
½ large beef stock cube, or 1 small one, dissolved in 350ml (12fl oz) hot water
1.5kg (3lb) mixed lean minced beef and pork, or 1.5kg (3lb) lean minced beef
1 onion, grated
90g (3oz) sun-dried tomatoes, chopped
1½ tsp salt
¾ tsp freshly ground black pepper
2 eggs, beaten
1 tsp chopped fresh marjoram, or ½ tsp dried marjoram
2 tbsp freshly grated Parmesan
1 tbsp lightly toasted breadcrumbs
60ml (2fl oz) red wine, for basting the meatloaf
Filling
1 egg
2 tsp chopped fresh flat-leaf parsley
pinch of salt
freshly ground black pepper, to taste
½ tsp butter or olive oil
4 slices boiled ham

PREPARATION

1 Preheat the oven to 180°C/350°F/gas 4.
2 Soak the bread in the stock, then squeeze it dry, reserving the liquid. Shred the dampened bread and combine it with the remaining polpettone ingredients except the toasted breadcrumbs and wine. Use your hands to mix it well.
3 Make the frittatine. In a small bowl, beat the egg with the parsley, salt and pepper. Heat the butter or oil in a 23cm (9in) omelette pan or frying pan. Add half of the egg mixture, tilting the pan so that it covers the surface entirely. When the egg is set, about 30 seconds, turn it and allow it to set on the reverse side, about 15 seconds. Transfer to a plate and make the second omelette. Allow them to cool.
4 Meanwhile, scatter the breadcrumbs on a dry work surface. Spread the meat mixture over the crumbs, using your hands to form a 30 x 45cm (12 x 18in) rectangle about 1cm (½in) thick.
5 Cover the rectangle with ham slices, then with the frittatine, laying them side by side to cover the whole surface of the meat mixture. Working from the long edge, roll the polpettone into a long, narrow, sausage-like loaf (see page 164).
6 Place the loaf in an ungreased baking dish and pour half of the reserved stock into the dish. Bake in the centre of the oven for 15 minutes, then add the remaining stock. Cook for a futher 20 minutes, basting from time to time with the pan juices. Add a tablespoon or two of water if necessary – there should be sufficient juice for basting and for serving.
7 Add the wine to the dish and return the meatloaf to the oven for 15 minutes. Allow it to settle for 15 minutes before slicing. Serve with the pan juices or Salsetta Rossa Cruda (see page 139).

BISTECCA ALLA FIORENTINA

Chargrilled steak in the style of Florence

This is one of the best meat dishes Italy has to offer. Ideally, the steak should be chargrilled over the white embers of a hardwood (oak or olive) fire, which produces little smoke. If this is impracticable, cook it over coals.

INGREDIENTS

4 x 250g (8oz) beef rib steaks on the bone, cut 3.5–5cm (1½–2in) thick, excess fat trimmed
sea salt and freshly ground black pepper, to taste
highest quality cold-pressed extra-virgin olive oil
4–8 rosemary sprigs, optional

PREPARATION

1 Prepare a barbecue using dry hardwood such as oak, if possible, or charcoal; do not use chemical starter fuels. It is ready when the embers or coals are white and glowing. Position a grill rack approximately 5cm (2in) above the embers or coals and allow it to preheat.
2 Place the steaks on the sizzling-hot grill rack. Cook them until they are well charred on one side, 2–3 minutes for medium to medium-rare. Turn the steaks and cook them on the reverse side for 2–3 minutes. Transfer them to warm plates.
3 Sprinkle each steak with salt and pepper and drizzle with a little olive oil. Garnish with the rosemary and serve immediately.

SCHMORBRATEN

Sour pan-roasted beef in the style of Alto Adige

I have always been fond of beef cooked this way. We never had a name for it when I was growing up, but I realized years later, when my travels took me to the Tyrol, that it was actually Schmorbraten, a signature dish of Alto Adige. The cooking traditions of that region are more Austrian than Italian, as this dish illustrates. It is best made 2 or 3 days in advance. Serves 6.

INGREDIENTS

1 piece of beef sirloin, about 1.5kg (3lb)
3 large carrots, cut diagonally into 1cm (½in) slices
2 large onions, halved and thinly sliced
3 tbsp olive oil
175ml (6fl oz) full-bodied dry red wine or beer
1 tsp salt
Marinade
250ml (8fl oz) red wine vinegar
600ml (1 pint) water
4 bay leaves

PREPARATION

1 Combine the meat, vegetables and marinade in a large bowl. Place a plate over the meat and on top of this put a weight of at least 2kg (4lb). Refrigerate for 48 hours, turning the meat occasionally.
2 Discard the marinade. Pat dry the meat to prevent it from splattering when it cooks. Rinse the vegetables under cold water.
3 Heat the oil in a heavy-based pan. Add the meat and sauté on all sides for 10 minutes to seal in the juices (the meat will not actually brown).
4 Add the wine or beer and allow it to evaporate. Stir in the vegetables, 250ml (8fl oz) of water and the salt. Cover partially and cook over a medium-low heat until tender, about 2 hours, stirring the vegetables and turning the meat occasionally.
5 Cut the meat into very thin slices and serve hot with the vegetables.

PEPERONATA CON CARNE DI MAIALE

Pork and peppers in the style of Basilicata

Here is a good, simple dish that can be served with Purè di Patate (see page 129), or tossed with short-cut pasta – 500g (1lb) pasta is sufficient for this amount.

INGREDIENTS

1.5kg (3lb) pork tenderloin or pork cutlets from the leg, cut into 5mm (¼in) thick slices and trimmed of fat
125ml (4fl oz) corn oil
2 onions, halved and very thinly sliced
2 large cloves garlic, finely chopped
2 tbsp red wine vinegar
2 tbsp chopped fresh rosemary, or 1 tsp dried rosemary
1 tsp salt
large pinch of freshly ground black pepper
2 red and 2 yellow peppers, cored, deseeded and cut into 2.5cm (1in) squares

PREPARATION

1 Cut the pork into strips approximately 1cm (½in) wide and 5cm (2in) long.
2 Warm half the oil in a deep frying pan and add the onion and garlic. Sauté over a medium heat until the onion is translucent, about 4 minutes. Add the pork and increase the heat to high. Sauté quickly until excess liquid evaporates from the meat, about 5 minutes, stirring occasionally.
3 Reduce the heat to medium and add the vinegar. Sauté until the vinegar evaporates, about 2 minutes. Add the rosemary and 250ml (8fl oz) of water.
4 Cover the pan and simmer until the meat is tender, stirring occasionally and adding more water, if necessary, to prevent the meat from drying out. Tenderloin and high quality leg cutlets will cook in 15–20 minutes. Tougher meat will require lengthier cooking – up to 45 minutes. Add salt and pepper.
5 Meanwhile, heat the remaining oil in a separate frying pan. Add the peppers and cook, partially covered, until tender, about 15 minutes.
6 Transfer the peppers to the pan with the pork, toss well, and serve immediately.

ARISTA FIORENTINA CON PATATE

Florentine loin of pork with pan-roasted potatoes

In Tuscany, roast pork is part of the landscape. It is a common sight to see street stalls selling luscious porchetta, spit-roasted suckling pig sliced and sandwiched between two thick slices of bread. Arista, a tender cut from the loin end, is another speciality. In and around Florence, the flavourings are invariably rosemary and garlic; in Umbria, fennel is used. Buy only the tender centre loin, and ask the butcher to give you the bones. The traditional accompaniment is boiled cannellini beans dressed with olive oil, but roast potatoes are also good. Serves 6.

INGREDIENTS

1 boneless centre loin-end pork roast, about 2kg (4lb), or 1 unboned centre-cut loin roast, about 3kg (6lb)
6 large cloves garlic, cut into slivers
8 rosemary sprigs
20–25 small potatoes, peeled and parboiled for 5 minutes, optional
sea salt, to taste
Rub
2 tbsp extra-virgin olive oil
coarsely ground black pepper, to taste
2 tbsp finely chopped fresh rosemary, or
3 tsp crushed dried rosemary

PREPARATION

1 Bring the meat to room temperature. Combine the rub ingredients and massage the surface of the meat with it. Using a small sharp knife, make 1cm (½in) deep incisions all over the roast. Slip the garlic slivers into the cuts. If desired, at this point the pork can be covered, refrigerated and left to marinate overnight.
2 Preheat the oven to 180°C/350°F/gas 4.
3 Set the joint fat-side up on a rack in a large roasting pan, arranging the detached bones underneath. Slip the rosemary sprigs in between the bones. Roast the pork for about 30 minutes, then baste it with the pan juices.
4 Continue to cook the pork for a further 25 minutes, then, if using potatoes, place them around the joint and cook for 45 minutes longer, or until the internal temperature of the pork reads 65°C/150°F, basting every 20 minutes or so. Turn the potatoes halfway through cooking.
5 Remove the pan from the oven and sprinkle the joint and the potatoes with salt then cover with foil. Allow the joint to rest for 15 minutes – the meat will continue to cook as it rests.
6 Skim the fat from the pan juices and serve them hot with the meat.

AGNELLO ALLA SARDA

Roast leg of lamb my mother's way

Nothing reminds me more of my childhood, and of Sardinian cuisine, than lamb roasted over the embers of a hardwood fire. The method is simple and the results utterly delicious. An indoor wood-burning oven is not a feature of the average modern kitchen, but an outdoor barbecue can be substituted. It is essential to start the fire with kindling rather than chemical fire-starter, which affects the flavour and aroma of the meat. Serves 8.

INGREDIENTS

1 leg of lamb, about 3kg (6lb), trimmed
Rub
3 large cloves garlic, finely chopped
2 tsp finely chopped fresh rosemary, or
½ tsp crushed dried rosemary
20g (¾oz) chopped fresh flat-leaf parsley
90ml (3fl oz) extra-virgin olive oil
½ tsp coarse freshly ground black pepper
sea salt, to taste

PREPARATION

1 Bring the lamb to room temperature. Combine the ingredients for the rub. With a small, sharp knife, make shallow, evenly spaced incisions on all sides of the leg then work in the rub mixture (see page 164). Transfer the lamb to a roasting pan and allow it to stand at room temperature for 2 hours.
2 Preheat the oven to 200°C/400°F/gas 6 or prepare a barbecue, using dry hardwood such as oak, if possible, or charcoal.
3 If using a barbecue, check that the embers or coals are white and glowing. Arrange most of the fuel around the edges of the grill to produce indirect heat, leaving a few coals in the centre. Transfer the lamb to the grill and cover, turning occasionally, until the internal temperature of the thickest part of the leg registers 54°C/130°F for medium-rare, 45–60 minutes. If roasting in an oven, reduce the oven temperature to 180°C/350°F/gas 4 and roast the lamb until the thickest part of the leg comes up to temperature or until cooked to taste, about 1 hour.
4 Transfer the lamb to a serving platter and leave to rest for 10 minutes. Skim the fat from the pan juices. Sprinkle the lamb with sea salt, carve and serve immediately with the pan juices.

COSTOLETTE D'AGNELLO IMPANATE

Pan-fried breaded lamb chops

Veal chops are often breaded and fried, but in Liguria, tender young lamb rib chops are used instead. The rosemary-scented coating is especially delicious.

INGREDIENTS

olive oil for frying
60g (2oz) plain flour for dredging
freshly ground black pepper, to taste
1 heaped tsp crushed dried rosemary
3 eggs
45g (1½oz) breadcrumbs
12 small rib lamb chops, fat trimmed
salt, to taste
1 lemon, cut into wedges, to serve

PREPARATION

1 Pour as much olive oil as necessary to reach halfway up the sides of the chops in a heavy frying pan. Warm the oil over a medium-high heat until hot enough to make the meat sizzle upon contact with it, without burning the coating.
2 Place the flour, pepper and rosemary on a plate. Beat the eggs lightly in a shallow bowl. Sprinkle the breadcrumbs on a separate plate.
3 Just before you are ready to cook, dredge the chops in the flour, shaking off excess. Dip each chop into the egg mixture, and then in the crumbs. Slip the chops into the oil immediately. Do not crowd the pan, or the chops will not cook properly. Cook until golden on both sides but still pink in the middle, about 5 minutes in total.
4 Drain the chops on kitchen paper, sprinkle with salt and serve immediately with lemon wedges.

VARIATION

Costolette di Vitello alla Salsa di Pomodoro Crudo e Rucola (Veal chops with fresh tomato and rocket sauce). Coat 500g (1lb) of veal chops in the above breadcrumb mixture, omitting the rosemary. To make the sauce, combine 60ml (2fl oz) of extra-virgin olive oil, 1 finely chopped garlic clove, ¼ teaspoon of salt and plenty of freshly ground black pepper with 500g (1lb) of deseeded and chopped fresh, ripe tomatoes. Chop 60g (2oz) of washed and dried rocket leaves then toss with the other ingredients. Leave the sauce to stand at room temperature for 30 minutes to allow the flavours to blend. Fry the chops until golden and cooked through but still tender, about 4–5 minutes on each side. Spoon over a little of the sauce, passing the remainder at the table. Serves 2.

SPEZZATINO DI VITELLO IN UMIDO CON LIMONE E PINOLI

Braised veal with wine, lemon and pine nuts

Lemon is often used in cooking veal because its sharpness provides a counterpoint of flavour without overwhelming the delicate character of the meat. This dish is designed for an economy cut of veal that will stand up to lengthy cooking. Slow braising produces enough gravy for 250g (8oz) of short-cut pasta, such as farfalle, or Purè di Patate (see page 129) makes an excellent side dish.

INGREDIENTS

1.25kg (2½lb) veal shoulder steaks, 1–2.5cm (½–1in) thick
4 tbsp flour, for dredging
30g (1oz) unsalted butter
2 tbsp sunflower or corn oil
125ml (4fl oz) dry white wine
1 sprig fresh thyme, or ¼ tsp dried thyme
500ml (16fl oz) chicken stock
2 x 5cm (2in) strips lemon zest
½ tsp salt
1 tbsp pine nuts, coarsely chopped
¼ tsp freshly ground white or black pepper

PREPARATION

1 Cut each steak in half and remove any excess fat. If there is bone, include it in the dish as it will add flavour and its marrow can be eaten like a miniature *osso buco*. Spread the flour on a large plate.
2 Heat the butter and oil together in a deep frying pan. Meanwhile, dredge the veal in flour and when the butter and oil are hot, add the steaks to the pan. Brown them on both sides for about 8 minutes.
3 Stir in the wine and thyme. Allow the wine to evaporate, about 3 minutes, then pour in about 90ml (3fl oz) of stock. Adjust the heat to medium-low, cover the pan and simmer gently. Continue to add stock, about 60ml (2fl oz) at a time, every 10 minutes or so, or as needed. Stir occasionally.
4 Cook the veal for 1–1½ hours, depending on the toughness of the meat. Halfway through, add the lemon zest. Sprinkle the salt and pine nuts into the pan juices 15 minutes before the meat has finished cooking. Remove the pan from the heat, stir in a little pepper, and serve.

UCCELLETTI SCAPPATI

Veal rolls stuffed with prosciutto and fontina

Literally "little birds", these bundles of tender veal stuffed with cheese and sage are typical of Roman cooking. It is very important to use thin, high-quality veal slices cut from the leg. There is plenty of delicious gravy, which can be served with 125g (4oz) of fresh tagliatelle (see page 166), or dried egg noodles. Alternatively, Purè di Patate (see page 129) is an ideal accompaniment.

INGREDIENTS

*8 slices, about 750g (1½lb) veal escalopes cut from the leg, about 1cm (⅜in) thick
8 fresh sage leaves, or ½ tsp dried crumbled sage
8 slices prosciutto crudo or ham
90g (3oz) fontina or provolone, shredded
30g (1oz) unsalted butter
2 tbsp olive oil
60g (2oz) plain flour for dredging
125ml (4fl oz) dry white wine
salt and freshly ground black pepper, to taste*

PREPARATION

1 Lightly pound the veal (see page 164).

2 Put a fresh sage leaf or a tiny sprinkling of dried sage on each piece of veal. Cover each piece of meat with a slice of prosciutto or ham, trimming the edges if necessary. Sprinkle about 1 teaspoon of cheese evenly over each slice of ham.

3 Starting at one of the short ends, roll up the veal slice tightly and secure with two cocktail sticks. Prepare each slice in the same way.

4 Heat the butter and oil in a large frying pan.

5 Just before you are ready to cook the rolls, dust them with flour. When the butter and oil are hot, slip the rolls into the pan. Sauté gently until browned all over, 8–10 minutes.

6 Stir in the wine, salt and pepper. Use a wooden spoon to dislodge any bits of meat stuck to the base of the pan. Allow the wine to evaporate, about 3 minutes. Stir in 125ml (4fl oz) of water and reduce the heat to low. Cover and simmer until the meat is tender, about 40 minutes. If necessary, add a little more water. Check the seasoning and serve.

POLLO ALLA CACCIATORA
Chicken hunter's style

The term alla cacciatora, "hunter's style", describes a dish based on game, lamb or chicken that is cooked slowly in a tomato-based sauce. This is my mother's recipe. Its rich sauce contains giblets and livers, making it particularly appealing, and wine vinegar adds a lovely piquancy. Serve with Polenta (see page 169) or toasted bread. Serves 4–6.

INGREDIENTS

1.75kg (3½lb) chicken, cut up, including giblets
6 chicken livers
150g (5oz) wild or 250g (8oz) cultivated mushrooms
100ml (3½fl oz) extra-virgin olive oil
approximately 90g (3oz) plain flour
2 large cloves garlic, bruised
1 onion, chopped
1 large carrot, chopped
1 large celery stalk with leaves, chopped
1 tbsp chopped fresh flat-leaf parsley
3 tsp chopped fresh rosemary, or ½ tsp dried rosemary
2½ tbsp wine vinegar
500g (1lb) fresh or canned tomatoes, skinned, deseeded and chopped, plus 90ml (3fl oz) juice or water
salt and freshly ground black pepper, to taste

PREPARATION

1 Remove excess fat from the chicken. Trim any fat or membranes from the giblets and livers and finely dice. Wash and dry the chicken pieces.
2 Clean the mushrooms with a soft brush or cloth; do not wash them. Trim their stems, discarding any that are woody. Cut the caps into quarters, if large, then slice them across.
3 Heat 60ml (2fl oz) of oil in a frying pan. Spread the flour on a plate. When the oil is hot, dredge the chicken pieces in flour and slip them immediately into the oil. Fry them in batches to avoid crowding, if necessary. When all the pieces are golden-brown, about 15 minutes, transfer them to a platter and set aside. Wash and dry the pan.
4 Warm the remaining oil in the pan with the garlic, pressing down on the cloves to release their juices. When the garlic begins to colour, add the onion, carrot, celery and parsley. Increase the heat slightly and cook for 5 minutes, stirring occasionally.
5 Add the rosemary, giblets and livers and brown them for 2–3 minutes. Add the mushrooms, cook for 4 minutes then stir in the vinegar, the tomatoes and tomato juice or water and salt to taste.
6 Transfer the chicken to the sauce, stirring to coat the pieces thoroughly. Cover partially and cook gently until the chicken is tender and juicy, about 25 minutes. Sprinkle with pepper and serve.

Garlic

Flour

Extra-virgin olive oil

Wild mushrooms

Chicken livers

Chicken with giblets

Onion

Carrot

Celery with
leaves

Flat-leaf parsley

Rosemary

Wine
vinegar

Plum tomatoes
and juice

Salt

Black
pepper

POLLO IN TEGAME

Pan-roasted chicken with rosemary and garlic

My mother usually made this simple but succulent pan-roasted chicken for Saturday or Sunday supper and served it with homemade egg noodles. Because the chicken is cooked in a covered pan over slow, steady heat, plenty of richly flavoured gravy is produced — enough for 250g (8oz) of noodles. It is also good served with Purè di Patate (see page 129) or loose Polenta (see page 169).

INGREDIENTS

1 roasting chicken, about 1.75kg (3½lb)
2 tbsp extra-virgin olive oil
2 tbsp red or white wine vinegar, or cider vinegar
½ tsp salt, or to taste
Inside rub
1 sprig fresh rosemary, or ½ tsp crushed dried rosemary
2 large cloves garlic, bruised
freshly ground black pepper, to taste
Outside rub
2 tbsp extra-virgin olive oil
1 large clove garlic, finely chopped
1 tsp fresh finely chopped rosemary, or ½ tsp crushed dried rosemary
plenty of freshly ground black pepper
½ tsp sweet paprika

PREPARATION

1 Wash the chicken well and dry it thoroughly inside and out using kitchen paper. Combine the ingredients for the inside rub and spread it around the cavity. Then mix the ingredients for the outside rub and work it into the chicken skin.

2 Select a deep, heavy-bottomed pan wide enough to accommodate the chicken. Warm the oil over a medium heat and when it is hot enough to make the chicken sizzle, add the bird to the pan. Immediately lower the heat to medium-low to prevent the rub from burning, and brown the chicken lightly on all sides, 10–12 minutes. Use tongs or two large spoons to turn the chicken.

3 Add the vinegar and use a wooden spoon to dislodge any bits of skin or rub that are stuck to the base of the pan. Cover the pan and cook the chicken over a low heat for about 1 hour, turning it occasionally. It is essential to keep the pan tightly covered to prevent the juices evaporating. However, should the chicken appear dry, add up to 60ml (2fl oz) of water in the last 30 minutes of cooking.

4 Take the pan off the heat and sprinkle the chicken with salt, turning it so that it is seasoned evenly. Allow the chicken to settle in the pan, covered, for about 10 minutes. Carve the chicken and serve it hot with its pan juices.

PETTI DI POLLO IMPANATI

Breaded chicken breast cutlets

This is a classic preparation of chicken breast cutlets that is light and elegant, but very easy. The cutlets can be served hot or at room temperature. Cold, they are excellent for the picnic basket.

INGREDIENTS

4 boneless chicken breasts, partially frozen
1 tsp freshly grated Parmesan
pinch of freshly grated nutmeg
1 tsp grated onion
salt and freshly ground black pepper, to taste
2 eggs, beaten
90g (3oz) lightly toasted white breadcrumbs
60g (2oz) unsalted butter
2 tbsp olive oil
1 lemon, cut into wedges, to serve

PREPARATION

1 Slice each breast section across into three slices to make very thin, even cutlets.

2 Beat the Parmesan, nutmeg, onion, salt and pepper with the egg and marinate the cutlets in the mixture for up to 3 hours.

3 Spread the breadcrumbs on a piece of waxed paper or on a plate. Heat the butter and oil in a frying pan until hot enough to make the chicken sizzle. Just before frying, dip each cutlet into the crumbs, making sure they are covered completely. Sauté the chicken over a medium heat until golden on the outside but still tender and moist within, 2–3 minutes on each side. Drain on paper towels.

4 Serve the cutlets, squeezing a little lemon juice over them at the table.

VARIATIONS

• Substitute turkey breasts for chicken breasts to make **Petti di Tacchino Impanati**.

• For a variation with fontina and ham **(Petti di Pollo Impanati alla Piemontese)**, prepare the chicken breasts according to the recipe, omitting lemon juice. Preheat the oven to 200°C/400°F/ gas 6. Arrange the cooked cutlets in a baking dish and top them with 60–90g (2–3oz) of sliced ham. Cover the ham with 90–125g (3–4oz) of shredded fontina. Bake at the top of the oven until the cheese melts, about 5 minutes. Serve immediately.

POLLO ALLA MARENGO
Chicken Marengo

Pollo alla Marengo commemorates the Battle of Marengo, being the dish that was served up to Napoleon on the eve of his victory over the Austrians on Lombard soil in June 1800. Some say that the general's cook created the dish from the few ingredients that were to hand; others claim the dish included crayfish, tomatoes and eggs and was created by somebody else entirely. Whatever, this dish became Napoleon's preferred pre-battle dinner and he resisted all later attempts to dress it up with truffles and spirits. My version of this superb dish includes wine and mushrooms. Accompany with plenty of fresh bread or rice. Serves 4–6. Illustrated on page 121.

INGREDIENTS

1.75kg (3½lb) chicken, cut-up
1 tbsp extra-virgin olive oil
30g (1oz) unsalted butter
2 large cloves garlic, bruised
1 onion, chopped
1 carrot, chopped
1 celery stalk with leaves, chopped
2 tbsp chopped fresh flat-leaf parsley
150g (5oz) mushrooms
2–3 tbsp olive oil
150ml (¼ pint) dry white wine
2 tbsp flour
350ml (12fl oz) good chicken stock
salt and freshly ground white or black pepper, to taste

PREPARATION

1 Remove excess fat from the chicken. Use the blunt side of a chef's knife to break the bottom of the leg bone. Divide each breast in half.
2 Heat the extra-virgin olive oil and butter in a casserole. Add the garlic and sauté gently for about 3 minutes until it begins to colour and release its juices. Add the onion, carrot, celery and half the parsley. Sauté until softened, then set aside.
3 Meanwhile, clean the mushrooms with a soft brush or cloth; do not wash them. Trim their stems, discarding any that are woody. Cut the caps into quarters, if large, and then slice.
4 Heat the ordinary olive oil in a frying pan. When it is hot enough to make the chicken sizzle, add the pieces (in batches if necessary) and brown them on all sides, about 15 minutes. Transfer to the casserole with the sautéed vegetables.
5 Drain the oil from the frying pan, return the pan to the heat and add the wine. Allow the alcohol to evaporate, about 3 minutes, using a wooden spoon to dislodge any bits of meat stuck to the pan. Meanwhile, mix the flour with just enough water

to make a paste then stir it into the frying pan. Add the stock and stir to make a smooth sauce.
6 Pour the liquid mixture into the casserole and seaon with salt, stirring thoroughly. Cover the pot, leaving a small gap. Cook over a medium-low heat for 20 minutes, stirring occasionally. Finally, stir in the remaining parsley and plenty of pepper.

CONIGLIO ALLA VENETA
Rabbit in the style of the Veneto

Here is a way of cooking rabbit that is also successful with chicken. A great deal of flavour is derived from the liver, heart and kidneys of the animal, which are chopped and added to the sauce, but you can make do with just the liver. Plenty of rich sauce is produced. In the Veneto, such gamy dishes are typically served with Polenta (see page 169), but buttered noodles, plain rice or Purè di Patate (see page 129) are also good.

INGREDIENTS

1.5kg (3lb) rabbit, including liver, heart and kidneys, cut-up
60g (2oz) flour for dredging
2 tsp chopped fresh rosemary, or
¾ tsp dried rosemary
freshly ground black pepper, to taste
30g (1oz) unsalted butter
1 tbsp olive oil
1 large clove garlic, bruised
½ tsp salt
zest of 1 lemon
125ml (4fl oz) dry white wine

PREPARATION

1 Wash and dry the rabbit pieces. Remove any excess fat. Chop the liver, heart and kidneys.
2 Spread the flour on a plate and mix in half the rosemary and plenty of pepper.
3 Place the butter, oil and garlic in a large frying pan and sauté the garlic until golden. Remove it and set aside. Just before you are ready to fry the rabbit, dredge each piece lightly in flour. Slip the pieces immediately into the pan and cook for 10–12 minutes – fry them in batches if necessary. Transfer the browned rabbit pieces to a dish.
4 Add the liver, heart and kidneys to the pan and sauté for 30 seconds. Return the rabbit to the pan, add the salt, remaining rosemary, lemon zest and wine. Allow the wine to evaporate, about 3 minutes.
5 Pour in 125ml (4fl oz) of water, bring to the boil, then reduce the heat to low. Simmer gently, partially covered, until the rabbit is cooked through but still moist, about 15 minutes, then serve.

ANATRA ALL'ARANCIA
Roasted duck with orange
sauce, Tuscan style
(page 124)

POLPETTONE FARCITO
Meatloaf stuffed with ham
and parsley frittatine
(page 110)

POLLO ALLA MARENGO
Chicken Marengo
(page 119)

STUFATO DI CERVO
Venison casserole

Anna Amedolara Nurse is a legend in New York food circles. She cooks with great gusto, and her friends have many an anecdote to tell about her food. One such story came from a relative who was at Anna's home when her husband, Gene, returned from a hunting trip with a prize deer. Anna lost no time: she moved her guests to the sidelines, covered the floor with a cloth and butchered the animal on the spot while her company looked on in amazement. Considering this story, I decided that Anna's venison recipe must be shared. Here it is.

INGREDIENTS

*125ml (4fl oz) olive oil
1kg (2lb) boneless venison leg or shoulder,
cut into 3.5cm (1½in) cubes
125g (4oz) pancetta or blanched bacon, diced
1 onion, chopped
2 cloves garlic, finely chopped
1 celery stalk, diced, plus 2 tbsp chopped celery leaves
1 carrot, diced
30g (1oz) chopped fresh flat-leaf parsley
1 bay leaf
½ tsp chopped fresh thyme, or ¼ tsp dried thyme
pinch crushed dried red chillies
3 fresh ripe tomatoes, or 250g (8oz) canned drained
tomatoes, skinned, deseeded and chopped
125ml (4fl oz) dry white wine
250ml (8fl oz) Meat Broth (see page 72) or good stock
salt and freshly ground black pepper, to taste*

PREPARATION

1 Heat the olive oil in a deep frying pan or cooking pot until hot enough to sear the meat. Add the venison to the pan in batches and allow it to brown, about 10 minutes. Transfer the meat to a plate then drain off all but 3 tablespoons of the oil.
2 Reheat the oil and add the pancetta, onion, garlic, celery, carrot, herbs and chillies to the pan, using a wooden spoon to loosen any bits of meat stuck to the bottom of the pan. Cover and cook gently until the vegetables are translucent, 8–10 minutes.
3 Remove the lid and stir in the tomatoes. Sauté for 2 minutes, then add the wine and broth and raise the heat to medium. Allow to come to the boil then quickly reduce the heat to medium-low.
4 Return the venison to the pan, cover and cook until thoroughly tender, about 40 minutes, stirring occasionally. Stir in the salt and pepper. Transfer the venison to a warm platter. Return the pan to the heat and simmer the gravy until reduced and thickened slightly, 4–8 minutes. Pour the gravy over the venison and serve.

QUAGLIE SAPORITE
Savoury braised quails

Small game birds are an immensely popular food in Italy. They are cooked in many ways – larded and spit-roasted, pan-roasted with wine, wrapped in aromatic leaves and boiled, cooked in parchment and even baked whole into pies. Quail are prized for their delicate meat; unlike many game birds, their tender flesh makes them ideal for sautéing. Serves 2.

INGREDIENTS

*30g (1oz) unsalted butter
1 tbsp sunflower or vegetable oil
30g (1oz) pancetta or lean bacon, finely chopped
45g (1½oz) flour for dredging
freshly ground black pepper, to taste
2 quail, each about 175g (6oz), split into quarters
livers and gizzards from the quails, if available, chopped
1 small onion, grated
6 fresh sage leaves, chopped, or ¾ tsp dried crumbled sage
salt, to taste
125ml (4fl oz) dry white wine
175ml (6fl oz) Chicken Broth (see page 73) or good stock*

PREPARATION

1 Heat the butter and oil in a large, preferably non-stick frying pan. Add the pancetta and sauté until lightly coloured, 1–2 minutes.
2 Meanwhile, place the flour and pepper on a sheet of waxed paper or plate and dredge the quail sections in the flour. Transfer them to the frying pan and sauté until they are browned all over, about 10 minutes. Transfer them to a dish.
3 Add the liver and gizzards, if available, and the onion and sage to the pan. Sauté until the onion softens, about 3 minutes.
4 Stir in a little salt and the wine, using a wooden spoon to dislodge any bits of meat stuck to the pan. Allow the alcohol to evaporate, about 4 minutes. Pour in the broth and bring it to a simmer.
5 Return the quail sections to the pan. Braise them gently, partially covered, until cooked through, 20–25 minutes, turning them once. Serve hot, perhaps accompanied by sautéed mushrooms or loose Polenta (see page 169).

FARAONA RIPIENA

Pan-roasted guinea fowl with bread and
sun-dried tomato stuffing, Sardinian style

Guinea fowl is a very popular bird in central Italy,
and in Sardinia too. These birds cannot be raised in cages
because they roost in trees, and their meat has a
great deal more flavour than chicken. Because of their
low fat content, guinea fowl are best cooked with
moisture, either pot-roasted, or in the oven
al cartoccio, sealed in paper or foil. This Sardinian
stuffing is also used for boiled chicken. Serves 6.

INGREDIENTS

2 guinea fowl, each about 1kg (2lb)
freshly ground black pepper, to taste
4 tbsp extra-virgin olive oil
125ml (4fl oz) dry red or white wine
3 carrots, quartered
2 onions, quartered
½ tsp salt
250ml (8fl oz) Chicken Broth (see page 73)
or good stock
Stuffing
6 sun-dried tomatoes preserved in oil or dry
250g (8oz) packed 2-day old very thinly sliced Italian or
French bread, crusts removed
2 tbsp chopped fresh flat-leaf parsley
⅛ tsp saffron strands, or 1 sachet (130mg)
saffron powder
125ml (4fl oz) Chicken Broth (see page 73)
1 egg
½ tsp salt, or to taste
freshly ground black pepper, to taste
1 tbsp oil from sun-dried tomatoes
or extra-virgin olive oil

PREPARATION

1 Make the stuffing. If using tomatoes preserved in oil, drain and chop them. If they are the dry variety, first soak them in hot water until they are tender, about 20 minutes. Combine the chopped tomatoes with the bread and parsley.

2 Heat the saffron strands, if using, in a small frying pan until they start to colour and release their flavour, about 15 seconds. Pulverize them with the back of a spoon.

3 Lightly beat together the broth, egg, saffron strands or powder, salt, pepper and oil. Pour this mixture over the tomato, bread and parsley and toss everything together.

4 Wash the guinea fowl inside and out with cold water then sprinkle pepper into the cavities. Fill the birds with the stuffing mixture and close the cavities securely using a needle and thread. Pat dry the skin with kitchen paper.

5 Heat the olive oil in a large heavy-based pan over a medium-high heat and add the birds. Sauté until the birds are nicely browned on all sides, about 10 minutes. Use tongs to turn them so you avoid puncturing the skin. Add the wine to the pan and allow the alcohol to evaporate, about 3 minutes. Remove the guinea fowl and set them aside.

6 Add the vegetables, stirring to coat them with the juices. Return the birds to the pan, setting them on their backs. Add the salt and half the broth to the pan and cover partially.

7 When the broth begins to simmer, reduce the heat to low and cook the guinea fowl until tender, approximately 1¼ hours, stirring occasionally and adding more liquid, if necessary, to keep the birds and vegetables moist. Do not turn the guinea fowl. Make a cut in the leg joint to see if the juices run clear. If not, continue to cook, partially covered, for 10–15 minutes longer. Do not overcook or the flesh will be dry. Remove the pan from the heat.

8 Allow the guinea fowl to settle for 15 minutes before serving them. Skim the fat from the pan juices, remove the trussing thread and serve the birds split down the middle, leaving the stuffing intact. Surround them with the vegetables and pour over the pan juices.

ANATRA ALL'ARANCIA

Roasted duck with orange sauce, Tuscan style

This is one of many dishes taken to France by Caterina de' Medici's cooks. Traditional recipes call for aquavit, but brandy may be used. The orange and honey baste gives the duck a deep golden-brown skin. Serves 4–6. Illustrated on page 120.

INGREDIENTS

1 duck, about 3kg (6lb)
salt, to taste
5 oranges
15 cloves
125ml (4fl oz) brandy
3 tbsp honey or sugar
1½ tbsp flour

PREPARATION

1 Preheat the oven to 200°C/400°F/gas 6.
2 Wash the duck inside and out and cut out excess fat from the cavity. Dry the cavity of the duck and sprinkle it with salt. Keep the skin wet.
3 Press two of the oranges against the work surface to soften them. Using a small knife, puncture the oranges and push in the cloves. Place the oranges in the cavity of the duck. Puncture the skin of the duck then close the cavity with small skewers.
4 Place the duck on a rack in a roasting pan breast-side down and roast it for 30 minutes.
5 Meanwhile, remove the zest from two of the remaining oranges, taking care to leave behind the pith. Squeeze the juice from the oranges – there should be about 250ml (8fl oz) – and strain. Mix it with the brandy, honey or sugar and ½ teaspoon of salt. Cut the zest into matchstick strips, soak in boiling water for 1 minute then drain and set aside.
6 Remove the duck from the oven and lower the temperature to 180°C/350°F/gas 4. Drain all the fat from the pan and pierce the duck skin again to release fat. Baste the duck with some of the orange juice mixture. Return to the oven and cook for 1 hour, basting every 20 minutes or so.
7 Turn the duck breast-side up so that it browns nicely on both sides and cook for a final 30 minutes.
8 Remove the duck from the oven and make an incision in the leg joint. If the juices do not run clear, cook the duck for 10–15 minutes longer. Lift the duck from the pan and allow it to stand.
9 Skim the fat from the pan juices. In a small pan, combine the flour with a little orange juice mixture then stir in the remaining juice mixture, the zest and pan juices. Heat until thickened, 8–10 minutes, stirring frequently. Serve the duck with the sauce, surrounded by slices of the remaining orange.

ROGNONCINI CON PISELLI

Sautéed kidneys with peas and shallots

Here is a delicate and simple dish in which kidneys are at their best. I like to serve it with rice, or simply with plenty of good bread to soak up the sauce.

INGREDIENTS

500g (1lb) fresh lamb or veal kidneys
salt, to taste
125g (4oz) frozen and thawed or fresh shelled peas
30g (1oz) unsalted butter
1 tbsp olive oil
2 shallots, chopped
1 tbsp chopped fresh flat-leaf parsley
½ tsp chopped fresh marjoram, or ¼ tsp dried marjoram
2 tbsp dry white wine
freshly ground white or black pepper, to taste

PREPARATION

1 Soak the kidneys for 30 minutes in cold water to which 1 teaspoon of salt has been added. Meanwhile, if using fresh peas, blanch them in salted boiling water for 1½ minutes. Drain and rinse in cold water then set aside.
2 Remove any membranes from the kidneys and trim any fat. Cut them into 5mm (¼in) slices.
3 Heat the butter and oil with the chopped shallots. When the shallots are soft, add the kidneys and sauté them over a high heat for several minutes just until they lose their pinkness. Take care not to overcook them, or they will lose their delicacy.
4 Reduce the heat and add the parsley, marjoram, wine and salt to taste. Continue to sauté, allowing the wine to evaporate, 2–3 minutes. Stir in the blanched or thawed peas. Sauté for 3 minutes, add a good sprinkling of pepper and serve immediately.

FEGATO ALLA VENEZIANA
Venetian-style sautéed calves' liver

The Venetians are famous for this dish. It is no ordinary treatment of liver and onions. The secret to its success lies in sweating the onions until they are almost melted, and in sautéing the paper-thin liver so rapidly that its tenderness and delicacy are retained. Choose very fresh, light pink liver from a young calf. While it is not traditional to do so, and may be considered heresy by Venetians, I sometimes add a drop of balsamic vinegar to each slice of liver at the table. Serve with polenta crostini or plain Polenta with butter (see page 169).

INGREDIENTS

4 tbsp corn or sunflower oil
1kg (2lb) onions, halved and sliced as thinly as possible
750g (1½lb) calves' liver, partially frozen
salt and freshly ground black or white pepper, to taste

PREPARATION

1 Heat 3 tablespoons of oil in a large non-stick frying pan. Add the onions, turn the heat to medium-low, stir, then cover the pan. Cook the onions until completely soft, about 30 minutes, stirring occasionally to prevent them browning.
2 Meanwhile, use a very sharp knife to cut away the tough outer skin of the liver. Slice the liver on the diagonal into paper-thin strips. Cut out any hard tubes you may find. Set the pieces aside.
3 Transfer the onions to a dish. Warm the rest of the oil in the pan over a medium-high heat. Place as many pieces of liver as possible in the pan without crowding. Sauté the liver quickly on both sides, just until it changes colour (less than half a minute); do not allow it to brown. Transfer it to a dish and return the onions to the pan just to heat through.
4 Pile the onions on to a warm serving dish, arrange the liver on top, season well and serve.

TRIPPA IN UMIDO
Stewed honeycomb tripe

This is the first dish I ever cooked without help. I was nine when dinner responsibilities were left to me due to the unusual absence of my mother, who gave me the instructions for this recipe, probably because she knew it was one of my favourites. We served it with Polenta (see page 169) scattered with Parmesan. I recommend you do the same.

INGREDIENTS

1kg (2lb) honeycomb tripe, washed and trimmed of fat
salt, to taste
3 tbsp olive oil
2 large cloves garlic, finely chopped
1 onion, chopped
1 large celery stalk with leaves, chopped
1 large carrot, chopped
2 fresh bay leaves, bruised but left whole
90g (3oz) tomato purée
125ml (4fl oz) dry white wine
freshly ground black pepper, to taste

PREPARATION

1 Slice the tripe into strips about 5cm (2in) long and 2.5cm (1in) wide and rub salt into each piece. Wash the strips in cold water, rinse and pat dry.
2 Heat the oil in a large pot and add the garlic, onion, celery, carrot and bay leaves. Sauté gently until the vegetables soften, about 7 minutes.
3 Add the tripe and sauté over a medium heat for 5–10 minutes, stirring occasionally. Lower the heat and stir in the tomato purée. Add the wine and the pepper and leave to simmer for 2–3 minutes.
4 Add 350ml (12fl oz) of water and a teaspoon of salt. Partially cover the pot and simmer gently until the tripe is tender, 1–1¼ hours. Add a little more water if it starts to dry out. There should be abundant, thick gravy. Taste for salt before serving.

SALSICCIE CON CIME DI RAPA
Sausages with bitter broccoli, Apulian style

Few things are as contentedly mated as sweet Italian sausages and peppery bitter broccoli greens. Kale can be used successfully, though it is inauthentic.

INGREDIENTS

500g (1lb) fresh sweet Italian pork sausages
1kg (2lb) cime di rapa (bitter broccoli) or kale
90ml (3fl oz) extra-virgin olive oil
4 large cloves garlic, finely chopped
½ tsp salt, or to taste

PREPARATION

1 Cook the sausages as described on page 164. Cover them and take off the heat.
2 Trim and peel the stems of the greens. Cut the leaves and stems across into 7cm (3in) pieces and wash well. Bring a pan of water to the boil and parboil the greens for 5 minutes. Drain well.
3 Warm the oil and garlic together in a large frying pan until the garlic has softened, about 2 minutes.
4 Add the greens and the salt to the frying pan. Cover and cook gently, stirring occasionally, until tender but not mushy, about 5 minutes. Serve the greens immediately alongside the sausages.

VEGETABLE DISHES

The traditional Italian diet is based on the products of the local landscape. The heart of every village, town and city is the market where the opulent red of tomatoes and peppers, the vibrant greens of herbs and the stunning colours of golden squashes and purple cabbages dazzle the eye. The Italian way of cooking vegetables is straightforward, aiming to make food taste of itself, so the raw ingredients must be absolutely fresh. The Italian for vegetable dishes, *contorni*, means "surroundings", but vegetables are never relegated to side-dish status on the Italian table. Some of the recipes in this chapter are simple in their composition. The more complex dishes, prepared in larger quantities, might be served as main courses.

INVOLTINI DI CAVOLO
Stuffed cabbage

When I think back to my childhood and the dishes I loved the most, many come to mind. But the ones for which I have a particular fondness are the fortifying winter dishes. My mother always served stuffed cabbage as a main course, but the tartness given the dish by sour pickles makes it into a lovely starter for 8. Balsamic vinegar, my own touch, rounds out the flavours nicely.

INGREDIENTS

24 leaves from a green cabbage
salt, to taste
10 small gherkin pickles, thinly sliced lengthways
2 bay leaves
2 tbsp balsamic vinegar
Filling
100g (3½ oz) long-grain rice
375g (12oz) lean minced beef
375g (12oz) lean minced pork
1 egg
1 small onion, grated
2 tbsp chopped fresh flat-leaf parsley
1 tsp ground allspice
1 tsp salt
½ tsp freshly ground black pepper
Sauce
2 tbsp extra-virgin olive oil
1 small celery stalk with leaves, finely chopped
1 small onion, grated
1 large clove garlic, finely chopped
625g (1¼lb) canned drained tomatoes, chopped

PREPARATION

1 Slice off the protruding tip of the central rib of each cabbage leaf so that they will lie flat. Have ready a large bowl half-full of cold water.

2 Bring 2 litres (3½ pints) of water to the boil in a large pot. Add 2 teaspoons of salt. Drop in the leaves a few at a time and cook until just tender, 3–4 minutes. Transfer them to the cold water. Reserve the cooking water. Remove the leaves from the cold water and dry them with a clean tea towel.

3 Combine the ingredients for the filling with 2 tablespoons of water, mixing thoroughly. Place 2 teaspoons of filling in a cylindrical shape at the base of each leaf, across the spine. Begin to roll up the leaf, folding in the sides as you work to make a neat package. If you have any leftover stuffing, make small meatballs out of it.

4 Secure each bundle with a cocktail stick. Place the bundles side-by-side in a heavy-bottomed pan, slipping the sliced gherkins in between. Tuck the bay leaves into the pan.

5 In a bowl, combine the ingredients for the sauce and stir in 500ml (16fl oz) of cabbage cooking water. Pour the sauce over the cabbage bundles and simmer gently, partially covered, until the sauce is thickened and the rice tender (make a small cut in one of the parcels to test), about 1½ hours.

6 Use a slotted spoon to transfer the bundles to a serving plate. Reheat the sauce, moistening it with cabbage water if necessary. If it is runny, simmer it uncovered until reduced. Taste for salt, sprinkle in the vinegar and simmer for another 2 minutes. Spoon the sauce over the cabbage and serve hot or at room temperature, with additional rice if desired.

Cavolo alla Parmigiana
Stewed cabbage with pancetta and vinegar, Parma style

This recipe was given to me by Paola Rinaldini, who with her husband runs a small farm and winery in the Parma countryside. The cabbage, flavoured with pancetta and vinegar, is stewed very slowly so that the flavours become concentrated as the cabbage cooks down to a creamy consistency. Signora Rinaldini serves this dish with the famous cotechino sausage, and it is indeed a splendid match for any pork or game dish. Serves 6.

INGREDIENTS

2 tbsp vegetable oil or olive oil
90g (3oz) pancetta, sliced and finely diced
1 onion, quartered and thinly sliced
1 tbsp tomato purée
3 tbsp red wine vinegar
1kg (2lb) cabbage, shredded
1 tsp salt

PREPARATION

1 Heat the oil, add the pancetta and sauté until it begins to colour. Add the onion and sauté gently until softened, about 4 minutes.
2 Dissolve the tomato purée in 60ml (2fl oz) of water, stir it into the pan, then pour in the vinegar. Add the cabbage and salt and toss with a wooden spoon. Pour in 250ml (8fl oz) of water and stir.
3 Increase the heat to medium-high and cook until the cabbage begins to sweat, about 6 minutes, tossing frequently. Reduce the heat to low, cover, and cook until the cabbage has an almost creamy consistency, about 1½ hours, stirring occasionally. If it seems dry, add a little more water, but no more than a teaspoon or two at a time. Serve hot.

Patate Fritte
Fried potatoes

On the Italian table, fried potatoes are something special – nothing like the greasy, mass-produced potato chips of some fast food restaurants. The secret lies in using good potatoes and olive oil, and in the method, which is to slice them thinly and dry them well. Salting them before frying ensures crispness. Illustrated on page 107.

INGREDIENTS

500g (1lb) boiling potatoes, peeled
freshly ground sea salt, to taste
olive oil
4 large cloves garlic, unpeeled and cut in half
freshly ground white or black pepper, to taste

PREPARATION

1 Wash the potatoes and dry them well. If they are large, cut them in half. Using a sharp chef's knife, cut the potatoes into very thin slices. Blot them between two clean cotton tea towels to absorb the potato moisture. Transfer them to dry towels and sprinkle lightly with salt. When they begin to produce more moisture, blot them again.
2 Pour olive oil into a frying pan to a depth of 1.5cm (¾in) and heat. Add the garlic, fry until golden, then remove. Slip the potatoes in rapidly one by one to prevent the slices from sticking to each other. Fry them in batches to avoid crowding the pan. Sauté until they are golden-brown on both sides then drain on kitchen paper. Transfer to a warm platter and sprinkle with pepper. Serve hot.

"Gâteau" di Patate
Potato "cake"

This Neapolitan treatment of potatoes produces a layered "cake" of sorts. The mozzarella creates a generous middle layer, which serves as a lovely oozy contrast to the potatoes.

INGREDIENTS

1.5kg (3lb) boiling potatoes, scrubbed but unpeeled
125g (4oz) unsalted butter, plus butter for greasing
250ml (8fl oz) warm milk
2 eggs, lightly beaten
3 tbsp freshly grated pecorino or Parmesan
5 tbsp breadcrumbs, lightly toasted
250g (8oz) mozzarella, diced
125g (4oz) prosciutto or Italian salami, finely diced
large pinch of paprika

PREPARATION

1 Preheat the oven to 180°C/350°F/gas 4.
2 Boil the potatoes until tender, then drain. When they are cool enough to handle, peel them and pass them through a potato ricer, or use a potato masher. Leave to cool slightly, then mix in the butter, milk, eggs and 1 tablespoon of grated cheese.
3 Butter a baking dish and sprinkle in half of the breadcrumbs, making sure they coat the surface entirely. Tap out any excess crumbs.
4 Spoon half of the potato mixture into the dish, spreading it evenly. Top with the mozzarella, 1 tablespoon of grated cheese and the prosciutto or salami, then cover with the rest of the potato.
5 Sprinkle the top with the leftover breadcrumbs, the final tablespoon of grated cheese and a little paprika. Bake for 30 minutes. If the top isn't golden-brown, place the dish under the grill for a few minutes. Allow to settle for 10 minutes and serve.

PATATE AL FORNO

Scalloped potatoes baked in milk

Serves 6.

INGREDIENTS

1.25kg (2½lb) potatoes, scrubbed but kept whole
45g (1½oz) unsalted butter, plus butter for greasing
250g (8oz) soured cream blended with 2–3 tbsp milk
½ tsp salt
45g (1½oz) freshly grated Parmesan
250ml (8fl oz) milk

PREPARATION

1 Boil or steam the potatoes until they are half-cooked, 20–30 minutes, according to size. Drain them thoroughly and allow to cool completely. Peel them and cut them across into approximate 5mm (¼in) slices.

2 Preheat the oven to 200°C/400°F/gas 6.
3 Butter a baking dish that will comfortably hold the potatoes. Arrange a layer of potatoes in the dish then dot with butter and smear with some of the thinned soured cream. Sprinkle with some of the salt, then scatter a little of the Parmesan on top.
4 Repeat the process, layering until all of the potatoes are used up and distributing butter, cheese and salt evenly between the layers (leave a little butter and Parmesan for scattering on the top). Pour the milk over all, and finish with little pieces of the remaining butter and a sprinkling of Parmesan. Cover the dish tightly with foil.
5 Bake the dish on the top rack of the oven for 20 minutes. Take off the foil and continue baking until the potatoes are golden-brown on top, another 5–10 minutes.
6 Remove the dish from the oven and allow it to settle for 10–15 minutes before serving.

PURE DI PATATE
Puréed potatoes

The Italian version of puréed potatoes goes one step beyond what is called mashed potatoes. After the potatoes are mashed, they are returned to the pan while first butter, and then hot milk – as much as the potatoes will absorb – are beaten into them. The result is creamy, light and fluffy. Only include Parmesan if it is compatible with the main dish. Serves 6.

INGREDIENTS

750g (1½lb) boiling potatoes, scrubbed but kept whole
60g (2oz) unsalted butter, cut into thin slices
salt, to taste
175ml (6fl oz) hot milk
30g (1oz) freshly grated Parmesan, optional
freshly ground white pepper, to taste

PREPARATION

1 Boil the potatoes until tender, about 30 minutes, then drain. Take care not to puncture the potatoes' skins too often during cooking or they will absorb too much water. Rinse the pan.
2 When the potatoes are just comfortable to handle, peel them and pass them through a potato ricer into the saucepan, or use a potato masher, pressing out all lumps.
3 Place the saucepan over a heat diffusing mat, if available, or over the lowest possible heat. Add the butter and salt, stirring constantly as you work to prevent the potatoes on the bottom of the pan from becoming scorched. Using an electric beater or whisk, beat in the hot milk a little at a time.
4 Remove the pan from the heat, adjust for salt and beat in the Parmesan, if using, and pepper.

FAGIOLINI E PATATE ALL' ISTRIANA

Green beans and potatoes, Istrian style

This dish was made for me by Lidia Bastianich after one of our vegetable-hunting trips in the Lecce market. Among our finds were creamy-fleshed baby yellow potatoes and freshly picked buttery green beans that complement each other beautifully in this earthy and tasty dish. Serves 6.

INGREDIENTS

500g (1lb) baby yellow new potatoes, unpeeled
750g (1½lb) green beans, trimmed
salt, to taste
90ml (3fl oz) extra-virgin olive oil
6 large cloves garlic, thinly sliced
freshly ground black pepper, to taste

PREPARATION

1 Scrub the potatoes well and cut the green beans in half. Bring a large pan of water to the boil and cook the potatoes until three-quarters tender, 15–20 minutes (test them with a skewer).
2 Add the green beans and 2 teaspoons of salt to the pan. Cook until the green beans are tender but not mushy, 8–10 minutes, then drain. When the potatoes are cool enough to handle, peel them and set them aside.
3 Warm all but 1 tablespoon of the olive oil in a frying pan with the garlic. Fry the garlic until it begins to colour, but do not let it brown. Add the potatoes and green beans, using a wooden spoon to mix them thoroughly and pressing down to half mash them. Continue to sauté until the potatoes begin to acquire a golden crispness, 5–7 minutes.
4 Remove the pan from the heat and stir in the remaining oil. Check the seasoning and sprinkle over plenty of pepper. Serve hot or warm.

VARIATION

Sprinkle the finished dish with 1 tablespoon of chopped fresh flat-leaf parsley and 125g (4oz) of bacon, cut into julienne strips and fried until crisp.

FAGIOLINI AL POMODORO

Green beans with tomato and garlic

Illustrated on page 56.

INGREDIENTS

500g (1lb) green beans, trimmed
salt, to taste
3 tbsp extra-virgin olive oil
2 large cloves garlic, chopped
500g (1lb) fresh or canned drained tomatoes, skinned, deseeded and chopped
3–4 large fresh basil leaves, torn into small pieces, or 1 tbsp chopped fresh flat-leaf parsley
freshly ground black or white pepper, to taste

PREPARATION

1 Bring a saucepan of water to a rolling boil. Add the beans and 2 teaspoons of salt. Cook the beans until almost tender, 7–9 minutes, then drain.
2 Meanwhile, heat the olive oil in a frying pan and add the garlic. When the garlic begins to colour, stir in the tomatoes and basil or parsley. Simmer the sauce for 5 minutes, then check the seasoning.
3 Add the cooked beans to the sauce and simmer gently until the beans are thoroughly tender, 10–15 minutes. Sprinkle with pepper and serve warm or at room temperature.

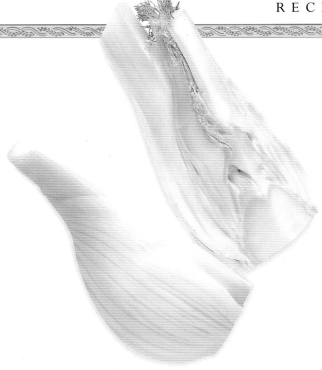

SCAROLA IN PADELLA CON FAGIOLI
Sautéed escarole with beans

The origins of this dish are in hearty southern Italian peasant cooking, which makes use of a great variety of leafy greens. Escarole, chicory or cime di rapa *(bitter broccoli) can be used.* Cime di rapa, *with its agreeable bitter taste, is especially complemented by the creaminess of the beans, but it is hard to find. Boiling rather than steaming the greens not only sweetens them, but sets their vibrant colour. This makes a good vegetarian meal or side dish for sausage or pork. Serves 6.*

INGREDIENTS

750g (1½lb) escarole, chicory or cime di rapa
(bitter broccoli)
salt, to taste
3 tbsp extra-virgin olive oil
2 cloves garlic, chopped
pinch crushed dried red chillies
*300g (10oz) dried cannellini beans, rehydrated
and cooked (see page 161)*

PREPARATION

1 If using escarole or chicory, slice off the bottom of the stalk. Place the leaves in a large bowl and soak for 15–20 minutes. If using bitter broccoli, trim the ends of the stalks then peel off the skin from the tough lower stalks. Rinse thoroughly in cold water then drain. Cut or tear the greens into approximate 7cm (3in) pieces.
2 Bring a large pan of water to a rolling boil. Add the greens and 1 tablespoon of salt to the pan. Bring back to the boil, cover partially and cook for another 5 minutes.
3 Meanwhile, place the olive oil, garlic and chilli in a frying pan. Turn the heat to low and sauté gently until the garlic just starts to colour (do not let it brown), about 5 minutes.
4 Drain the cooked greens, leaving some water still clinging to the leaves, and transfer them and the drained beans to the frying pan. Toss them over a medium heat until heated through. Check for salt, stir, cover and cook gently, until tender, about 5 minutes, before serving.

VARIATION

Friarelli (Greens sautéed with pancetta, garlic, onion and chilli, Campanian style). Cook the greens as above. Warm the oil, then add the garlic, chilli, 30g (1oz) sliced, finely diced pancetta and 1 small onion to the pan. Sauté until the garlic, onion and pancetta begin to colour. Add the greens and beans and proceed as above. Illustrated on page 57.

FINOCCHI GRATINATI
Baked fennel

Illustrated on page 57.

INGREDIENTS

6 fennel bulbs
salt, to taste
30g (1oz) unsalted butter
3 tbsp freshly grated Parmesan
90g (3oz) fontina cheese, shredded

PREPARATION

1 Trim the tough bases of the fennel bulbs. Cut off the tough stalks and feathery leaves, reserving them for some other dish, and cut away any blemished parts. Quarter the bulbs lengthways.
2 Place the fennel bulbs in a saucepan with just enough water to cover and add salt – 1 teaspoon per 1.25 litres (2 pints). Bring the water to the boil and cook the fennel until almost tender, 6–7 minutes, then drain.
3 Preheat the oven to 220°C/425°F/gas 7.
4 Arrange the fennel wedges in a baking dish. Scatter the butter and cheeses on top. Bake in the middle of the oven until the cheese melts and forms a golden crust, about 25 minutes. Serve hot.

VARIATION

Prepare and parcook the fennel wedges as described in steps 1 and 2. Place the boiled fennel in a baking dish and cover lightly with Besciamella (see page 136). Sprinkle with the butter and cheeses and bake as directed above. This method is used for many precooked vegetables, particularly asparagus, onions and cauliflower.

ASPARAGI ALLA PARMIGIANA

Asparagus, Parma style

Serves 8.

INGREDIENTS

1kg (2lb) tender asparagus
salt, to taste
60g (2oz) unsalted butter
60g (2oz) freshly grated Parmesan
freshly ground white pepper, to taste

PREPARATION

1 Preheat the oven to 220°C/425°F/gas 7.
2 Trim the ends of the asparagus and peel away the skin at the end of each stalk (see page 161).
3 In a frying pan large enough to take the whole length of the asparagus, bring enough water to cover the asparagus to the boil. Add salt – 1 teaspoon per 1.25 litres (2 pints) of water. Lower the asparagus into the water and boil until tender but not mushy, about 6 minutes.
4 Drain the asparagus immediately and plunge it into iced water to arrest cooking.
5 Butter a baking dish that will comfortably accommodate the asparagus in two or three layers. Scatter pieces of butter over each layer of asparagus, sprinkle generously with Parmesan and season with pepper.
6 Bake the dish in the middle of the oven until the Parmesan is just beginning to melt, approximately 15–20 minutes, then serve immediately.

ZUCCHINI ALLA CASALINGA

Steamed courgettes with butter and onion

This good and simple dish is something I often make when young courgettes are in season. The natural sweetness of the courgettes, the large proportion of onion and the creamy butter combine to create a delightfully sweet dish. It is best served warm or at room temperature, or even made a day ahead of serving. Serves 6.

INGREDIENTS

1kg (2lb) fresh, young courgettes, no more than 175–250g (6–8oz) each
1 large onion, finely diced
30g (1oz) unsalted butter
2 tbsp extra-virgin olive oil
¾ tsp salt, or to taste
1 tsp chopped fresh thyme, or ½ tsp dried thyme, or 1 tsp finely shredded fresh basil leaves

PREPARATION

1 Wash the courgettes and trim both ends. Slice them in half lengthways and then horizontally into slices approximately 1.5cm (¾in) thick.
2 Place the courgettes, onion, butter and olive oil in a heavy-based lidded pan, leaving a small opening for steam to escape. Cook over a medium heat until the courgettes are tender but not falling apart, about 15–20 minutes. Stir them frequently during cooking and if there is excess water, remove the lid during the last 5 minutes of cooking. If the courgettes seem dry, cover the pot completely and reduce the heat.
3 When the courgettes are cooked, add the salt and herbs and toss thoroughly. Allow to cool to room temperature before serving.

MELANZANE AL FUNGHETTO

Aubergine with mushrooms, garlic and herbs

This tasty dish is very straightforward to prepare. I like to serve it as an accompaniment to chicken or other fowl, or lamb.

INGREDIENTS

750g (1½lb) medium-small aubergines
salt, to taste
250g (½lb) cultivated mushrooms
4 tbsp extra-virgin olive oil
1 onion, chopped
2 large cloves garlic, finely chopped
½ tsp chopped fresh marjoram, or ¼ tsp dried marjoram
1 tbsp chopped fresh flat-leaf parsley
freshly ground black pepper, to taste

PREPARATION

1 Wash the aubergines and cut off the stems and navel ends; do not peel them. Cut into approximate 2.5cm (1in) cubes. Sprinkle the aubergine cubes lightly with salt and place them in a colander, set a weighted plate on top (a heavy can is ideal) and leave to drain for at least 40 minutes before rinsing with cold water. Pat dry with clean kitchen paper.
2 Meanwhile, clean the mushrooms with a brush or cloth; do not wash them. Trim the stems and slice the mushrooms lengthways.
3 Warm the olive oil in a non-stick frying pan. Add the onion and garlic and sauté over a medium heat until they soften, about 4 minutes.
4 Transfer the aubergine to the pan and sauté for 10 minutes, stirring frequently to prevent sticking. Add the sliced mushrooms and herbs and continue to fry, stirring constantly, until tender, 4–5 minutes. Sprinkle with salt and pepper and serve.

CARCIOFI RITTI

Tuscan-style stuffed braised artichokes

This is a particularly good way to serve artichokes. It is substantial enough for an antipasto, but it is also an appealing accompaniment for pork or lamb. Serves 3.

INGREDIENTS

6 artichokes, about 250g (8oz) each
1 tbsp freshly grated Parmesan
3 tbsp extra-virgin olive oil
2 cloves garlic, finely chopped
60g (2oz) capocollo (see page 27) or prosciutto, finely chopped
3 tbsp chopped fresh flat-leaf parsley
2 tbsp lightly toasted breadcrumbs
¼ tsp salt
good pinch of freshly ground pepper

PREPARATION

1 Prepare the artichokes for stuffing (see page 160).
2 Preheat the oven to 190°C/375°F/gas 5.
3 Select a baking dish in which the artichokes will fit snugly. Combine the Parmesan, 2 tablespoons of oil, the garlic, capocollo or prosciutto, parsley, breadcrumbs, salt and pepper in a small bowl.
4 Use a teaspoon to fill each artichoke with the stuffing. Place the artichokes and their stems in the baking dish and pour 175ml (6fl oz) of water and the remaining oil into the bottom of the dish.
5 Cover the dish with foil. Bake until the artichokes are tender, about 40 minutes. Check them occasionally and add more water if the dish gets too dry. Leave to cool for 15 minutes before serving.

PISELLINI CON PROSCIUTTO

Baby peas with prosciutto, Roman style

INGREDIENTS

60g (2oz) unsalted butter
1 small onion, finely chopped
60g (2oz) prosciutto in a thick slice, finely diced
1.5kg (3lb) fresh baby shell peas (unshelled weight), or
500g (1lb) frozen baby peas
1 tbsp chopped fresh flat-leaf parsley
125ml (4fl oz) Chicken Broth (see page 73) or water
salt and freshly ground black pepper, to taste

PREPARATION

1 Melt the butter in a frying pan. Add the onion, increase the heat to medium and sauté until softened but not coloured, 4–5 minutes.
2 Stir in the prosciutto and cook for 1–2 minutes to marry the flavours. Add the peas, parsley and broth or water. Cover and cook gently until the peas are tender and most of the liquid has evaporated, about 15 minutes, stirring occasionally.
3 Season to taste and serve immediately.

CONDIGGION

Summer vegetable salad, Ligurian style

Serves 6. Illustrated on page 56.

INGREDIENTS

4 yellow or red peppers, roasted, skinned and deseeded
(see page 160), and cut into 1cm (½in) wide strips
1 small seedless cucumber, peeled and thinly sliced
2 sweet vine-ripened tomatoes, cut into eighths
20 black or green olives, halved and pitted
10 anchovies in olive oil, drained and cut into small pieces
2 tbsp small capers, drained
1 tsp chopped fresh oregano, or ½ tsp dried oregano
salt and freshly ground black pepper, to taste
4 hard-boiled eggs, quartered
extra-virgin olive oil

PREPARATION

1 In a salad bowl, combine the roasted peppers, cucumber, tomatoes, olives, anchovies, capers, oregano and seasoning to taste.
2 Toss lightly, then lay the eggs over the salad and dress with the olive oil just before serving.

INSALATA RUSSA ALLA PIEMONTESE

Russian salad in the style of Piedmont

The Russian salad was long ago assimilated into Italian cuisine, though a simpler combination of vegetables is used in the Italian version than in the true original. The hard-boiled eggs may be left out, but I think they add a great deal to the composition. Serves 6.

INGREDIENTS

750g (1½lb) boiling potatoes, scrubbed
2 carrots, scraped
2 medium beetroot
150g (5oz) fresh or frozen peas
1 tbsp vinegar
1 hard-boiled egg
1 tbsp olive oil
1 quantity Maionese (see page 140)

PREPARATION

1 Place the potatoes in a pot, cover with cold water and bring to the boil. Add the carrots to the pot. Cook the vegetables until tender (the carrots will cook more quickly and should be lifted out and set aside to cool). When the potatoes are cooked, drain and peel them, then set aside to cool.
2 Meanwhile, wash the beetroot and remove their stems but not the base of the stem. Avoid piercing the flesh. Place them in a pot and cover with cold water. Cook until a sharp knife inserted through the beetroot comes out easily, about 25 minutes.
3 Cook the peas in boiling salted water until tender but not mushy, 2–5 minutes, depending on type and size. Drain and rinse in cold water.
4 Drain the cooked beetroot and leave to cool completely. Peel them and remove the stems. Cut the flesh into dice, place in a bowl and cover with cold water. Pour in the vinegar (this prevents the beetroot from "bleeding"). Allow to soak for 5 minutes then drain thoroughly.
5 Dice the potatoes and carrots and cut the hard-boiled egg into slightly smaller dice.
6 Combine the vegetables and egg in a serving dish and mix with the olive oil. Add the mayonnaise, toss everything together and serve.

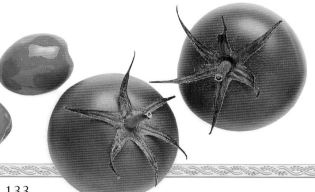

133

INSALATA DI PANE RAFFERMO E PEPERONI
Bread salad with roasted peppers

There are several famous Italian bread salads, such as Tuscan panzanella *and Apulian* cialed, *that should be made with only the best tomatoes. However, in this salad, the primary ingredients are excellent all year round. Its success depends on the quality of the bread: it should contain no sugar, eggs or seeds, and it must be chewy and substantial, not light and airy, in order to stand up to the dressing. An unsalted, sturdy peasant bread is perfect, but it must be firm — about 4 days old. Don't be afraid to add more pepper: a dressing with plenty of bite is a lovely contrast to the sweetness of roasted peppers.*

INGREDIENTS

2 large red peppers, or a combination of
red and yellow peppers
500g (1lb) sturdy white Italian bread or peasant bread
125ml (4fl oz) extra-virgin olive oil
3 tbsp wine vinegar
1 small red or white onion, quartered and very finely sliced
1 spring onion, including green tops, finely sliced
2 tbsp pitted and sliced sharply flavoured green olives
1 tbsp chopped fresh oregano, or 1 tsp dried oregano
½ tsp salt
¼ tsp freshly ground black pepper, or more to taste

PREPARATION

1 Roast the peppers (see page 160). When they are cool enough to handle, cut them lengthways in half. Remove the stem, lift off the skin, then scrape out all of the seeds.
2 Meanwhile, remove and discard all the crusts from the bread and cut it into bite-sized cubes.
3 To make the dressing, combine the oil, vinegar, 125ml (4fl oz) of water, the onions, olives, herbs, salt and pepper in a small bowl. Leave the mixture to marinate for 10 minutes to allow the flavours to blend thoroughly.
4 Cut the peppers into 5cm (2in) strips. Transfer the bread cubes and pepper strips to a salad bowl. Pour over the dressing, toss well and check the seasoning. It is best served within several hours.

VARIATION

To make a summer version of this salad, substitute firm Italian-style wholemeal bread for white bread. Omit the red peppers and olives and replace with two diced vine-ripened tomatoes, 1 teaspoon of chopped fresh oregano, or half a teaspoon of dried oregano, and 2 tablespoons of torn fresh basil leaves. Adjust the quantities of oil and vinegar according to taste.

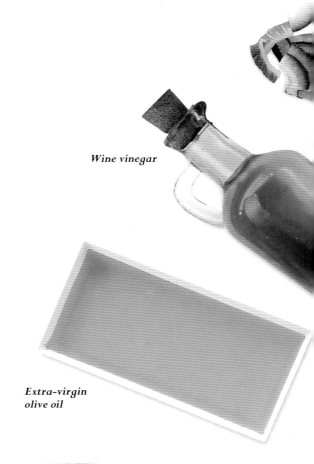

Wine vinegar

*Extra-virgin
olive oil*

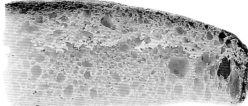

Italian bread

Red and yellow peppers

Red onion

Spring onion

Green olives

Oregano

Salt

Black
pepper

SAUCES

Italian *salse* are a simple affair in comparison to those of the classic French kitchen, which require lengthy simmering, straining and reduction. The foundation of many sauces is the cooking liquid from the dish, often enriched by wine. Few sauces that are made separately are butter-based, and cream is rarely used. The basic ingredient is often olive oil to which pounded nuts, herbs, cheese or breadcrumbs are added for body and flavour. As for tomato sauces, I have no doubt that there are as many varieties as there are cooks in Italy. Quickly cooked, they preserve the inherent flavour of the tomatoes. Some are not cooked at all, but combine sun-ripened tomatoes with fruity olive oil, thickened with herbs, capers or olives. The sauces in this chapter have a multitude of purposes.

BESCIAMELLA

Béchamel sauce

The origins of this white sauce have long been disputed between the Italians and the French. Its name is supposed to derive from the Marquis de Béchamel, maître d'hôtel to Louis XIV, but its place in northern Italian cuisine predates its appellation. Béchamel is as fundamental to Italian cooking as tomato sauce. It acts as a binding for fillings and croquettes; it is indispensable in baked lasagne; it moistens vegetable gratins, and is a foundation for other sauces. If it is to be used as a binding, the consistency should be made thicker by long simmering. The recipe below is for a pouring sauce.

INGREDIENTS

550ml (18fl oz) milk
60g (2oz) unsalted butter
3 tbsp plain flour
¼ tsp salt

PREPARATION

1 Heat the milk to just below boiling point; keep it warm.
2 Melt the butter in a heavy-based saucepan over a low heat. Add the flour and stir with a wooden spoon or whisk to remove lumps. Heat the flour and butter paste through, stirring continually, for about 2 minutes. Do not allow it to brown.
3 Add the warm milk one tablespoon at a time, stirring constantly. Begin to add several tablespoons at a time, still stirring, then slowly trickle in the remaining milk. If lumps appear, you may be adding the milk too quickly, or the heat may be too high. Should this occur, turn off the heat and stir vigorously, pressing the lumps against the side of the pan.
4 When all the milk has been added, simmer the sauce over a low heat for another 15 minutes, until it is thick enough to coat the back of a spoon. Add the salt during the last 10 minutes of cooking. Béchamel sauce may be kept covered in the refrigerator for up to 4 days.

VARIATIONS

For pasta dishes, add a pinch of nutmeg with the salt. For vegetable casseroles and other dishes, add 1 bay leaf to the milk before heating it and remove it when the sauce is finished.

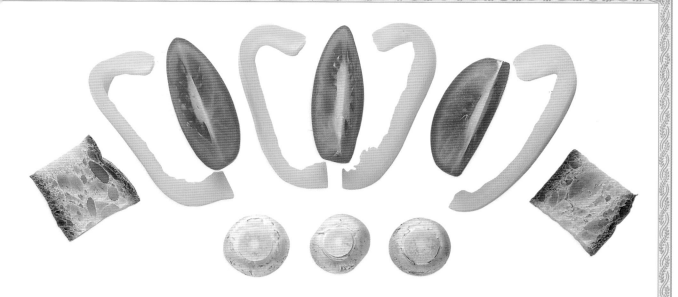

BAGNA CAÔDA

Hot anchovy sauce in the style of Piedmont

This garlicky sauce, literally "hot bath" in the regional dialect, is served straight from the cooking pot and used for dipping vegetables in — particularly cardoons, peppers and celery — or thin slices of sturdy bread. It also makes a good sauce for thin spaghetti, or if there is a little bit of leftover sauce at the bottom of the pan, you can scramble eggs in it. It is usually made with an equal proportion of butter to olive oil, but you can vary the quantities. Makes about 250ml (8fl oz), enough for 250g (8oz) of pasta.

INGREDIENTS

*6 large cloves garlic, finely chopped
milk
90ml (3fl oz) extra-virgin olive oil
125g (4oz) anchovy fillets in olive oil
125g (4oz) unsalted butter
shavings of white or black truffle, or ¼ tsp truffle oil,
optional*

PREPARATION

1 Place the garlic in a small bowl and cover with milk. Set aside for about 2 hours to soften the garlic's strong flavour, then drain off the milk and rinse the garlic under cold water.
2 In a small saucepan over a very low heat, combine the oil, the anchovies in their oil and the garlic. Use a wooden spoon to mash the anchovies.
3 When the anchovies have dissolved into the oil, stir in the butter and truffle shavings or truffle oil, if desired, and leave to melt.
4 Pour the sauce into a fondue pot; keep the heat under the sauce very low. Serve at once with a selection of vegetables and robust bread.

SUGO DI POMODORI FRESCHI

Fresh tomato sauce

Authentic Italian tomato sauces, with their pungent sweetness and depth of flavour, are impossible to replicate without vine-ripened Mediterranean plum tomatoes, and it is far better to use good canned plum tomatoes than the ubiquitous artificially ripened variety. This simple sauce makes the most of good, fresh summer tomatoes. It can be used with pasta, and is particularly good with seafood.

INGREDIENTS

*1.25kg (2½lb) fresh, sweet, mature vine-ripened plum tomatoes, skinned, deseeded and chopped
75ml (2½fl oz) extra-virgin olive oil
4 cloves garlic, bruised
½ small onion, sliced into fine half-moons
1 tbsp chopped fresh flat-leaf parsley
½ tsp sea salt
6 large fresh basil leaves, shredded
freshly ground black pepper, to taste*

PREPARATION

1 Place the tomatoes in a colander over a bowl and allow to drain for about 5 minutes.
2 Warm the olive oil and garlic together in a pan, pressing on the bruised garlic to release its juices. When the oil is hot, add the onion and parsley and sauté just until the garlic begins to colour lightly and the onion is softened, about 2 minutes.
3 Discard the tomato juice and add the tomatoes and salt. Use a potato masher to crush the tomatoes finely. Bring the sauce to a simmer then reduce the heat and continue to simmer, stirring occasionally, until thickened, about 20 minutes.
4 Add the shredded basil and pepper and check for salt before serving.

SALSETTA ROSSA ALLA LIGURE

Uncooked tomato sauce with black olives

*This tomato sauce is particularly suitable for fish.
The best tomatoes to use here are the sweet, vine-ripened
Italian "plum" variety. The next best are other tasty
vine-ripened varieties that are available during the
summer when farm stands sell fresh produce.
Cherry tomatoes are often good, and widely available,
although they require a little more work to skin
and deseed than other tomatoes.*

INGREDIENTS

*750g (1½lb) fresh vine-ripened tomatoes, skinned,
deseeded and chopped
1 small clove garlic, finely chopped
1 anchovy, mashed, optional
60g (2oz) pitted black olives, sliced
15g (½oz) torn or chopped fresh basil
60ml (2fl oz) extra-virgin olive oil
½ tsp salt, or to taste
freshly ground black pepper, to taste*

PREPARATION

1 Place the tomatoes in a colander over a bowl
and allow to drain for about 30 minutes.
2 Discard the tomato juice and mix together the
tomatoes with all the other ingredients, adding
pepper to taste. Allow to stand for 1–3 hours
before using to give the flavours time to develop.

SUGO DI POMODORO

Tomato sauce

*A basic cooked tomato sauce with countless applications,
this is ideal with pasta. For use in baked dishes or
as a foundation for other sauces, it is best to pass the
sauce through a food mill (see page 159) or sieve,
which produces a smooth purée. Makes enough
for 1kg (2lb) of pasta.*

INGREDIENTS

*1kg (2lb) canned plum tomatoes in juice
75ml (2½fl oz) extra-virgin olive oil,
plus extra to serve
2 large cloves garlic, bruised
1 onion, finely chopped
1 small carrot, finely chopped
1 tbsp chopped fresh flat-leaf parsley
½ tsp salt, or to taste
4 large fresh basil leaves, chopped*

PREPARATION

1 Drain the tomatoes, reserving their juice for
another use. If the sauce is not to be passed
through a food mill or sieve, scoop out the excess
seeds. Crush or mash the tomatoes and set aside.
2 Warm the oil and garlic together in a pan,
heating gently until the garlic is golden,
1–2 minutes. Add the onion, carrot and parsley
and continue to sauté until softened but not
coloured, about 10 minutes.
3 Add the tomatoes, salt and basil. Simmer gently
until a uniformly thick sauce forms and the oil
collects on the surface, 20–25 minutes. Remove
the sauce from the heat.
4 If you are not straining the sauce, discard the
garlic cloves. For added flavour, an additional
tablespoon of extra-virgin olive oil may be stirred
into the sauce before serving.
5 To strain the sauce, allow it to cool slightly then
place a food mill over a pan and pass the sauce
through it, including the garlic cloves, if desired.
Press out as much pulp as possible. Return to the
heat just long enough for the sauce to warm
through. Stir in an additional drizzle of extra-
virgin olive oil for added flavour, if desired.

VARIATION

For a creamy tomato sauce, add 2 tablespoons of
mascarpone, or 60ml (2fl oz) of double cream to
the strained tomato sauce. Return to the heat just
to heat through, but do not allow to boil.

SALSETTA ROSSA CRUDA
Uncooked red sauce

This is one of the several traditional sauces that accompany the classic boiled dinner (meat or fish). It can also be used as a topping for pasta, but grated Parmesan should not be added. The sauce can only be as good as the tomatoes used, which must be sweet, flavoursome and vine-ripened. It is best made up to several hours before serving.

INGREDIENTS

750g (1½lb) mature, vine-ripened plum tomatoes, skinned, deseeded and chopped
6–8 large fresh basil leaves, finely shredded
60ml (2fl oz) extra-virgin olive oil
1 small clove garlic, finely chopped
½ tsp salt
¼ tsp freshly ground black pepper

PREPARATION

1 Place the tomatoes in a colander over a bowl and allow to drain for about 30 minutes.
2 Discard the tomato juice and combine the tomato flesh with the basil, oil, garlic, salt and pepper. Cover and leave for at least 1 hour, and up to 3 hours, before serving.

VARIATION

Replace the garlic with 1 tablespoon of grated red onion and 1 tablespoon of capers. Thicken with a tablespoon of dry breadcrumbs, if desired.

SALSA VERDE
Green sauce

Salsa verde, "green sauce", a piquant olive-oil-and-herb-based sauce, is the classic accompaniment to simple meat and fish dishes. It also goes well with grilled prawns or chicken, or with potatoes of any kind. The addition of bread makes a thicker sauce for a variation in texture. Use only white Italian or French bread made without sugar.

INGREDIENTS

60ml (2fl oz) freshly squeezed lemon juice, or wine vinegar (if serving with meat)
1 small clove garlic, finely chopped
30g (1oz) chopped fresh flat-leaf parsley
2 tbsp grated sweet white onion or spring onion
3 tbsp small capers, drained and rinsed
1 tsp Dijon mustard
125ml (4fl oz) extra-virgin olive oil
freshly ground salt and black pepper, to taste

PREPARATION

1 In a small bowl, combine the lemon juice, garlic, parsley, onion, capers and mustard. Gradually beat in the oil using a fork.
2 Season with salt and pepper to taste. Set aside at room temperature for 1–2 hours to marinate. It can be made up to one day in advance and kept at room temperature until ready to serve.

VARIATIONS

• **Salsa Verde con Peperoncini** (Green sauce with little green peppers). Add 1 finely chopped miniature pickled green Italian pepper and 1 mashed cooked egg yolk to the basic mixture.
• **Salsa Verde alla Mollica di Pane** (Green bread sauce). Add 1 teaspoon of well-mashed anchovy fillet and 2 tablespoons of finely chopped gherkins or sour pickles to the basic mixture. Soak 1 slice of white Italian or French bread, crusts removed, in a little water. Squeeze out as much water as possible then pulp the bread in a food processor. Use a fork to blend it with the other ingredients. This sauce can be made up to one day in advance and kept at room temperature until ready to serve.
• **Salsa Verde al Rafano** (Green horseradish sauce). Substitute good red wine vinegar for the lemon juice; omit the garlic, onion or spring onion and capers; reduce the parsley to 2 tablespoons and the olive oil to 60ml (2fl oz) and add 4 tablespoons of grated fresh or bottled horseradish to the sauce.

PEPERONATA
Sweet pepper sauce

This cooked sauce, which includes sweet peppers, is especially compatible with beef and pork. Its flavour is improved if it is made in advance up to step 5. Allow it to cool, leaving out the remaining tablespoon of olive oil and the parsley until just ready to serve. It can be prepared 2–3 days in advance and stored tightly covered in the refrigerator.

INGREDIENTS

750g (1½lb) mature, vine-ripened plum tomatoes, or canned drained tomatoes, skinned, deseeded and chopped
1 red and 1 yellow pepper
4 tbsp extra-virgin olive oil
1 small onion, finely chopped
2 cloves garlic, finely chopped
pinch crushed dried red chillies
2 tbsp chopped fresh flat-leaf parsley

PREPARATION

1 Place the tomatoes in a colander over a bowl and allow to drain for about 5 minutes.
2 Using a vegetable peeler, peel the skin off the peppers. Alternatively, place them under a hot grill, turning them until blackened all over (see page 160). Allow to cool slightly then lift off the skin. Cut them in half lengthways and remove their cores and seeds. Cut the halves into 1cm (½in) wide strips, then cut the strips into small dice. Set aside.
3 Warm 3 tablespoons of oil in a frying pan over a medium-low heat. Sauté the onion and garlic until soft and translucent, stirring occasionally.
4 Add the crushed chilli and diced peppers and continue to sauté gently until the peppers begin to soften, 10–12 minutes. Add the tomatoes, discarding the juice, cover, and simmer gently, stirring occasionally, until the peppers are thoroughly tender, 5–8 minutes.
5 Remove from the heat and stir in the parsley and the remaining tablespoon of olive oil. Serve hot, warm, or at room temperature.

VARIATION

Mandorlata di Peperoni (Pepper and almond sauce in the style of Basilicata). In this variation, which is particularly suited to fish, the sauce is embellished with ground almonds. Add 1 teaspoon of red wine vinegar to the tomatoes, omit the parsley and stir in 45g (1½oz) of blanched, ground, untoasted almonds just before serving.

MAIONESE
Mayonnaise

Mayonnaise has a great many uses in the Italian kitchen. Homemade mayonnaise using fresh eggs and good olive oil is a far cry from the commercial product. The procedure for making mayonnaise with a food processor is simple, as long as all the utensils and ingredients are at room temperature before you begin. Classic mayonnaise is made with only the yolk of the egg, but I use the whole egg, which produces lighter mayonnaise with a higher protein content (the yolk is nearly pure fat while the white is pure protein). Makes about 250g (8oz).

INGREDIENTS

125ml (4fl oz) vegetable oil
60ml (2fl oz) extra-virgin olive oil
1 egg, at room temperature
½ tsp salt, or to taste
1 tsp Dijon mustard
2 tbsp freshly squeezed lemon juice, or to taste
sprinkling of freshly ground white pepper

PREPARATION

1 Mix the oils together in a small jug.
2 Crack the egg into the blender jug and add the salt. Beat lightly and briefly.
3 Drizzle in 2 tablespoons of the combined oils. Blend on high speed for 10 seconds. Pour in the remaining oil in a thin, steady stream. It is critical that the oil be added slowly and gradually in order for the mayonnaise to emulsify.
4 Stop the blender and scrape the inside of the jug so that the ingredients can be mixed in thoroughly. Add the mustard, lemon juice and pepper and blend again. Use immediately or cover tightly and refrigerate for up to a week.

VARIATIONS

• ***Maionese Verde*** (Green mayonnaise). Add 1 finely chopped small pickled green Italian pepper, 2 tablespoons of finely chopped fresh flat-leaf parsley, 1 tablespoon of chopped capers, freshly ground black pepper and half an anchovy fillet, well mashed, to the basic mayonnaise. Mix together with a wooden spoon. Serve with boiled beef (see page 110), boiled chicken (see page 73), boiled fish (see page 50), or on hard-boiled eggs.
• ***Maionese Tonnata*** (Tuna mayonnaise). Blend 1 tablespoon of freshly squeezed lemon juice and 100g (3½oz) drained canned tuna in olive oil into the basic mayonnaise. Use over cold boiled sliced veal, on hard-boiled eggs, or on sliced tomatoes. Sprinkle drained small capers over the sauce.

PESTO

Pounded basil and pine nut sauce

It is said that Genoa, where this sauce originated, produces the best pesto because of the superior fragrance of Italian Riviera basil. The flavour of the olive oil and the blend of cheeses used are at least as important: Parmesan provides depth and complexity, and can be used alone, while pecorino adds intensity and sharpness. The unctuous quality of pesto necessitates a sturdy pasta cut to support it; trenette, eggless fettuccine and potato gnocchi are used in Genoa. Suitable dried pastas are spaghetti, linguine and bucatini. Makes enough for 500g (1lb) of pasta.

INGREDIENTS

75g (2½oz) fresh basil leaves, solidly packed
3 cloves garlic, roughly chopped
45g (1½oz) pine nuts, lightly toasted
125ml (4fl oz) extra-virgin olive oil
½ tsp salt
pinch of freshly ground black or white pepper
45g (1½oz) freshly grated Parmesan
20g (¾oz) freshly grated pecorino
30g (1oz) unsalted butter, at room temperature

PREPARATION

1 Put the basil, garlic, pine nuts, oil, salt and pepper into a food processor and blend for about 20 seconds to make a smooth purée. Make sure that all the ingredients are evenly ground.

2 Transfer to a bowl and, using a wooden spoon, beat in the grated cheeses and butter (you can use the food processor for 10 seconds, but the texture will not be as good).

3 If using the pesto as a pasta sauce, place it in the serving bowl. Add 2 tablespoons of the cooking water from the pasta to the pesto and blend. Toss the drained pasta with the pesto sauce.

Note: Pesto can be made in advance, transferred to a glass jar, topped with a little olive oil and covered with clingfilm, which should be pressed directly on to the surface. It will keep refrigerated for several months, or frozen for up to 3 months. The flavour will be better if the garlic, cheese and butter are omitted until the pesto is needed. Beat them in up to several hours before serving.

Black pepper

Parmesan   Pecorino   Butter

Salt

Olive oil

Pine nuts

Garlic

Basil

DESSERTS

Italians usually reserve desserts for celebrations. An exception to this custom is the consumption of little pastries or *biscotti* with espresso for breakfast or at mid-day. Religious feasts bring confections that invariably have symbolic meaning and in every region the diversity of sweet dishes is astonishing. They are often bestowed with charming whimsical names, such as *coscie di monache*, "nun's thighs", *chiacchiere di monache*, "nun's chatter" and *suspirus*, "sighs". The desserts in this chapter represent the types of sweets more usually made in the home.

CRESPELLE DOLCI CON LE MELE
Sweet apple crêpes

Thin, delicate crespelle *(see page 89) can have sweet as well as savoury stuffings. This apple filling is simple and very good. Makes 20 crêpes.*

INGREDIENTS

1.5kg (3lb) apples
125g (4oz) granulated sugar
⅓ tsp ground cinnamon
60g (2oz) unsalted butter, plus butter to grease
60ml (2fl oz) Cognac or brandy
1 quantity Crespelle (see page 89), with the zest
of 1 lemon added to the batter, optional
icing sugar, to dust

PREPARATION

1 Peel, halve and core the apples. Cut them into thin slices and place in a large bowl. Add the sugar and cinnamon and toss well.
2 Heat the butter in a large shallow frying pan. Add the sliced apples and sauté until they are a rich golden colour, about 10 minutes. Pour in the Cognac and toss everything together. Cook over a medium heat until the alcohol is evaporated, the apples are tender and the juices have reduced slightly. Allow to cool and make the crêpes.
3 Preheat the oven to 190°C/375°F/gas 5.
4 Lightly butter two large baking dishes. Place a rounded tablespoonful of filling at one end of each crêpe. Brush a little apple liquid along the inside edge of the crêpe, fold it over, then press to seal. Repeat with the remaining crêpes, then place them in the dishes, leaving a little space around each one.
5 Bake the crêpes for about 15 minutes, then remove them from the oven and leave to settle for 10 minutes. Sprinkle with icing sugar and serve.

ZUPPA INGLESE
Italian trifle ("English soup")

Zuppa inglese *is one of Italy's most popular desserts. This is the version I grew up with. It is best made a day ahead, up to step 4. Serves 6. Illustrated on page 150.*

INGREDIENTS

12 savoiardi biscuits or sponge fingers, split
3–4 tbsp raspberry jam
60ml (2fl oz) dry sherry or rum
2 egg yolks
3 tbsp sugar
1 heaped tbsp cornflour
pinch of salt
2.5cm (1in) strip of lemon zest
350ml (12fl oz) milk
12 strawberries, 8 sliced and 4 left whole
500ml (16fl oz) double or whipping cream
dash of vanilla extract
small piece of frozen plain chocolate, to decorate

PREPARATION

1 Select a wide glass bowl. Spread the insides of the savoiardi biscuits with jam and arrange them in the bowl. Sprinkle over the sherry or rum and set aside.
2 In a small pan off the heat, beat the yolks with 2 tablespoons of sugar. Mix in the cornflour. Stir in the salt, lemon zest and milk. Place over a very low heat and stir constantly until you have a custard thick enough to coat the spoon, about 7 minutes.
3 Pour the custard over the biscuits and arrange a layer of sliced strawberries on top of the custard.
4 Whip the cream, adding the remaining sugar and a dash of vanilla, then spread it over the fruit.
5 Use a vegetable peeler to pare chocolate shavings on to the whipped cream. Decorate with the whole strawberries and chill before serving.

ZABAIONE

Zabaione with Marsala

While zabaione has become a popular dessert, in Italy it is also considered a restorative. I remember my uncle Aldo, a serious athlete, whipping up then downing straight zabaione for an energy boost. It can be eaten as it is or combined with whipped cream, and it is excellent with baked fruit desserts or fresh strawberries.

INGREDIENTS

3 egg yolks
3 tbsp sugar
3 tbsp dry Marsala or Vin Santo, if available
200ml (7fl oz) chilled whipped double cream, sweetened with 1½ tbsp icing sugar, optional

PREPARATION

1 Pour water to a depth of 5cm (2in) into a double boiler or pan, bring to the boil then leave to simmer.
2 Meanwhile, place the eggs, sugar and Marsala in the cold insert of a double boiler, or in a large shallow heatproof bowl, and whisk thoroughly.
3 Fit the insert into the double boiler, or position the bowl over the pan, making sure it does not touch the water. Beat until light, pale and velvety. The mixture is ready when it is thick enough to coat the back of a spoon. Do not allow it to overheat.
4 Remove the zabaione from the heat. It can be eaten as it is, or left to cool then folded into the chilled cream. Pour it into glasses and serve at once.

COPPA ORESTE

"Oreste's goblet" mascarpone dessert

This wonderful dessert originated in the Oreste restaurant in Modena.

INGREDIENTS

12 large amaretti biscuits
3 tbsp brandy
2 eggs
60g (2oz) sugar
250g (8oz) softened mascarpone cheese
15g (½oz) plain chocolate shavings, to decorate

PREPARATION

1 Put three amaretti in each of four wide goblets. Sprinkle the brandy over the biscuits.
2 Beat together the eggs and sugar until pale then beat in the mascarpone until smooth and creamy. Spoon the mixture into the glasses then chill in the refrigerator until firm, about 2 hours. Sprinkle with the chocolate shavings and serve immediately.

MONTE BIANCO

Chestnut and chocolate "white mountain"

This dessert is named after Mont Blanc, whose frosty white peaks are within view of Lombardy, where the dish originates. It is often made without chocolate, but I prefer this version, which was taught me by my friend Flavia Destefanis. Use fresh chestnuts if available as canned ones don't have quite the depth of flavour.

INGREDIENTS

500g (1lb) fresh chestnuts or drained canned chestnuts
500ml (16fl oz) milk
pinch of salt
150g (5oz) sugar
5cm (2in) piece of vanilla pod, or ½ tsp vanilla extract
15g (½oz) unsalted butter
4 tbsp cocoa powder, or 175g (6oz) plain chocolate, melted
2 tbsp Cognac or rum, optional
500ml (16fl oz) chilled double whipping cream
4 tbsp icing sugar, plus extra to sweeten purée if necessary
60g (2oz) crystallized violets, or 30g (1oz) chopped toasted almonds, optional

PREPARATION

1 Chill the bowl and whisks for whipping the cream in the refrigerator.
2 If using fresh chestnuts, soak them in a bowl of warm water for 30 minutes. Score an "x"-shape on the flat side of each chestnut, avoiding piercing the flesh, then put them in a pot, cover with water and bring to the boil. Reduce the heat and simmer, partially covered, until tender, about 40 minutes. Drain the chestnuts, cover them with warm water to keep them soft, and begin to peel them.
3 Place the peeled or canned chestnuts in a pan with the milk. Add the salt, sugar and vanilla. Bring to the boil then lower the heat to medium and cook the chestnuts until they are starting to disintegrate, about 20–30 minutes. If the milk is becoming syrupy, add a little more. Drain the chestnuts, discarding the vanilla pod, and reserve the milk.
4 Purée the chestnuts, butter, cocoa or chocolate and Cognac or rum in a food processor, or pass the mixture through a potato ricer or food mill, adding up to 4 tablespoons of reserved milk to moisten it.
5 Taste the purée and add a little icing sugar if required. Chill for at least an hour.
6 Pass the mixture through a ricer or food mill again directly on to a serving plate, spiralling inwards to create an airy mound of purée.
7 Place the chilled cream in the bowl with the icing sugar and whip it into soft peaks. Spoon some cream over the mound and scatter the violets or almonds on top. Serve with the remaining cream.

LATTE ALLA PORTOGHESE
Orange flan

This dessert takes its name from the typical Portuguese custard flan. Custards are popular in Italy, too. I especially like this delicate orange-flavoured version. Serves 12.

INGREDIENTS

*8 extra-large eggs
2 tsp vanilla extract
finely grated zest and the juice of 1 small
orange, about 60ml (2fl oz)
560g (1lb 2oz) caster sugar
1 litre (1¾ pints) milk
pinch of salt
candied orange peel to decorate, optional*

PREPARATION

1 Preheat the oven to 180°C/350°F/gas 4.
2 Have twelve 175g (6oz) oven-proof custard cups or a 30cm (12in) ring mould to hand.
3 Beat the eggs. In a separate bowl, combine the vanilla, orange zest and juice, 175g (6oz) of sugar, the milk and the salt. Combine this mixture with the eggs, then put it through a sieve.
4 Heat the remaining sugar in a large pan over a medium-low heat until it melts and caramelizes. Do not allow it to burn.
5 Carefully pour the caramelized sugar into the individual cups or the ring mould, coating the bottom and sides evenly. Work quickly while the caramel remains liquid – if it starts to set, reheat it. Allow the caramel to cool and harden.
6 Pour the custard into the cups or ring mould over the caramel. Place the cups or mould in a 5cm (2in) deep baking dish. Pour boiling water into the dish to within 1cm (½in) of the top of the cups or mould and slide it into the oven. Bake the large flan for about 1 hour and the individual ones for 45 minutes–1 hour, or until a skewer comes out clean (test during the last 15 minutes of cooking).
7 Allow the flan to cool for 10 minutes, then refrigerate it until cold (3–4 hours). Invert the flan(s) on to a plate. The caramel will form a lovely sauce around the firm custard. Decorate the top with pieces of candied orange peel if desired.

CROSTATA DI CREMA DI LIMONE
Nick Malgieri's Ligurian lemon tart

My friend Nick Malgieri, a master pastry chef and cookery writer, found this recipe during his travels. Pasta frolla, the classic sweet Italian pastry, forms the crust. Like the lemon tart of Nice, it has a distinctive dark top. Serves 12.

INGREDIENTS

Pasta frolla
250g (8oz) plain flour
75g (2½oz) sugar
½ tsp baking powder
¼ tsp salt
125g (4oz) unsalted butter, cut into small pieces
2 large eggs (size 1)

Filling
250g (8oz) sugar
45g (1½oz) plain flour
8 eggs
2 tsp lemon zest
125ml (4fl oz) lemon juice
500ml (16fl oz) double cream

PREPARATION

1 Combine the flour, sugar, baking powder and salt either by hand or in a food processor. Rub in the butter until you have a fine crumb-like consistency.
2 Add the eggs and beat everything together until the mixture forms a ball of dough. Wrap the dough in clingfilm and chill in the refrigerator.
3 Preheat the oven to 160°C/325°F/gas 3.
4 Grease a 25 x 5cm (10 x 2in) round cake tin. Roll the dough to a thickness of 5mm (¼in), keeping it approximately the size of the tin, and line the tin.
5 Beat the sugar and flour together in a mixing bowl, then whisk in the eggs, two at a time. Next, whisk in the lemon zest, juice and double cream.
6 Pour the filling into the tin and bake on the lowest rack of the oven for about 1 hour, or until the crust is golden and the filling has set. Leave to cool, then cover and refrigerate before unmoulding.

PIZZA DOLCE PASQUALE
Neapolitan sweet Easter pizza

This traditional Easter sweet is really cheesecake in a biscuit-like crust. Serves 6–8. Illustrated on page 151.

INGREDIENTS

Pastry
125g (4oz) unsalted butter, at room temperature
60g (2oz) sugar
1 small egg, beaten
175g (6oz) plain flour, or more if necessary

Filling
3 tbsp sultanas, or chopped candied peel
1 tbsp Grand Marnier or Anisette
1.25kg (2½lb) whole-milk ricotta
2 extra-large eggs
60g (2oz) double cream
125g (4oz) sugar
⅛ tsp salt
grated zest of 1 orange
slices of candied fruit, optional, to decorate

PREPARATION

1 Cream the butter and sugar until very light in colour and texture. Gradually beat in the egg until the mixture is creamy and smooth.
2 Sift the flour into the butter and sugar. Stir by hand, just until the flour is absorbed. Shape the dough into a thick disc, adding up to 60g (2oz) more flour if necessary to make a workable dough. Wrap in clingfilm and chill for at least 5 hours.
3 Roll out the dough, fit it into a 23–25cm (9–10in) tart tin and chill for another hour.
4 Soak the sultanas in the liqueur for 30 minutes.
5 Preheat the oven to 190°C/375°F/gas 5.
6 Beat the ricotta with the eggs until you have a smooth, even mixture. Beat in the cream, then the sugar, salt, orange zest, sultanas and the liqueur.
7 Pour the filling into the crust and bake for 1 hour and 15 minutes, or until a skewer comes out clean. Decorate with candied fruit and serve chilled.

PESCHE RIPIENE
Baked stuffed peaches from the Piedmont

INGREDIENTS

6 large fresh sweet, ripe peaches, halved and stoned
18 amaretti, crushed, about 150g (5oz), or more to bind
1 tbsp unsalted butter, melted, plus butter to grease
1 egg yolk
1 tsp sugar, or to taste
1 tsp Cognac or brandy

PREPARATION

1 Preheat the oven to 190°C/375°F/gas 5.
2 Scoop out the pulp from each peach half, leaving 5mm (¼in) of the peach shell intact. Chop the pulp.
3 Combine the amaretti, 2 teaspoons of butter, the egg yolk, sugar and Cognac with the peach pulp.
4 Fill the peach halves with the mixture. Place them in a buttered baking dish and brush the edges of the peach shells with the remaining butter. Bake them in the middle of the oven, uncovered, until thoroughly cooked, about 30 minutes.

PERE RIPIENE CON CREMA PASTICCIERA

Stuffed poached pears with custard sauce

This is one of my mother's tried and true dessert recipes, her own "fantasia". Ginger is not commonly used in Italian cooking and baking, but it is a splendid flavour match with the pears. For 2 people.

INGREDIENTS

3 green pears (not too ripe)
juice of half a lemon
125ml (4fl oz) dry sherry
1 slice fresh ginger
1 tbsp honey or sugar
Custard
5 tsp sugar
1 egg yolk
1 heaped tbsp cornflour
250ml (8fl oz) milk
small pinch of salt
2.5cm (1in) strip of lemon zest
Filling
60g (2oz) crushed amaretti or macaroons
1 tbsp raisins, chilled and chopped
pinch of ground cinnamon

PREPARATION

1 Peel and halve the pears. Remove the seeds and surrounding membrane, being careful not to scoop out any of the flesh. Leave the stems intact. Sprinkle the pear halves with lemon juice to preserve their colour and place them in a pan, hollow part down, without overlapping them.

2 Pour 250ml (8fl oz) of water and the sherry over the pears. Add the ginger and honey or sugar. Cover the pan, bring to the boil, then lower the heat and cook the pears until they are firm but not mushy, about 5 minutes. With a slotted spoon, transfer them to a baking dish, reserving 1 tablespoon of liquid, and allow to cool.

3 Meanwhile, make the custard. Place the sugar and egg yolk in a saucepan and beat for a few minutes until creamy. Beat in the cornflour and 2 tablespoons of milk using a wooden spoon.

4 Place the pan over a low heat and gradually add the rest of the milk, the salt and lemon zest. Stir constantly until the mixture is simmering gently and is thick enough to coat a spoon. Remove from the heat, cover and keep warm.

5 Combine the amaretti, raisins, cinnamon, 2 tablespoons of custard and the reserved pear liquid. Stuff the pears and turn them on to a serving plate. Drizzle with warm custard, sprinkle with cinnamon and serve immediately.

Sugar

Honey

Fresh ginger

Dry sherry

Lemon juice

Pears

Egg yolk

Cornflour

Milk

Salt

Lemon zest

Amaretti

Raisins

Cinnamon

FRAPPE
Sweet fried pastry ribbons

There are many versions of these light, ribbon-like pastries that are typically made for celebrations. In Tuscany they are called cenci, *"tatters"; in Perugia,* frappe, *"fringe"; and in Liguria,* bugie, *"lies". A variation is even mentioned in a 13th-century Emilian manuscript. In my grandmother's Apulian version, the dough includes olive oil and the pastries are soaked in a honey syrup, but I prefer this, my mother's version. Serve with icing sugar, or with Salsetta d'Uva Passa (right) and make plenty, because once you start eating them, you can't stop. Serves 10–15. Illustrated on page 150.*

INGREDIENTS
500g (1lb) plain flour
30g (1oz) chilled unsalted butter, cut into small pieces
1 whole egg and 2 yolks, beaten together
150g (5oz) sugar
¼ tsp salt
250ml (8fl oz) dry sherry or dry vermouth
corn or other vegetable oil for shallow frying
icing sugar, to dust

PREPARATION

1 Sift the flour and rub in the butter either by hand or in a food processor fitted with a metal blade, until the mixture has become fine and crumbly. Transfer the mixture to a large pastry board.
2 Make a well in the centre of the mound. Beat together the eggs, sugar, salt and sherry in a separate bowl and pour the mixture into the well.
3 Using a fork, draw the dry ingredients into the liquid, always beating in the same direction. When the dough becomes pliable, begin to work it with your hands. If it is too soft, sprinkle in more flour, but do not make it too stiff. Divide it into four parts.
4 Work with one piece at a time, keeping the rest covered with a damp tea towel. Roll out the dough until it is paper-thin, or use a hand-cranked pasta machine to do so, working through all the settings.
5 Using a fluted pastry wheel or a knife, cut the dough into 2.5cm (1in) x 12cm (5in) strips. Tie the strips into loose knots or pinch short pieces in the middle to form bows. Spread them out on dry tea towels and cover them while you make the rest.
6 Heat the oil in a frying pan. When it is hot enough to make the dough sizzle, add the first batch of frappe and fry until golden on both sides. There should be plenty of space around each one so they cook quickly and evenly. Transfer them to kitchen paper and leave to drain.
7 Sprinkle the cooled pastries with plenty of icing sugar or drizzle them with raisin sauce and serve.

SALSETTA D'UVA PASSA
Raisin sauce with port wine

My paternal grandmother used to make this raisin syrup for lacing over cartadatte, *Apulia's counterpart of* frappe *(see left). Some of my friends like to serve it with their Christmas ham. The port is my own innovation, and I find it adds depth to the flavour.*

INGREDIENTS
500g (1lb) raisins
250ml (8fl oz) port wine
½ tsp cloves
½ tsp cinnamon
125g (4oz) honey

PREPARATION

1 Place the raisins in a pan with 750ml (1¼ pints) of water, cover and boil gently for 1 hour, lowering the heat once they start to simmer.
2 Strain the boiled raisins through a food mill or sieve. Return the syrup to the pan and add the port, spices and honey. Simmer for another 30 minutes then leave to cool before serving.

FICHI MANDORLATI
Dried stuffed figs, Apulian style

Stuffed figs are a speciality of Apulia. This variation, typical of Bari, is my favourite. The filling includes chocolate, which goes exceedingly well with almonds and figs, and bay leaves impart a beguiling aroma and flavour. Store them in sealed glass jars and leave for the scents and flavours to marry. Eat these little jewels with espresso or a glass of sweet dessert wine.

INGREDIENTS
50 soft, moist, unstrung dried figs, preferably Barese
50 whole unblanched almonds, roasted for 15 minutes
2 tbsp fennel seeds
175g (6oz) bitter chocolate, broken into small pieces
25 bay leaves

PREPARATION

1 Preheat the oven to 180°C/350°F/gas 4.
2 Make a slit in each fig. Place an almond, a pinch of fennel seeds and a sliver of chocolate in the centre of each fig then press the opening closed.
3 Place the figs on a baking sheet and bake until heated through and lightly coloured, about 20 minutes. Remove from the oven and leave to cool.
4 Place the figs in a glass jar between layers of bay leaves, sprinkling in any remaining fennel seeds. Seal and store in a cool place for 1–2 weeks before using.

BISCOTTI DELLA NONNA
Italian sesame biscuits

Because these biscotti are traditionally dunked into sweetened espresso, they are meant to be firm. Two versions of these popular biscuits are included. The first recipe produces a hard dunking biscuit. The variation, made with more butter, is richer and more cookie-like. Both versions will keep for 3 months or more in a sealed container in a cool, dry place. Makes 5 dozen.

INGREDIENTS

250g (8oz) sugar
60g (2oz) unsalted butter
3 large eggs (size 1)
1 tsp vanilla extract
425g (14oz) flour
¼ tsp salt
3 tsp baking powder
60ml (2fl oz) milk
150g (5oz) sesame seeds (toasted or untoasted)

PREPARATION

1 Preheat the oven to 180°C/350°F/gas 4.
2 Beat together the sugar and butter until very creamy – the more you beat, the better. Add the eggs and continue to beat for a few minutes by hand, or for a minute with an electric mixer.
3 Beat in the vanilla. Sift in the flour, salt and baking powder and beat again for several minutes by hand until you have a firm, well mixed dough. Wrap the dough in clingfilm and chill for 1 hour.
4 Spread the sesame seeds on a piece of waxed paper or plate. Dust your hands with flour and shape the dough into long ropes about 2.5cm (1in) across. Cut the ropes into 2.5cm (1in) pieces.
5 Brush the dough pieces with milk and roll them in the sesame seeds. Place them on greased baking sheets, leaving plenty of space between each one. Bake until golden, 15–20 minutes.

VARIATION

For a softer, crumblier biscuit, preheat the oven to 190°C/375°F/gas 5. Sift 500g (1lb) of plain flour, 250g (8oz) of sugar, 1 tablespoon of baking powder and ½ teaspoon of salt into a mixing bowl. Rub in 250g (8oz) of butter until the mixture resembles fine crumbs. Combine 2 lightly beaten eggs (size 1) with 125ml (4fl oz) of milk and 1 teaspoon of vanilla extract and stir them into the dry ingredients to make a soft dough. Wrap the dough in clingfilm and chill for 1 hour. Shape the dough into pieces as decribed above and brush with 60ml (2fl oz) of milk. Roll them in the sesame seeds and bake for 12–15 minutes, or until golden.

BISCOTTI CON PINOLI
Pine nut biscuits, Piedmontese style

Elisa De Rogatis gave me this recipe, which has been in her Piedmontese family for years. The lack of flour and butter strikes one as odd at first, but the preponderance of almond paste makes them really light. Makes 4–5 dozen. Illustrated on page 150.

INGREDIENTS

500g (1lb) almond paste
500g (1lb) sugar, plus 2 tbsp
45g (1½oz) fairly dry white breadcrumbs
5 large egg whites
1 tsp vanilla extract
375g (12oz) pine nuts

PREPARATION

1 Preheat the oven to 190°C/375°F/gas 5.
2 Combine the almond paste, sugar and breadcrumbs using two knives or a pastry cutter. Work the mixture until it is fine and crumbly.
3 Add the egg whites and vanilla and beat by hand just until the mixture is smooth and sticky.
4 Spread the pine nuts on a plate. Break off a walnut-sized piece of dough and roll it into an oval shape. Roll it in the pine nuts. Place the biscuits on baking sheets lined with parchment, leaving about 3.5cm (1½in) between each one.
5 Bake the biscuits until lightly golden, 12–15 minutes. Slip the parchment off the tray and leave for 2 minutes before peeling off the biscuits.

CROCCANTE DI MANDORLE
Sardinian almond brittle

This rustic sweet can be eaten with coffee, or crushed and used as an ice-cream topping. Illustrated on page 150.

INGREDIENTS

250g (8oz) sugar
250g (8oz) blanched almonds, lightly toasted and chopped
grated zest of a lemon
1 lemon, washed and dried, for spreading out the brittle

PREPARATION

1 Lightly oil a marble or wooden pastry board.
2 Place a heavy non-stick frying pan over a medium heat. Add the sugar and stir occasionally until caramelized. Stir in the almonds and lemon zest.
3 Working quickly, pour the mixture on to the board and use the whole lemon to spread it out to about 1cm (½in) thick. Allow it to harden and cool then break it into pieces and store in a sealed jar.

PIZZA DOLCE PASQUALE
Neapolitan sweet Easter pizza
(page 145)

MENU PLANNER

Here are menus that draw from eight regions of Italy. Each course is meant to be served separately, never on the same plate. The *antipasto*, if there is one (this course is often reserved for Sunday or feast days), arrives first. The *primo* follows. It may consist of a soup, a pasta or a risotto dish, but never more than one (soup and pasta would not be eaten at the same meal, for example). The *secondo*, second course, is one of meat or fish. The *contorno*, side dish, or *contorni*, may appear alongside the *secondo* or afterwards, as vegetables are never an afterthought, but instead a highlight in the whole menu scheme. There may be cheese to savour after the side dishes, but if not, there's always fruit to end the meal. Certain fruit are specialities of particular regions and I have therefore included fruit of note in each menu. *Dolci*, desserts, are rarely a part of everyday meals, but are included here to represent what might be prepared for a celebratory occasion. While this book does not concern itself with bread or wines, it should be remembered that both of these sacred foods are essential parts of the Italian meal.

·

LAZIO

ANTIPASTO
Involtini di Cavolo (see page 126)
Stuffed cabbage

·

PRIMO
Bucatini all'Amatriciana (see page 85)
Bucatini with tomato and bacon sauce

·

SECONDO
Uccelletti Scappati (see page 115)
Veal rolls stuffed with prosciutto and fontina

·

CONTORNO
Pisellini con Prosciutto (see page 133)
Baby peas with prosciutto, Roman style

·

FORMAGGIO
Mozzarella di bufala,
caciocavallo, provolone

·

FRUTTA
Fruit in season (melon, plums,
pears, peaches, figs)

·

DOLCE
Tiramisù (see page 58)
Chocolate and mascarpone "pick me up"

LIGURIA

ANTIPASTO
Melanzane Ripiene (see page 64)
Stuffed aubergine

·

PRIMO
Riso Arrosto (see page 95)
Roasted rice with sausage and artichokes

·

SECONDO
Costolette d'Agnello Impanate (see page 114)
Pan-fried breaded lamb chops

·

CONTORNO
Condiggion (see page 133)
Summer vegetable salad

·

FRUTTA
Fruit in season (figs, tangerines, oranges, grapes)

·

DOLCE
Crostata di Crema di Limone (see page 145)
Nick Malgieri's Ligurian lemon tart

APULIA

ANTIPASTO
Cozze Arracanati (see page 66)
Baked mussels

·

PRIMO
Ciceri e Tria (see page 86)
Salentine fettuccine with
chick-peas and onions

·

SECONDO
Taiedda (see page 108)
Baked fish fillets with vegetables,
potatoes and white wine

·

CONTORNO
Fagiolini al Pomodoro (see page 129)
Green beans with tomato and garlic

·

FORMAGGIO
Ricotta forte, pecorino, caciocavallo,
scamorza, provòle

·

FRUTTA
Fruit in season (loquats, pears,
quinces, figs, apricots)

·

DOLCE
Fichi Mandorlati (see page 148)
Dried figs stuffed with roasted almonds,
chocolate and fennel

Biscotti della Nonna (see page 149)
Italian sesame cookies

EMILIA

ANTIPASTO
Salumi
Cured meats – prosciutto, salame, culatello

·

PRIMO
Cappelletti in Brodo (see page 80)
Little pasta dumplings with meat and
cheese filling, cooked in broth

·

SECONDO
Petti di Pollo Impanati (see page 118)
Breaded fried chicken breast cutlets served
hot with wedges of lemon

·

CONTORNO
Asparagi alla Parmigiana (see page 131)
Asparagus, Parma style

·

FORMAGGIO
Parmigiano-reggiano
(A two-year-old Parmesan)

FRUTTA
Fruit in season (cherries, plums, pears,
apples, strawberries, raspberries)

·

DOLCE
Coppa Oreste (see page 143)
"Oreste's goblet" mascarpone dessert

Ciceri e Tria

Asparagi alla Parmigiana

PIEDMONT

ANTIPASTO
Castellana di Peperoni (see page 63)
Stuffed roasted pepper "sandwiches",
grissini (breadsticks)

•

PRIMO
Brodo di Manzo (see Manzo Lesso, page 110)
Beef broth

•

SECONDO
Gallinelle e Polenta (see page 52)
Poussin fricassee with wild mushrooms
and polenta

•

CONTORNO
Finocchi Gratinati (see page 130)
Baked fennel

•

FORMAGGIO
Toma, robiola, Gorgonzola

•

FRUTTA
Castagne Arrosto (see page 161)
Roasted chestnuts

•

DOLCE
Zabaione (see page 143)
Zabaione cream with Marsala

TUSCANY

ANTIPASTO
*Crostini con Fegatini di Pollo alla Salvia
(see page 70)*
Sautéed chicken livers with
sage on crostini

Carciofi Ritti (see page 132)
Stuffed braised artichokes

•

PRIMO
Minestrone Invernale (see page 42)
Winter vegetable soup

•

SECONDO
Arista Fiorentina con Patate (see page 113)
Florentine loin of pork with rosemary and
garlic and pan-roasted potatoes

•

CONTORNO
Fagioli in Stufa (see page 90)
Beans stewed with garlic and herbs

•

FORMAGGIO
Caciotta
(Young sheep's cheese with extra-virgin
olive oil and freshly ground black pepper)

•

FRUTTA
Fruit in season (grapes, quinces, plums,
peaches, strawberries)

•

DOLCE
Zuppa Inglese (see page 142)
Italian trifle ("English soup")

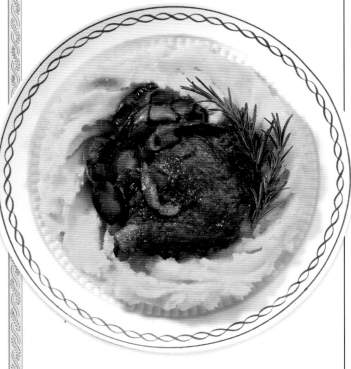

Gallinelle e Polenta

Zuppa Inglese

LOMBARDY

ANTIPASTO
Peperoni Ripieni (see page 64)
Peppers stuffed with rice and Gorgonzola

•

SECONDO
Risotto alla Milanese (see page 92)
Saffron risotto, Milanese style

Ossobuco alla Milanese (see page 54)
Braised veal shins, Milanese style

•

CONTORNO
Insalata Mista
Mixed green salad

•

FORMAGGIO
Grana, Gorgonzola (spread on bread with
unsalted butter), stracchino,
bel paese, taleggio

FRUTTA
Fruit in season (grapes, apples, pears)

•

DOLCE
Monte Bianco (see page 143)
Chestnut and chocolate "white mountain"

Peperoni Ripieni

SARDINIA

ANTIPASTO
Funghi Fritti alla Sarda (see page 63)
Crispy fried mushrooms

•

PRIMO
Polenta Pasticciata di Mia Nonna (see page 96)
My grandmother's baked polenta

•

SECONDO
Agnello alla Sarda (see page 113)
Roast leg of lamb with rosemary and garlic,
my mother's way

•

CONTORNI
Fagiolini
Boiled green beans dressed with
extra-virgin olive oil and lemon

Pinzimonio
Fresh radishes and sliced raw artichoke hearts
with an extra-virgin olive oil, salt and
black pepper dip

•

FORMAGGIO
Fior di Sardegna
(Semi-soft Sardinian pecorino cheese)

•

FRUTTA
Fruit in season (loquats, apricots, pears,
figs, pomegranates, cactus fruit)

•

DOLCE
Croccante di Mandorle (see page 149)
Almond brittle

Polenta Pasticciata di Mia Nonna

TECHNIQUES

*Italian cooking is, for the most part, informal and
straightforward. There are practically no complicated
culinary techniques, no lengthy preparation of reductions
and stocks. The only real necessity for the cook is to
know how to handle the raw ingredients. These photographic
step-by-step sequences are designed to demonstrate the
fundamental preparation techniques and to offer some
useful guidance on making the most of the ingredients that
are typically found in the Italian kitchen. The basic
recipes for fresh pasta, polenta and pizza and focaccia
dough may also be found in this chapter.*

EQUIPMENT

There is little sophisticated equipment in the Italian kitchen. Most tasks are accomplished with a good knife or mezzaluna and a chopping board. Pots and pans are simple, too. The traditional vessel is earthenware, which is superbly versatile. Copper or cast-iron cookware is also invaluable because it allows even cooking.

OTHER TYPICAL EQUIPMENT
Vegetable peeler, long-handled wooden spoons, sieves, wire whisk, baking stone and baker's peel, ladle, pastry brushes, blender, pepper mill, pestle and mortar, stove-to-oven pan and lidded frying pan.

KNIVES
The best types of blades are made of carbon steel, as they have a cleaner edge and can be sharpened more easily than those made of stainless steel. A large chef's knife with a straight edge for slicing and a paring knife for smaller tasks are essentials. A mezzaluna with a 25cm (10in) blade is indispensable for chopping.

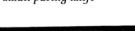

Straight-edged chef's knife

Small paring knife

Straight-edged cutting wheel

Fluted cutting wheel

*Mezzaluna
(half-moon cutter)*

PASTRY WHEELS
Sheets of fresh pasta and pastry dough can be cut with pastry wheels. Straight-edged wheels are used primarily for cutting pizza and focaccia. Flute-edged wheels make attractive edges on ribbon-style fresh pasta and stuffed pasta.

MEAT MALLET
A meat mallet with a blunt end and a textured metal end is used to tenderize meat and for flattening cutlets, chicken breasts and beef slices for stuffed meat rolls.

COLANDER
A sturdy, free-standing metal colander with large round holes is needed to drain pasta quickly (rapid draining is necessary to prevent pasta from continuing to cook after being removed from the heat).

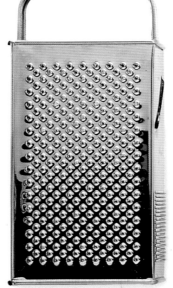

BOX GRATER
Choose a stainless steel grater. Use the smallest holes for grating nutmeg, the medium holes for hard cheese or to make breadcrumbs, and the larger holes for shredding softer cheese or vegetables.

PASTA MACHINE

The roller-type pasta machine is the only equipment that produces good homemade pasta as it both kneads the dough and rolls it into very thin sheets. Extrusion machines do not successfully accomplish these tasks. The heaviest, most sturdy machines are best because their rollers are better calibrated for rolling out the dough thinly and evenly. These machines are cranked by hand, or may have electric motors attached for automatic rolling.

Pasta machine

Separate cutting attachment

POTATO RICER

This is the best piece of kitchen equipment for transforming cooked potatoes into a smooth purée. It can also be used for other cooked ingredients, such as chestnuts. The ricer works like a garlic press, extruding the ingredient in very fine shreds.

DOUGH SCRAPER

A scraper is used for clearing the work surface of flour and dried dough that has stuck to it and would otherwise find its way into a ball of dough. Scrapers may also be made of plastic or metal.

WIRE MESH SPOON

This is a useful tool for retrieving food from a deep-fryer or from boiling water. It allows liquid to drain off quickly before the food is transferred to absorbent paper or served.

SPATULA

Use a rubber spatula to scrape clean the inside of a bowl while blending or mixing.

FOOD MILL (*Passatutto*)

No piece of modern electric equipment can replace the food mill (also called a "mouli"). It pushes through food, such as cooked tomatoes, puréeing while straining. (Blenders and food processors do a good job of puréeing, but do not hold back seeds or skin.)

Three discs can be inserted into the mill for varying degrees of fineness

Long-handled mesh spoon

PREPARING VEGETABLES

Vegetables are best eaten fresh, not frozen or canned, and this necessitates some preparation. Wilted or yellow leaves should be removed from greens. Bruises should be cut from fennel bulbs or celery. Carrots must be scraped and, if large, cored, and aubergines should be salted and drained to leach out bitter juices.

SKINNING TOMATOES

Blanch the tomatoes in rapidly boiling water for 30–45 seconds. Drain, then plunge them into cold water. Score the skin with a paring knife then lift it off with your fingers.

DESEEDING TOMATOES

Using a small sharp knife, cut out the tough core portion. Slice the tomatoes in half lengthways. Push out the seeds with your finger. The tomatoes may then be left to drain in a colander.

SKINNING PEPPERS

Place the peppers under a hot grill, turning them until the surface is blackened all over. Lift off the charred skin. Cut the peppers as described and scrape out the ribs and seeds.

PREPARING ARTICHOKES FOR STUFFING

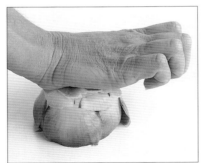

1 Slice off the stem of the artichoke. Using a paring knife, tear off the tough outer leaves. Cut across the head of the artichoke with a serrated knife, leaving about 3.5cm (1½in) of the base.

2 Trim the top of the base with kitchen shears. Turn the artichoke upside down on the work surface and bang it with the heel of your hand, forcing the leaves to spread open.

3 Reach into the centre of the artichoke to pull out the hairy choke (use a teaspoon if necessary). Spread the leaves open further to make room for the stuffing.

CLEANING MUSHROOMS

Use a soft cloth, brush or kitchen paper to remove any dirt. Do not immerse them in water as this spoils their texture. Remove their stems and trim off any woody parts. Wild mushrooms, such as porcini, may have to be washed quickly to rid them of earth or grit. They should be dried immediately and thoroughly.

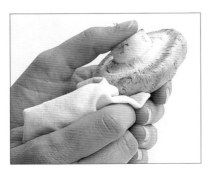

USING A POTATO RICER

To mash potatoes after cooking, peel them and pass through the potato ricer, one at a time, while they are still warm. This method gives a light, even-textured mass; a hand masher does not remove lumps, while a food processor makes cooked potatoes gluey.

SHAPING GNOCCHI

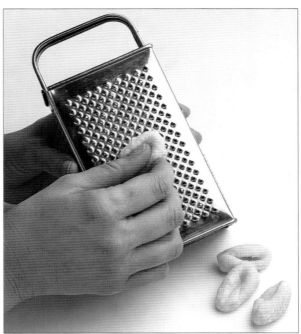

Take each piece of gnocchi dough between the thumb and forefinger and drag it down the face of the grater with the medium-sized holes, pushing your thumb into it as you do so to make a small, concave dumpling.

SOAKING & COOKING DRIED BEANS

To prepare beans, *place in a bowl, covering with cold water by 7cm (3in). Leave to stand for at least 4 hours, or overnight. Or, place in a pan with cold water to cover by 7cm (3in). Bring to the boil, cover and remove from the heat. Leave to stand for 1 hour. Drain and rinse. Place in a pan with water to cover by 7cm (3in). Bring to the boil, then reduce the heat. Simmer until tender, about 1 hour. Season only after cooking and drain well.*

To prepare chick-peas, *rinse well then place in a pan with 1.25 litres (2 pints) of water and ⅛ teaspoon of bicarbonate of soda per 200g (7oz). Cover and leave in a cool place for 12–15 hours. Drain and rinse. Place in a pan with 1.5 litres (2½ pints) of water. Bring to the boil, then reduce the heat. Simmer until tender, 1–1½ hours. Add 1 teaspoon of salt. Leave to stand for 15 minutes.*

TRIMMING ASPARAGUS

Cut the hard ends off the asparagus. Using a vegetable peeler, pare the thicker skin at the base end of each stalk to reveal the tender stalk underneath.

ROASTING CHESTNUTS

Wash the chestnuts and place them in a bowl with warm water to cover. Allow them to soak for about 30 minutes. Score an X-shape on the flat side of each chestnut, without penetrating the flesh (this prevents the chestnuts from exploding in the oven). Place the chestnuts in a roasting tin, scored side up. Roast until tender, 20–30 minutes depending on their size and freshness. Peel while still hot or warm, otherwise it will be difficult to remove the thin membrane that surrounds the nut.

PREPARING FISH AND SHELLFISH

Most Italian fish and seafood dishes are quite simple to prepare. Fish is generally kept whole as a great deal of flavour permeates the flesh from the head, bones and skin: scaling and gutting are therefore the only techniques usually needed. It is very important to rinse the cavity of the fish completely after gutting in order to remove any traces of entrails, which have a very bitter taste. Shellfish, too, must be scrupulously fresh and cleaned thoroughly before cooking.

SCALING AND GUTTING FISH

1 Draw the blunt side of a chef's knife along the body of the fish, working towards the head. Be careful not to tear the delicate flesh underneath.

Keep the knife at a right angle to the fish

2 Using a sharp chef's knife, make a slit up along the belly towards the gills, taking care not to insert the blade too far into the body.

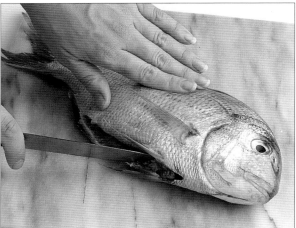

3 Ease out the innards with the point of the knife. Wash the fish well, inside and out, making sure that it is free of blood and any membranes.

CHOOSING AND PREPARING SALT COD

When buying salt cod, or *baccalà*, select meaty, white fillets, not thin dark pieces. The skinless and boneless variety eliminates tedious preparation techniques. Traditionally, preserved salt cod has a high salt content and is very dry. It should be soaked for two days, and the water must be changed twice a day. Today, salt cod is often preserved with less salt than in traditional methods, and the flesh is still somewhat soft. This greatly reduces the soaking time.

1 To rehydrate salt cod, soak it in cold water for 24 hours (see note left). Keep the bowl covered in the refrigerator and change the water twice.

2 Drain the salt cod and rinse it thoroughly in fresh, cool water. Pull off any skin and remove any remaining bones before cooking.

PEELING AND BUTTERFLYING PRAWNS

1 Remove the head of the prawn behind the gills then peel off the skin from the body (you may need to use a small sharp knife for larger species, such as Dublin Bay prawns).

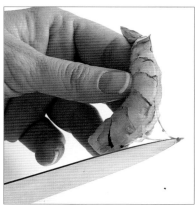

2 Make a deep cut along the prawn's back then, using the point of a knife, lift out the dark intestinal vein. Rinse under cold running water to remove any traces of intestinal matter.

3 Using your fingers, open up the prawn along the cut so that it can be opened flat like a book. Transfer the butterflied prawns to a bowl of iced salt water and leave to stand for 15 minutes.

SOAKING MUSSELS AND CLAMS

Mussels and clams must be purged of any sand or grit before cooking. Place them in a large bowl and leave to soak. Partially cover with a plate and refrigerate for several hours, or up to 48 hours, changing the water several times and adding flour or cornmeal with each change. After soaking, carefully sort through the shellfish. Discard any that have broken shells or that do not close when gently tapped (these are dead), then clean the shells thoroughly.

1 Cover the mussels and clams with cold water and add a handful or two of flour or cornmeal to plump them.

2 Scrub the shells to remove surface dirt. To debeard mussels, pull out any strands protruding from the shells.

PREPARING MEAT

If possible, try to procure organic or free-range meat that has been raised as naturally as possible. A good butcher will advise on choosing cuts of meat, but as a general rule, it is best to buy tender meat from young animals. Certain cuts, such as the fillet and small rib chops, are tender enough not to require any preparation. For traditional Italian-style veal cutlets *(costolette)*, choose chops from the small end of the rack as this is the most succulent cut. There are typical Italian-style meat cuts that require specific treatment. Veal escalopes *(scaloppini)*, for example, require flattening to even out the thickness and tenderize them. If you are boning joints of meat, save the bones to make meat broths or stocks.

TENDERIZING MEAT

Place the escalope or cutlet on a chopping board. Pound it lightly with the blunt side of a meat mallet to tenderize and flatten it, being careful not to break it.

TYING OSSOBUCO

Tie a length of kitchen string around the circumference of the shin piece to prevent the meat from falling off the bone during cooking.

ROLLING UP MEATLOAF

Working from the long edge of the mixture, very carefully roll the meatloaf, Swiss roll fashion, to make a long, narrow sausage-like loaf.

COOKING SAUSAGES

Fresh sausages are best eaten within 3 days of being made. The following technique of steaming and then browning fresh sausages, rather than frying them in oil, was taught me by an Italian sausage-maker, Ignacious Bonanno. It ensures the sausages stay moist and tender.

Select a large frying pan. Pour in water to reach 5mm (¼in) up the sides of the sausages and bring to the boil. Add the sausages and cover. When the water has evaporated and the sausages have browned on one side, turn them. If necessary, add a little more water in order to brown the sausages on all sides. Do not cut or pierce them. Cook until done on the inside and nicely browned, about 20 minutes.

APPLYING A RUB TO A MEAT JOINT

Using your hands, press the rub into the incisions on the joint, then work the remaining mixture into the surface flesh.

CUTTING UP A CHICKEN

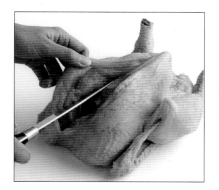

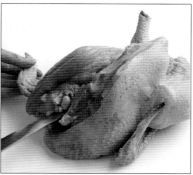

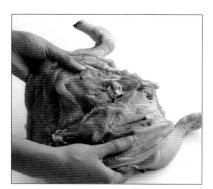

1 Using a very sharp chef's knife, cut along the breastbone towards the tail end. Work down the side of the breastbone to loosen the flesh.

2 Continue cutting down until the wing joint is reached. Slice through it then place the knife point in the wing socket and lever away the breast.

3 Cut downwards through the skin and flesh, then, using your hands, pull away the whole side of the chicken from the carcass.

4 Slice down through the leg joint and break it away from the main carcass. Cut away the whole side of the chicken.

5 Cut around the drumstick and thigh joint to separate it from the breast and wing. Chop off and discard the wing tips.

6 Divide the wing and breast piece, leaving a small piece of breast attached to the wing. Cut the drumstick from the thigh.

7 Repeat this process with the other side of the chicken. You will have 8 separate portions that can be used in a variety of dishes.

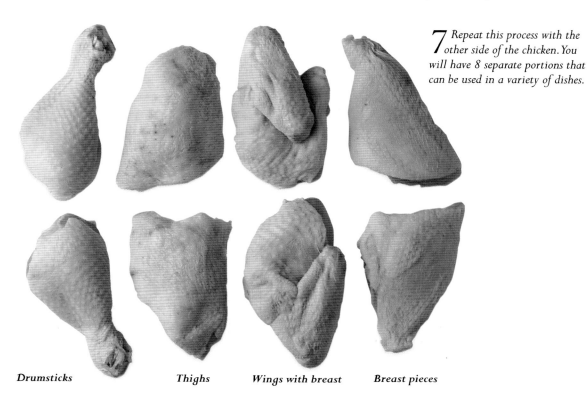

Drumsticks   **Thighs**   **Wings with breast**   **Breast pieces**

MAKING FRESH PASTA

Pasta is still made by hand throughout Italy, but it takes a great deal of practice to achieve light, delicate pasta. Hand-cranked or motorized roller-type pasta machines produce excellent results and are very easy to use. Extrusion machines and pasta attachments on food processors do not knead the dough sufficiently thoroughly. Below is a basic recipe for fresh pasta. The dough can be cut by machine or by hand into different shapes for loose or stuffed pasta.

PASTA FRESCA
Fresh egg pasta

Makes about 750g (1½lb);
enough for 4 standard servings

INGREDIENTS

300g (10oz) unbleached plain flour
⅛ tsp salt
3 large eggs (size 1)
1 tbsp vegetable oil

1 Combine the flour and salt directly on a large pastry board or work surface. Make a well in the centre of the flour. In a small bowl lightly beat the eggs with the oil and pour the mixture into the well.

2 Gradually draw in the flour from the inside wall of the well with a fork, beating in the same direction. Use your free hand to protect the outside wall of flour until the wet mixture is well integrated with the flour.

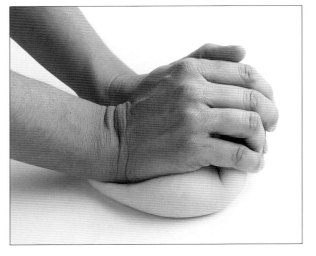

3 When the mixture becomes too stiff to work with a fork, use your hands to form it into a soft ball. With a pastry scraper, sweep up the flour left on the board and sieve it, discarding any dried-out dough pieces. Add enough of the flour to form a firm but very pliable dough.

4 Using the heels of your hands, flatten the dough ball and knead it from the middle outwards, folding it in half after working it each time. Knead both sides, keeping a round shape; do not let it rest. Cover the dough with an inverted bowl or slightly damp tea towel. Leave it to rest for 15 minutes–3 hours.

ROLLING PASTA BY MACHINE

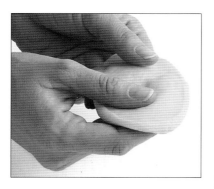

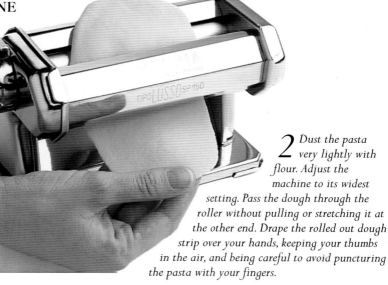

1 Attach the pasta machine to the work surface. Divide the dough into six equal portions. Use your hands or a rolling pin to flatten one piece of dough; keep the others covered.

2 Dust the pasta very lightly with flour. Adjust the machine to its widest setting. Pass the dough through the roller without pulling or stretching it at the other end. Drape the rolled out dough strip over your hands, keeping your thumbs in the air, and being careful to avoid puncturing the pasta with your fingers.

3 Fold the dough strip into thirds as you would a letter, overlapping the top third, then the bottom third over the middle portion to make a rectangular shape. Dust the dough strip very lightly with flour on one side.

4 Set the rollers at the next notch. Feed the dough through. Repeat the process of folding the dough into thirds, pressing out the air, flouring it lightly on one side and passing it through the second notch three times.

5 Feed the flattened piece of dough, narrow end first, through the machine's rollers at each of the remaining settings (see step 6). If the dough begins to stick at any point, dust it lightly with flour on both sides.

6 For all pasta cuts except fettuccine, pass the dough through every notch. For fettuccine, pass the dough through to the penultimate notch. When the sheet has passed through the rollers for the last time, collect it carefully in your hands and unfold to its full length, keeping your thumbs out of the way. Roll out each portion of dough in the same manner and lay on dry tea towels. Cover with dry tea towels until ready to cut.

The dough must dry slightly, for 10–15 minutes, before being cut

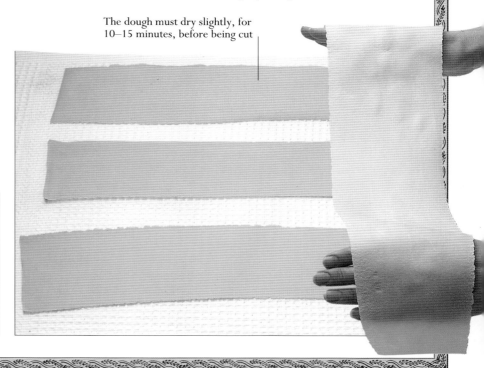

TIPS

• Keep dough not being worked covered at all times.

• Pinch the pasta together to mend any breaks.

CUTTING TAGLIATELLE

2 Collect the cut noodles at the base of the cutting attachment. Line four baking sheets with dry tea towels. Lay the noodles out to dry flat for 10–15 minutes, or for up to 3 hours.

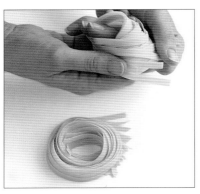

1 Fix the cutting attachment on to the machine. Take a strip of pasta dough (see page 167). It should now have a slight patina on the surface, but should

not be too dry as this makes cutting difficult. Cut the strips of dough in half across to shorten the strands. Pass each strip through the cutting attachment.

3 To make pasta nests, wrap a few strands loosely around your fingers, lay them flat and leave to dry. Store for up to 2–3 weeks in a clean container.

MAKING RAVIOLI

1 Roll out the pasta into 10cm (4in) wide strips, as described on page 167, passing the dough through every notch of the machine. Work with two strips at a time and set them side by side; keep the rest covered with a dry tea towel.

2 Place 1 teaspoon of filling at 5cm (2in) intervals along one strip of pasta. Use a clean brush to paint thin lines of egg white between the mounds of filling, so that each mound is surrounded by a square of egg white.

3 Cover the strip of pasta with the second strip. Using a pastry wheel or knife, cut the pasta into squares along the egg white lines. Press around each parcel to seal the edges. Repeat with remaining pasta strips.

MAKING POLENTA

Do not confuse ordinary cornmeal with polenta cornmeal. Italian "instant" polenta cooks in five minutes, but thickens so quickly that lumps easily form before it can be stirred properly. In the traditional method, the polenta is added to boiling water in a steady trickle. The following cold water method is just as effective and less tricky. Use a heavy-based pan that will conduct the heat evenly, and stir the polenta continuously with a long-handled spoon as it tends to bubble and splutter.

POLENTA
Basic polenta

This quantity serves 6 as an accompaniment.

INGREDIENTS

1.75 litres (2¾ pints) cold water
1 tbsp coarse salt
300g (10oz) coarse polenta cornmeal

PREPARATION

1 Combine the water and salt in a deep pan. Pour in the cornmeal, stirring constantly with a wooden spoon or whisk.
2 Place the pot over a medium heat. Continue to stir the polenta without interruption in the same direction (this prevents lumps from forming, and keeps the boiling temperature constant, which is important if the polenta is to be soft and creamy).

3 Continue to stir until the polenta is so thick that it begins to resist stirring and pulls away easily from the sides of the pan with the spoon or whisk, about 30 minutes.
4 Pour the polenta directly into a serving dish if eating straight away. Top with a generous lump of unsalted butter and the grated cheese of your choice (pecorino, Parmesan, ricotta salata or Gorgonzola are good choices). Loose polenta is also excellent served with Sugo di Pomodoro (see page 138) or Salsa Bolognese (see page 88). Alternatively, make polenta crostini (see below).

VARIATION

To make *Patùgoi a la Bàita* (milk polenta with smoked goat's cheese, Veneto style) substitute milk for water. Pour the cooked polenta into a serving dish and top with a large lump of unsalted butter and crumbled smoked goat's cheese.

MAKING POLENTA CROSTINI

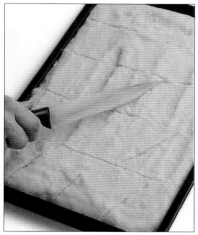

1 *Pour the cooked polenta into a lightly oiled baking tray or mould, or on to an oiled scratch-proof chopping board or work surface. Dip a palette knife in water and spread out the polenta. Leave to set, about 20 minutes.*

2 *Cut the cooled polenta into diamonds or squares, according to the recipe directions, and lift them out of the tray with the palette knife or a spatula. Proceed with the recipe, or grill or fry them (see step 3).*

3 *To grill, brush the polenta pieces with oil, place on a baking sheet under a hot grill and brown on both sides, 8–10 minutes. Alternatively, dredge the pieces in flour and fry in hot olive oil until golden. Drain on kitchen paper.*

PIZZA AND FOCACCIA DOUGH

The same basic recipe is used for pizza bases and focaccia. The initial mixing of the ingredients can be done by hand or in a food processor. See pages 68–70 for recipes for the different toppings and fillings. Probably no pizza in the world can match the famed pizzas of Naples. What makes the Neapolitan pizza crust so exceptional is the flavoursome wheat used in the flour, which is typically a high-gluten "00" flour that produces a chewy, but light and tender crust. Unbleached plain flour, preferably stone-ground, is a good substitute. The bases may be cooked on a traditional baking stone, but a baking sheet will also produce excellent, crisp bases.

PIZZA AND FOCACCIA DOUGH

INGREDIENTS

10g (½oz) fresh yeast, or 1 sachet active dry yeast
125ml (4fl oz) warm water
500g (1lb) unbleached plain flour, plus flour to dust
1½ tsp salt
250ml (8fl oz) cold water
2 tbsp extra-virgin olive oil, plus extra for brushing

PREPARATION

1 Combine the yeast and half the warm water. Leave to rest in a warm place for about 10 minutes, or until foamy.
2 Sift together 125g (4oz) of flour and the salt. Make a well in the centre of the flour. Add the remaining warm water, the cold water and oil to the yeast mixture and pour the liquid into the well.

3 Gradually stir the flour into the liquid until it is absorbed. Sift in another 250g (8oz) of flour. When the dough becomes too stiff to stir, form it into a ball with your hands. Proceed as shown opposite.

VARIATION

To make the dough in a food processor, prepare the yeast mixture as described in step 1. Place 375g (12oz) of flour and the salt in a food processor bowl and engage the motor for 30 seconds. Stir the remaining warm water, the cold water and oil into the yeast mixture then pour on to the flour. Process until a sticky ball of dough has formed, about 40 seconds. Transfer the dough to a lightly floured board and knead it with your knuckles for 3–4 minutes, sifting on to it as much of the remaining flour as is necessary to make a silky and elastic dough. Proceed as shown opposite, beginning with step 2.

PIZZA QUANTITIES AND BAKING TIMES

Pizza and focaccia should be cooked at 200°C/400°F/gas 6.
One quantity of pizza dough yields the following amounts:

Pizza type	Quantity	Cooking time
Roman-style pizza base – thickness: 2mm (⅛in)	2 x 35cm (14in) crusts 4 x 30cm (12in) crusts 8 x 20cm (8in) crusts	7 minutes 5 minutes 3–4 minutes
Neapolitan-style pizza base – thickness: 5mm (¼in)	2 x 30cm (12in) crusts 4 x 20cm (8in) crusts 8 x 15cm (6in) crusts	9–10 minutes 5 minutes 4 minutes
Focaccia base – thickness: 1cm (½in)	1 x 35cm (14in) x 45cm (18in) rectangular focaccia, or 1 x 30cm (12in) round focaccia	10–11 minutes

KNEADING AND SHAPING THE DOUGH

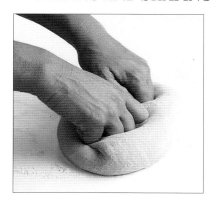

1 Transfer the dough to a lightly floured board. Knead it with your knuckles for 8–10 minutes, sifting on to it as much of the remaining flour as is needed to make a silky and elastic dough.

2 Place the dough in a lightly oiled bowl and brush it with oil. Cover the bowl with clingfilm or a clean tea towel. Leave to rise at room temperature until doubled in size, 1–2 hours.

3 Knock back the dough with your knuckles to expel the air. Lightly oil the baking sheet(s), or if using a pizza baking stone, place it in a hot oven and allow it to preheat.

4 Knead the dough for several minutes until it is elastic. If making more than one pizza, divide the dough into the number of portions desired. Keep covered until ready to shape.

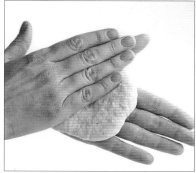

5 Using the palms of your hands, flatten the dough into a disc. Working from the centre outwards and turning it several times, press and stretch the dough with your fingers to make the base.

6 Transfer to the baking sheet(s), or a baker's peel or flour-dusted baking sheet if using a stone. Cover with clean tea towels. Leave to rise for 30 minutes then bake (see baking times opposite).

SHAPING FOCACCIA DOUGH

Proceed with the method above up to step 3, then turn to the main recipe (see page 70). The base may be dimpled before the topping is added.

Using your fingers, make indentations all over the focaccia base, creating little dimples to trap olive oil.

INDEX

AUTHOR'S ACKNOWLEDGMENTS
Above all, thanks to my mother, who
was my first introduction to fine
Italian cooking and style, and who is
my constant inspiration, and to my
tender, courageous and remarkable
children, Gabriella Leah and Celina
Raffaella, for whom I labour with love;
to Alex Barakov for helping me in
every way and with every task; to my
extraordinary editor, Lorna Damms,
and the exceptional team at Dorling
Kindersley; to my agent, Judith
Weber for her good work; to my
generous friend Flavia Destefanis for
her advice and contributions; to Anna
Amendolara Nurse for her recipes and
ever-present help; to Valerie Serra for
her kindness with recipe contributions
and assistance and to Elio Serra for
help with text, to Nancy Q. Keefe,
always, for leading me here; to Jack
Ubaldi for his advice about meat and
butchering; to Dun Gifford, Sara Baer-
Sinnott and Oldways for bringing me
to Apulia; to Alice Fixx and the
consortium of Parmigiano-Reggiano
cheese, especially Dr. Leo Bertozzi
and Renzo Cattabiani, for hosting me

in Emilia-Romagna; to Lidia Bastianich
for her kindness in allowing me to
reproduce her recipes; also to
La Molisana Pasta, Anna Teresa
Callen, Nick Malgieri, Anna Aldorisi,
Paul DuPont of Quebec, Pintelle of
Toronto; Anna Salerno, Gisella and
Cristiano Isidori, Andrea and Cathy
Baruffi, Professore Folco Portinari,
Ignacious Bonanno, Madhur Jaffrey,
Joanne Muir, Jenna Holst, Connie
Lozito, Carole Walter, Annette della
Croce Messina, Emily Balducci and
Nina and Andy Balducci for help with
research and recipe contributions.
I would also like to acknowledge the
following books, which were helpful
in my research:
La Cucina delle murge by Maria
Pignatelli Ferrante, *Puglia la tradizione
in cucina* by Angelina Stanziano and
Laura Santoro, *La cucina pugliese* by
Luigi Sada*, Guida gastronomica d'Italia*
by Felice Cùnsolo, *Guida all'Italia
gastronomica* by Massimo Alberini and
Giorgio Mistretta, *Treasures of the
Italian Table* by Burton Anderson, *The
Tuscan Cookbook* by Wilma Pezzini,
Italian Cuisine: Basic Cooking Techniques

by Tony May, *Ricette tradizionali della
Liguria: La cucina onegliese* by Lucetto
Ramella, *L'antica cucinieru genovese e
ligure, DOC Cheeses of Italy: A Great
Heritage* by Franco Angeli, *The
Complete Book of Fruits and Vegetables*
by Franceso Bianchini, Franceso
Corbetta and Marilena Pistoia,
and *Healing with Whole Foods* by
Paul Pitchford.

Dorling Kindersley would like to thank
Clive Streeter for his photographs and
Lyn Rutherford for preparing the food and
for hand modelling. Patrick McLeavey for
design work; Andy Whitfield for
photographic assistance and Amanda Grant
for assisting Lyn; Jo Brewer, Karen Ruane,
Dean Hollowood and Harvey de Roemer
for DTP work; Sarah Ponder for the
artworks; Tracey Beresford for editorial
help; David Roberts for the map on pages
8–9; Sarah Ereira for the index; Flavia
Destefanis for checking the Italian.

Many thanks also to the Elizabeth David
Cookshop, London, for loaning equipment.

Picture credits: Photography by Clive
Streeter except photographs of Julia della
Croce by Martin Merchant at Everett
Studios, New York.

10 040-717